SMALL-TOWN VALUES AND BIG-CITY VOWELS: A STUDY OF THE NORTHERN CITIES SHIFT IN MICHIGAN

SMALL-TOWN VALUES
AND BIG-CITY VOWELS:
A STUDY OF THE
NORTHERN CITIES SHIFT
IN MICHIGAN

MATTHEW J. GORDON

University of Missouri

Publication of the

American Dialect Society

•

Number 84

•

Published by Duke University Press

for the American Dialect Society

Library of Congress Cataloging-in-Publication Data

Gordon, Matthew J.
   Small-town values and big-city vowels : a study of the northern
cities shift in Michigan / by Matthew J. Gordon
      p. cm. — (Publication of the American Dialect Society ; no. 84)
   Includes bibliographical references.
   ISBN 0-8223-6478-6 (alk. paper)
      1. English language—Social aspects—Michigan. 2. English
language—Michigan—Pronunciation. 3. English language—
Phonology, Historical. 4. City and town life—Michigan. 5. Michigan
—Social conditions. 6. English language—Vowels. 7. Americanisms—
Michigan. 8. Linguistic change. I. Title. II. Series.

PE3101.M5 G67 2000
427'.9774—dc21

British Library Cataloguing-in-Publication Data available

For Lesley, who has stood by me throughout
with saintly patience, and for Zeke,
somewhat less patient, but no less faithful

CONTENTS

ACKNOWLEDGEMENTS

This volume reports on a sociolinguistic study of two Michigan communities. The report represents a revision of my 1997 dissertation completed at the University of Michigan. For help and inspiration of various kinds, I am indebted to the many people who were involved in my work and my studies there. My largest debt of gratitude is to the people of Paw Paw and Chelsea who graciously let me (and my tape recorder) into their homes and who shared with me much more of themselves than is captured in this report. Also, for guidance throughout this project, I would like to express my appreciation to my dissertation committee members: to Tom Toon, who was tremendously supportive to me throughout my years at Michigan, and most especially to Lesley and Jim Milroy, who opened my eyes to the study of language variation and change and gave me the analytical tools to approach such work. I owe special thanks to Pam Beddor, who played such a valuable role as teacher, scholar and friend in seeing me through my graduate studies and preparing me for an academic life. Among the other members of the Michigan faculty, there are many that helped shape my thinking though I am especially grateful to Jeff Heath and Rosina Lippi-Green. For friendship, feedback, and especially assistance in the lab, I thank my former fellow students Jimmy Harnsberger and Alicia Beckford. Among my family, I owe great thanks to my parents, all four of them, and even greater thanks to Lesley, my wife, whose faith in me has been a constant source of strength. Thanks also to Ron Butters for many helpful suggestions in revising this work and to Charles Carson, who tirelessly waded through even the swampiest bits of my manuscript and helped shape it into something presentable to a wider audience. Finally, this list would not be complete without recognizing the scholar whose name appears in this thesis more than any other: William Labov. While our thinking on certain matters related to this study may diverge at times, I know my work would not be the same, indeed much of it might not even be possible, if his contributions had not preceded mine, and I am very thankful for the trails that he has blazed.

1. THE NORTHERN
CITIES SHIFT

For over three decades sociolinguists and dialectologists have been researching a remarkable set of changes affecting the vowel systems in several varieties of American English. These changes are remarkable for their broad influence across both geographic and phonological space. As for the former, evidence of these changes has been documented as far east as New England and as far west as the Mississippi River, though most research has been focused on a few large cities including Chicago, Detroit, and Buffalo. In terms of phonological space, the impact is also great, with recent reports claiming that as many as six vowels are affected. Interestingly, the vowels at issue and the directions in which they are changing suggest a coordinated pattern in which movement of one vowel triggers movement in another, which in turn may trigger others in a sort of chain reaction. Traditionally, historical linguists have labeled this type of sound change a "chain shift," and because of its geographic context the present set of changes has come to be known as the Northern Cities Chain Shift or simply the Northern Cities Shift (NCS).[1] The vowels involved in the NCS and the changes they are reportedly undergoing are represented in figure 1.1.

The supposed relatedness of the vocalic changes in the NCS is quite evident in this diagram. When the changes are represented in this way, it appears that the basic movement of the NCS is a clockwise rotation with the vowels linked into a complete circuit. It is important to keep in mind, however, that the neat pattern presented in figure 1.1 provides a very simplified and abstracted picture of what is in actuality a rather complex phonetic situation. As the results of this study will show, this picture needs to be substantially elaborated; nevertheless, it serves here to provide some sense of the nature of the NCS changes.

The NCS is one of the most widely known examples of sound change currently in progress; however, it has attracted surprisingly

1

FIGURE 1.1
The Northern Cities Shift
(after Labov 1994, 191)

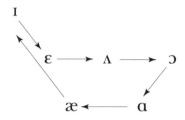

little substantive research, and there remain tremendous gaps in our knowledge of the shift. The present study attempts to narrow some of those gaps. Reported here are the findings of a project that examines the status of the NCS in two small towns in Michigan. In assessing this status, consideration is given to both the linguistic and social distributions of the variables associated with the NCS, as an attempt is made to better understand the factors that play a role in shaping this variation.

By way of orienting readers to the methods and goals of this study, this introductory chapter offers a general discussion of some of the central issues involved in this line of research, as well as a brief review of what is known about the NCS based on the work of previous investigators.

1.1. THE STUDY OF LANGUAGE CHANGE IN PROGRESS

To the delight of linguists and to the chagrin of almost everyone else, language is forever changing. The influence of change is felt throughout the language, in every arena, from phonology and morphology to syntax and semantics. Traditionally, however, much of the focus in historical linguistics has been placed on sound change. The reasons for this focus have to do in part with the nature of sound change, which seems to behave in a much more regular manner than other types of change, and with methodological considerations, such as the relative concreteness of sounds and the comfort of working within the clearly delineated realm of phonology. This focus has been remarkably fruitful and the field has made great advances in describing and working to understand the processes involved in sound change.

Describing the results of sound change is a relatively straightforward matter; however, getting at the details of how change is implemented has proven to be much more challenging. In fact, until quite recently linguists were content to deal with this issue only in the abstract. The kind of direct observation one would need to study the mechanism of change was felt to be an empirical impossibility. Sound change, it was held, proceeded by imperceptible degrees and, therefore, could only be detected after the fact. This was the view promoted by the neogrammarians and eventually adopted by American structuralists like Bloomfield and later Hockett (see discussion in Labov 1994, 43–72).

The last few decades have seen a renewed interest in studying the implementation of language change. This interest has been sparked in large part by the seminal paper of Weinreich, Labov, and Herzog (1968) and the pioneering methodologies of Labov and his colleagues. Among the "empirical foundations" laid out by Weinreich, Labov, and Herzog, their clear break with tradition in insisting that variation is a normal, in fact necessary, aspect of language was of central importance for future research:[2]

We will argue that nativelike command of heterogeneous structures is not a matter of multidialectalism or "mere" performance, but is part of unilingual linguistic competence. One of the corollaries of our approach is that in a language serving a complex (i.e., real) community, it is ABSENCE of structured heterogeneity that would be dysfunctional. [101]

Finding order in the apparent chaos of language variation has been a guiding principle in sociolinguistics at least since Labov's pioneering work on Martha's Vineyard (1963) and in New York City (1966). The connection between variation as a synchronic phenomenon and language change is perhaps obvious. Innovative forms do not simply replace older forms overnight; rather, the two forms coexist as competing variants for a period of time until eventually the older form disappears from use. A systematic exploration of the orderly heterogeneity in synchrony (where the forms compete) provides a platform from which one can make diachronic inferences. It is in this sense that Labov (e.g., 1972, 275) claims we can, *pace* the neogrammarians and structuralists, study language change in progress.

It should be noted that certain precautions must be taken before asserting that one has observed change in progress. For example, a critical datum for establishing a change is the evidence of significant generational differences in the use of the putative innovation, with older speakers using fewer of the new forms and younger speakers using more. This type of argument relies on "apparent-time" reasoning, in which the speech of different generations is taken as representative of different stages in the history of the language. Underlying such reasoning is the assumption that one's speech patterns do not change significantly over the course of one's life. There are, however, instances where such an assumption does not hold, where age-graded differences represent a stable pattern in which certain forms are associated with speakers of a certain age and are used only when one is in that period of life. In such cases, the distribution of forms across the generations may be indistinguishable from that produced while a genuine change is in progress.

To guard against misdiagnosis, Labov (1972, 275) recommends "obtaining at least one measurement at some contrasting point in real time." So, for example, in his 1963 Martha's Vineyard study, Labov was able to verify his apparent-time conclusions by consulting the records of the Linguistic Atlas of New England, which had been gathered 30 years earlier. Similarly, Milroy and Milroy (1985) supported their arguments for change in Belfast through comparison with the situation described over a century earlier by an elocutionist, David Patterson. The present project will also make use of such anchors in real time by incorporating evidence from linguistic atlas projects and various other studies from the nineteenth and early twentieth centuries.

1.2. THE DIFFUSION OF LINGUISTIC INNOVATIONS

Another issue central to this study is the question of how and why linguistic innovations are spread. Typically, changes spread in two dimensions, one linguistic and one social; that is, they make their way through both the language system, spreading from grammatical context to grammatical context, as well as through the social system, moving from speaker to speaker. Furthermore, along the latter dimension, the diffusion of changes takes place both within and across speech communities; that is, changes can spread vertically through a community from one social group to another, and they can spread horizontally from one location to another.

Understanding the processes involved in this social diffusion has been a central desideratum in variationist approaches to language change; yet, most of the research in this tradition has focused on the "vertical" dimension, and very few variationist studies examining the geographic diffusion of changes have appeared. Coincidentally, one of those few that was concerned with the geographic aspects of diffusion was a project dealing with the NCS: Callary's (1975) study of /æ/-raising in northern Illinois. This study is described more completely below. It is mentioned here because Callary reported an interesting geographic pattern, whereby the extent to which a community was affected by the change was correlated with the population size of that community, so that the larger the community, the more advanced its residents were in their adoption of the change.

An attempt to offer a more generalizable account of patterns like those observed by Callary was made by Trudgill (1983). Borrowing from the methodology of geography, Trudgill sets out to test a "gravity model" for the diffusion of innovations. This model derives from the fundamental idea that "the diffusion of an innovation is the result of the interplay of exposure to information about the innovation and factors leading to resistance to its adoption" (61). Trudgill describes a mathematical measure of the level of interaction between two population centers that is based on the populations of the two centers and the distance between them (75). Trudgill tested this gravity model on linguistic data from

Norway and East Anglia and found a reasonably good fit for the observed diffusion patterns. It seems, however, that a more sophisticated model is needed to adequately represent the complexities of sociolinguistic data. As Trudgill notes (1983, 83), attitudinal factors, such as prestige, should be taken into account,[3] as should internal linguistic factors, such as the structure of the linguistic system, since certain innovations may be more readily incorporated by some systems than by others. Of course, the quantification of such factors presents a much greater challenge than do measures of population and distance.

The diffusion patterns observed by Callary and Trudgill exemplify a common type of "hierarchical" diffusion in which innovations begin in large population centers and spread to other large population centers before trickling down to smaller centers. A rather different pattern is seen, however, with "contagious" diffusion, in which innovations are spread more uniformly across a region simply by contact among neighboring areas. Bailey et al. (1993) found that both patterns may obtain in the diffusion of linguistic innovations. Accounting for the spread of any particular change requires an understanding of the social meaning of that change, as different patterns are associated with elements serving different functions. As Bailey and his colleagues observed: "Features that reflect the imposition of external norms seem to diffuse hierarchically, whereas features that reaffirm traditional norms seem to spread contrahierarchically" (385). In actual fact the situation is often much more complicated and a single innovation may show characteristics of both types of diffusion. Such cases underscore the fact that the connection between linguistic form and social meaning is tenuous and frequently subject to reinterpretation (e.g., Labov 1966 on the changing prestige of (r) in New York).

The importance of social meaning in the diffusion of linguistic change is also stressed by Milroy and Milroy (1985), who found in their Belfast study that two changes similar in origin may function as social antonyms, depending on the groups with which they become associated. In order to understand why one group of speakers adopts some feature, we may consider why a different group does not adopt that feature. To begin to answer these questions, Milroy and Milroy appeal to the concept of social network. A community's social networks reflect its cohesion and the integration of its members. The degree to which speakers are integrated into a community affects their receptiveness to innovations, such that "a strong close-knit network may be seen to function as a conservative force, resisting pressures to change from outside the network," and conversely, "Those speakers whose ties are weakest . . . are most exposed to pressures for change originating from outside the network" (Milroy and Milroy 1985, 362). One of the benefits of this network-based approach is its generality. It provides a link between regional and social variation and suggests that the mechanism involved in diffusion of innovation through both geographic and social space is essentially the same.

1.3. CHAIN SHIFTING

As a final step in this general discussion of key issues, we examine the notion of chain shifting. The term "chain shift" describes a series of two or more related sound changes, the end result of which is a rearrangement of the phonetic realizations of the phonemes involved without the loss or gain of any phonemic contrast. Thus, chain shifts are distinguished from splits and mergers which add or subtract from a language's phonemic inventory. They are further distinguished from these other types of change in that they involve at least two (and often more) individual changes. Central to the definition of chain shifting (and to the controversy surrounding this notion) is the presumed interdependence of the participating elements. As seems clear in representations of putative chain shifts, such as that of the NCS shown in figure 1.1, the individual components appear to act in concert; the movement of one item sparks the movement of a second and so on.

Martinet (1952, 1955) distinguished two types of chain shifts on the basis of the relative chronology of the changes involved. In some cases, the movement of one sound creates an opening in phonological space into which another sound is drawn.[4] This type of shift is known as a "drag" or "pull" chain. In other cases, a sound begins to infringe on the area occupied by another sound, thus causing the latter to move in order to maintain its distance. Such cases are termed "push" chains. While nearly all linguists accept the existence of drag chains (though they may dispute the motivations behind them), there is a fair amount of controversy over the reality of push chains (see, e.g., Anttila 1972, 112; Vincent 1978, 411–12; Labov 1994, 199–200). Much of the disagreement on this issue is rooted in the inherent teleology of the push-chain scenario, a point discussed below.

The most comprehensive recent discussion of chain shifts is found in Labov's mammoth *Principles of Linguistic Change* (1994), in which no fewer than five chapters, spanning some 176 pages, are devoted to the topic. As the title of the book indicates, Labov's focus is on describing the wealth of phenomena associated with language change in terms of a small set of universal principles. With regard to chain shifting, Labov posits three such principles:[5]

  1. In chain shifts, tense nuclei rise along a peripheral track. [176]
  2. In chain shifts, lax nuclei fall along a nonperipheral track. [176]
  3. In chain shifts, back vowels move to the front. [116]

The term "peripheral" is used to refer to the relative position of a vowel in phonological space.[6] Specifically, a peripheral vowel is one whose nucleus is located closer to the outer edge of vowel space "in its mean and distribution than another vowel of the same height" (172). "Tense" and "lax" are also defined phonetically, as they are used as cover terms for "an abstract assembly of several phonetic features," including duration, peripherality, amplitude, and so on (174–75).

While the three general principles account for a great deal of the data on chain shifting, Labov believes they fail to capture the essential connectedness of all the elements in a shift. For this reason, he jettisons his three principles in favor of a single statement: "In chain shifts, peripheral vowels become less open and nonperipheral vowels become more open" (Labov 1994, 262). The introduction of the feature [± open] represents a change from a largely acoustic model to a wholly articulatory one, as a vowel's openness refers to the position of the highest point of the tongue body during its production. Such a change is motivated, according to Labov, by the elliptical shape of vowel space when viewed from an articulatory standpoint. This allows for a unity of the front/back and high/low dimensions on a single scale and, therefore, connects Principles 1 and 2 to Principle 3 (258–64).

A comprehensive assessment of Labov's principles is beyond the scope of the present discussion; however, the application of his statements to the specific problem of the Northern Cities Shift merits comment. In addition to the general principles, Labov (1994, 121–37, 166–218) presents a typology consisting of four basic patterns of chain shifting. The NCS is offered as the prime example of Labov's Pattern 2, which is reproduced here as figure 1.2. Labov's Pattern 2 illustrates each of his original three principles of chain shifting. A low back vowel is fronted (Principle 3), a low front tense vowel is raised (Principle 1), and front lax vowels fall (Principle 2).

A comparison of figure 1.2 with the diagram of the NCS presented above as figure 1.1 reveals a good deal of similarity. Low back /ɑ/ is fronted, while /æ/ is raised and high front /ɪ/ is lowered. There are, however, elements of the NCS that are not represented in Pattern 2, and it is not clear whether Labov's principles can account for them. For example, the movement of /ɔ/ involves both lowering and fronting (in addition to unrounding). Since /ɔ/ is a back vowel, its fronting is predicted by Principle 3; however, because it is structurally defined as a member of the tense class of

FIGURE 1.2
Labov's Pattern 2 Chain Shift
(after Labov 1994, 125)

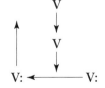

vowels (Labov 1994, 163), its lowering runs counter to the predictions of Principle 1. Labov's solution to this contradiction is to attribute the behavior of /ɔ/ to a "basic chain-shifting principle" based on Martinet (1955):

When the phonetic space between two members of a subsystem is increased by the shifting of one member (the leaving element), the other member will shift its phonetic position to fill that space (the entering element). [Labov 1994, 184]

This principle raises questions about the falsifiability of Labov's claims by providing a wild card to be played whenever other principles do not apply. Even if we ignore the ad hoc nature of the statement, it is not clear that it should apply in the present situation. The principle purports to govern the relationship between "two members of a subsystem"; however, the vowels in question are not clearly from the same subsystem. By Labov's own classification (1994, 163), the leaving element /a/ is a member of the class of short vowels, while /ɔ/ is a long or tense ingliding vowel.[7] Furthermore, the application of the "basic chain-shifting principle" in this case relies on a chronology in which /a/ was shifted before /ɔ/, though, as will be discussed below (§§1.4.4.2 and 6.1.3) the relative ordering of these elements is not at all clear.

Much more problematic for Labov's account is the backing behavior of /ɛ/ and /ʌ/. None of the original three principles provides for any backing; and, since the center section of vowel space is omitted from Labov's scale of openness (1994, 258), it is unclear whether his slimmed-down single-principle version holds. We are left with an empirical question of whether [ʌ] can be shown to be more open than [ɛ], and [ɔ] more open than [ʌ].[8] If so, then perhaps Labov's principle can be upheld in these cases; however, we might still ask why, in their inevitable pursuit of openness, these nonperipheral vowels did not simply fall in a straight line. This question is given added significance by the fact that in some cases it seems that /ɛ/ is in fact lowering directly to a more [æ]-like vowel (see §3.1.1). Labov suggests that this lowering was the main tendency in the early stages of the NCS, but that the distribution of /ɛ/ began to overlap with that of the freshly fronted /a/ . The result was a "reorientation" of /ɛ/ as it began to shift toward [ʌ] (Labov 1994, 196). This description has a teleological ring to it and raises questions about the underlying motivation for chain shifting.

Chain shifts have frequently been put forward as evidence of functionally motivated sound change. The most passionate proponent of this idea was Martinet, who viewed the fact that such shifts result in the preservation of phonemic contrasts as evidence that they are either consciously or unconsciously designed to promote the communicative function of language (1952, 126). The functionalist approach does have a certain intuitive appeal, though it does not always fare so well with the evidence, and Martinet's views have met with criticism from various fronts (e.g., King 1967; Lass 1978).

While a full review of the antifunctionalist responses is beyond the scope of this report, one alternative account proposed by Labov (1994, 569–99) certainly deserves mention. At the heart of Labov's argument is the concept of probability matching, a phenomenon which leads animals, including humans, to adjust the variation in their behavior to match some observed frequencies in their environment (see Labov 1994, 580–83, for examples). Probability matching offers a mechanism whereby patterns of stable variation get reproduced with each new generation of language learners. Because language-change situations typically involve gradual shifts in the frequency of variants, we might also suppose that probability matching plays a role here. Conveniently, Labov (1994, 586–88) illustrates the operation of this process with an example from the NCS, and this example is paraphrased here.

Suppose that a token of /ɑ/ is fronted so that it appears within the usual range of /æ/. In such a case, there is a chance that this item will be misinterpreted as an /æ/ token (e.g., *black* heard for *block*) or possibly not recognized at all (e.g., *drap* heard for *drop*). In either of these two cases, that token, because it was not identified as a token of /ɑ/, cannot influence the listener's conception of the acoustic profile of /ɑ/, a profile which is drawn on the basis of probability matching to the observed variation and which might include, for example, a sense of the mean frequency values for the first and second formants. Such cases of misunderstanding are predicted to have a conservative impact on the system, retarding any fronting of /ɑ/.

If, however, the same fronted token of /ɑ/ appears after the distribution of /æ/ has moved forward and up, it is more likely to be correctly interpreted as an instance of /ɑ/. The listener may still fail to recognize the intended word, but he/she is less apt to misidentify it as an /æ/ token. When the fronted token is correctly interpreted, it stretches the listener's conception of the acoustic range of /ɑ/ to include variants that are more fronted. As a result of this adjustment, listeners refigure their sense of what an average /ɑ/ sounds like, with the new average representing a more fronted pronunciation. Here, then, the mechanism works to promote innovation.

It is important to note that probability matching is a purely mechanical process that "proceeds without conscious attention" (Labov 1994, 597). Labov's appeal to such a mechanism is in keeping with his general defense of the neogrammarian conception of sound change as a process that operates blindly and advances by phonetically gradual steps.

While Labov has provided a rather concrete alternative to the functionalist view of language change, there are still many open questions. Perhaps most problematic for this account is the fact that it describes a mechanism that can only operate in cases of drag chains. The example outlined above clearly shows that probability matching will only promote the movement of vowels into empty spaces. When the phonological space surrounding a vowel is occupied, the mechanism serves to preserve the distance between that vowel and its neighbors. Labov (1994, 588) suggests that this explains the behavior of /ɛ/ in the NCS as, "an earlier pattern of descent of /e/ [= /ɛ/] to [æ] led to an overlap with advancing /o/ [= /ɑ/], and a gradual shift of the movement of /e/ toward the back." The probability matching mechanism may explain why the descent of /ɛ/ was rebuffed, but the vowel should have met with the same fate when it shifted to the back. Labov's own chronology (1994, 195) places /ɛ/-backing before /ʌ/-backing, and he identifies these two steps as forming a push chain. How could /ɛ/ have infringed upon [ʌ] space before /ʌ/ had abandoned it? If we accept the reality of push chains, as Labov does, then we must continue to search for a means of explaining them. Whether this means can be found in mechanical processes like probability matching or in more functionalist notions remains to be seen.

1.4. PREVIOUS RESEARCH ON THE NORTHERN CITIES SHIFT

Despite its large-scale impact both geographically and phonologically, the NCS has attracted very little attention in the way of primary research. The shift seems to have been generally accepted as a prime example of change in progress; yet, it has not been subjected to the kind of comprehensive study typified by Labov (1966) or Trudgill (1974). Our knowledge of the NCS is based on rather restricted sets of data produced by a handful of researchers.

Although the first linguist to recognize the NCS pattern was Ralph Fasold, who gave evidence of changes involving /æ/, /ɑ/, and /ɔ/ in an unpublished paper in 1969 (Labov 1994, 178), Labov has clearly been the most active figure in researching the shift and relating it to broader issues of language change. Much of Labov's theoretical approach to chain shifting is presented in his 1994 book, but his primary empirical work on the NCS appears in the study by Labov, Yaeger, and Steiner (1972). That study presented quantitative results and detailed phonetic analyses of the NCS changes and certainly made a major contribution to the study of the shift, though it should be borne in mind that their objective was rather more sweeping: "to discover the general principles which constrain, govern and promote sound change by the direct observation of change in progress" (1). The NCS, then, serves as one of several examples discussed in pursuit of this higher goal, rather than as a central focus of investigation. An important part of this goal is methodological, an affirmation of the claim that sound change can indeed be observed directly. This led, it seems, to a concentration on how sound change is implemented at the level of individual speakers. We see this focus reflected in the presentation of data, for which maps (plots of the frequencies of the first and second formants) of individual vowel systems are the preferred method, and in the sample of speakers. The Northern Cities data are based on a total of 25 speakers from three locations: 12 from Detroit (using materials from Shuy, Wolfram, and Riley 1968), 9 from the Buffalo area (including Rochester and the small town of Chili), and 4 from Chicago. While the Detroit and Buffalo groups contained older, middle-aged, and adolescent speakers, the oldest Chicago speaker was 22 and the others were 18, 16, and 11. Obviously, Labov and his colleagues make no claims of representativeness. This sample and the analysis derived from it seem designed to illustrate rather than establish the NCS as a change in progress. There is a fair amount of discussion dealing with internal linguistic factors affecting the shift, but very little information is given about its social distribution.

Some of the research gap regarding the social profile of the NCS has been filled by later researchers. Most prominent among these is Penelope Eckert (1987, 1988, 1989a, 1991, 2000), whose work is based on two years of participant observation carried out in a suburban Detroit high school. Rather than focusing on individual speakers and their vowel systems, Eckert used standard quantitative reasoning to correlate participation in the shift with categories of group identity (i.e., speaker variables). In her work Eckert has explored gender-based differences as well as variation associated with the primary social division in the school that separates "Jocks" from "Burnouts."[9] Eckert's research has greatly advanced our understanding and appreciation of the NCS, but it has been, nevertheless, rather limited in scope, examining only adolescents in a single geographic area.

In addition to the work of Labov and Eckert, there has been other research on the NCS, though the foci of these studies have been even more narrow. For example, Herndobler (1977, 1993) investigated a working-class community in Chicago and surveyed the speech of 82 informants covering a wide range of ages. However, the breadth of this sample of speakers was not matched by the coverage of linguistic matters. Herndobler provides data on only two changes involved in the shift (the raising of /æ/ and the fronting of /ɑ/), and she leaves unaddressed all questions about the linguistic conditioning of these changes. A more thorough discussion of phonological conditioning is offered by Callary (1975), who explored the geographic diffusion of the NCS by surveying the speech of 18 young women (first-year college students), each from a different county in northern Illinois. Callary's linguistic data are, nevertheless, severely limited because he examined only a single element in the NCS, the raising of /æ/. This limitation also applies to the study by Knack (1991), who examined the lowering and fronting of /ɔ/. Knack was interested in the linguistic consequences of ethnic identity and compared Jewish and non-Jewish speakers in Grand Rapids, Michigan, though she restricted her sample to middle-aged adults.

As might be expected, based on the limited scope of much of the previous research described here, there are many aspects of the NCS that are not well understood or even well documented. Nevertheless, some important findings have been reported, and these are summarized in the following discussion as a means of providing a sense of the current state of knowledge about the NCS.[10] This discussion is organized around four of the main types of issues relevant to the study of the shift (indeed, of any sound change): phonetic and phonological matters (§1.4.1), the question of the geographic range of the NCS pattern (§1.4.2), issues related to the social distribution of the shift (§1.4.3), and historical evidence of the changes (§1.4.4).

1.4.1. PHONETIC AND PHONOLOGICAL ISSUES. Chief among the issues of concern in the study of the NCS are the very fundamental questions of how the vowels are changing (i.e., what phonetic realizations are associated with the variation) and how these changes are conditioned (i.e., what linguistic factors promote the shifting). These issues have been addressed by previous investigators, though they appear to be far from settled.

Preliminary steps toward a phonetic description of the NCS changes were taken above with the depiction of the shift in figure 1.1. According to that diagram, which is based on Labov's (1994, 191) representation, the NCS involves six vowels, whose movements can be described as follows:

(æ) This low front vowel is fronted and raised resulting in variants near [ɛ] or even [ɪ], sometimes accompanied by an inglide, i.e., [ɛə] or [ɪə].[11]

(ɪ) This high front vowel is lowered to something near [ɛ].

(ɛ) This mid front vowel is backed to something near [ʌ].

(ʌ) This mid central vowel is backed and often rounded, resulting in variants near [ɔ].

(ɔ) This mid back rounded vowel is lowered, fronted, and unrounded to approach [ɑ].

(ɑ) This low back unrounded vowel is fronted to [a] and sometimes as far as [æ].

These descriptions, like the diagram presented as figure 1.1, portray the NCS changes as interlocking elements participating in a kind of vocalic circle dance. Each vowel is described as shifting away from one vowel and toward another. It must be noted, however, that descriptions such as these do not provide a complete account of the variation demonstrated by the NCS vowels, and, in fact, it seems the phonetic reality is much more complicated than is suggested by the abstract pattern described above. This point is illustrated by the findings of the present study reported below (chaps. 3 and 4), but some evidence on this issue has been described by other researchers.

The most-discussed case illustrating a more complicated phonetic picture involves the mid front (ɛ), which, in addition to the backing portrayed above, has also been described as exhibiting a lowering tendency. In fact, Labov, Yaeger, and Steiner (1972) originally described the movement of (ɛ) as one of lowering to something near [æ]. Later, this description was modified, in part due to Eckert's research, which showed a trend toward backing of (ɛ). Labov (1994, 196) interpreted these directional differences as representing a diachronic development in the shift where the initial lowering of (ɛ) has been replaced by a backing rule. Eckert (1991), on the other hand, suggested that the difference of lowering versus backing of (ɛ) is characteristic of a synchronic Chicago versus Detroit distinction, though she did not present evidence to support this claim.[12] It appears more likely that both lowered and backed variants are available to speakers in both cities, though the sociolinguistic patternings of these variants may differ by location. Eckert (1991), in fact, demonstrates that this is indeed the case in the Detroit area, and such findings are also reported here (see §3.1.3.2).

A very similar case of apparently multidirectional shifting is seen with high front (ɪ). According to the standard account (as shown in fig. 1.1), (ɪ) undergoes lowering to "mid or even lower mid position" (Labov 1994, 188). While many speakers do exhibit this lowering tendency, others tend more toward centralization of (ɪ) (see, e.g., Labov, Yaeger, and Steiner 1972, figs. 13 and 14; Labov 1994, 191–92). This centralizing tendency was not addressed in these works; however, in recent conference presentations (e.g., 1997), Labov has modified his representation of the NCS to incorporate a more centralizing trajectory for (ɪ), though this centralization is still accompanied by lowering and seems to result in variants approaching [ʌ].

Similarly versatile directional tendencies are found with the movements of almost all of the other NCS variables. Thus, (ɑ), which is usually fronted to something approaching [æ], is also occasionally raised to [ʌ]. With (ɔ), too, there are occasional fronted tokens near [ʌ], instead of the more usual [ɑ] and [a] variants, and for (ʌ), the backing tendency, which usually gives forms near [ɔ], may be supplemented by either raising or lowering, leading to [ʊ] or [ɑ] tokens (Eckert 1989a, 260–61).

While these variations from the pattern that is usually felt to characterize the NCS may represent minor tendencies in terms of their frequency of appearance, they are, nevertheless, of great significance to the interpretation of the NCS as a chain shift. It seems much more difficult to argue for a coordinated series of changes with the divergent trajectories described in the previous two paragraphs (as well as in the present results) than with those depicted in figure 1.1. As is discussed below (chap. 6), the conception of the NCS as a chain shift has, it seems, been accepted rather uncritically. This may have led investigators to disregard potentially interesting variation that does not accord with the chain-shift model, including not only variation shown by the vowels thought to be involved in the NCS, but also variation shown by those elements not (yet) recognized as part of the shift.[13]

Another issue fundamental to the study of sound change is how the variation is conditioned phonologically. Although the NCS appears to be an unconditioned change in the traditional sense that all allophones of the relevant phonemes are potentially subject to shifting, phonological contexts do play a conditioning role by influencing the rate at which various allophones are shifted. For example, it was reported by Labov, Yaeger, and Steiner (1972, 81) that the raising of (æ) was strongly favored when the vowel appeared before nasals (e.g., *hand, man, ham*). On the other hand, such raising was found to be disfavored when the vowel followed a liquid consonant (e.g., *lap, black, grand*). Other key findings from earlier studies regarding how particular environments affect the shift are discussed in fuller detail below (chap. 5).

It should be noted that, as with many aspects of the shift, coverage of the issue of phonological conditioning has been spotty. Previous researchers have restricted their investigation to only a few of the NCS variables. Even the most thorough account of phonological conditioning, that offered by Labov, Yaeger, and Steiner (1972), provides such information on the movements of only (æ), (ɑ), and (ɔ), and of these three, the raising of (æ) commands by far the greatest attention. In addition, investigators have typically conceived of conditioning environments in very narrow terms and have focused primarily on the effects of following consonants. While there is evidence to suggest that following consonants do play a role, other potential factors should also be explored, including most especially preceding contexts, which in the present study are found to play an important conditioning role for all elements in the NCS (see results in chaps. 3 and 4).

As this discussion makes clear, there are still many questions related to phonetic and phonological aspects of the NCS that remain open. Even issues as seemingly fundamental as the directionality of the shifting vowels have not been completely settled. Other issues only slightly less fundamental, such as the linguistic factors involved in conditioning the changes, have received very little coverage, and attempts to gain a clear understanding of them are hampered by a basic lack of documentation. The methods used in the present study were designed, in part, as a reaction to this situation, and they include the application of a consistent analytic framework to the investigation of each of the six NCS variables.

1.4.2. GEOGRAPHY OF THE NCS. The Northern Cities Shift, as the name implies, is generally conceived of as an urban phenomenon, and, with the exception of Callary (1975), all major studies have investigated speakers in and around large cities. Furthermore, the cities participating in the shift are not randomly distributed, but rather appear to fit a well-established dialectological pattern. They are all located within the Northern dialect region, which is one of three large speech areas first delimited by Kurath (1949), and which includes upstate New York, Michigan, Wisconsin, and the extreme northern areas of Pennsylvania, Ohio, Indiana, and Illinois.

The geographic range of the NCS has not been determined with any precision. Labov (1994, 185) notes that the shift "has been observed in all the major cities in the Northern dialect area, from the White Mountains in Vermont westward: Rochester, Syracuse, Buffalo, Cleveland, Detroit, and Chicago." Evidence from Laferriere's (1977) study of Boston, which is discussed below (§1.4.4.1), suggests that the shift, or at least the raising of /æ/ associated with the shift, may be operating even further to the east than Labov observed. On the western frontier, Callary's (1975) study found (æ)-raising all the way to the Mississippi River, and recent work from the ongoing Phonological Atlas of North America project at the University of Pennsylvania suggests that aspects of the NCS can be heard as far west as the Dakotas (Labov 1996).

While the NCS seems to be primarily an urban phenomenon, this does not mean it is restricted to major cities. It may be "more concentrated in the larger metropolitan areas," as Wolfram and Schilling-Estes (1998, 138) suggest, but the influence of the shift is certainly felt in communities of various sizes throughout the region. Interestingly, population size does appear to be a factor in determining the progress of the shift, as it seems to be spreading through a hierarchical diffusion. As noted earlier (§1.2), Callary

(1975, 156) found that "the height of /æ/ is directly correlated with the size of the community in which the informant was raised"; that is, the larger the community, the higher the vowel.[14] Of course, Callary's findings are based on an investigation of only a single element in the NCS and rely on a rather limited sample of speakers; still, if they are found to be generalizable, they may offer insight into the mechanisms at work in the propagation of this and other linguistic changes.

1.4.3. SOCIAL DISTRIBUTION OF THE NCS. Also important to consider in assessing the current state of knowledge about the NCS are questions of how it is distributed in the social structures of the communities in which it is found. Social factors can and do play a role in the diffusion of language change, even though in traditional historical linguistics they have not received the same consideration as linguistic factors. Innovations may spread through a community from one speaker to another or from one social group to another, just as they may spread though a language from one context to another or one item to another. Sociolinguists often study the influence of social factors by appealing to "speaker variables," including age, gender, social class, and ethnicity. To varying degrees, each of these four factors has been examined in previous studies of the NCS.

In the investigation of a putative change in progress, such as the NCS, we might expect that ample attention would be paid to the matter of speakers' ages. As noted earlier (§1.1), synchronic studies frequently rely on age data as apparent-time evidence to establish the presence of change. It is surprising, therefore, that so few data dealing with the age distribution of the NCS are available. In fact, only two major studies have sampled speakers from a broad range of ages. The most comprehensive of these two was the study by Herndobler (1977), whose 82 speakers covered an age range from 7 to 95. Herndobler grouped these speakers by generation and provided comparative data across three groups. Herndobler's results are rather surprising, however, because, while the oldest group of speakers showed, as expected, the lowest rates of use of the innovative forms, the highest rates were found not among the youngest group but among the middle generation (Herndobler 1977, 146, 155). This pattern held consistently for both variables Herndobler studied, the raising of (æ) and the fronting of (ɑ), and across both speech styles she examined, free conversation and reading style. These findings seem to raise serious questions about the interpretation of the NCS as a change in progress, though Herndobler does not address this issue. This kind of bell-shaped pattern shown in her data is often indicative of a stable age-graded variable (Trudgill 1988). It has been suggested that such a distribution may be related to the fact that the middle generation of speakers typically differs from both the younger and older generations in that they are active in the workforce and, therefore, more subject to the pressures of the "linguistic marketplace" (see discussion by Chambers 1995 and §5.2.3 below).

The only other source to incorporate data from a broad age distribution is the report by Labov, Yaeger, and Steiner (1972). Their sample ranged from 8 to 89 years, but with only 25 subjects total, each age group discussed contained relatively few speakers.[15] Given this small sample, it is not surprising that there are several apparent discrepancies regarding the age distribution in this study. For example, an 81-year-old rural speaker from Chili, New York, was found to be more advanced in his (æ)-raising than "many younger speakers from the city" (79).[16] There are also cases where older and younger speakers differ with regard to the phonological conditioning of a change (see the discussion of (ɔ); 118–19) and even cases where older speakers show changes that are not present among younger speakers (see the discussion of (ɪ) and (ɛ); 121). Anomalies such as these as well as the problems raised by Herndobler's data indicate that the issue of the age distribution of the NCS is far from settled.

A second important speaker variable in any study of language variation is gender. Linguistic differences between men and women have been documented in languages and speech communities around the world. In language-change situations, numerous studies have reported females leading males in the use of innovative forms (see Labov 1990).[17] For the most part this is the pattern that has been observed with the NCS. Thus, for example, Eckert (1989a) found significant differences between boys and girls in the use of three out of the five NCS variables that she studied, (æ), (ɑ), and (ɔ), and in all three cases the girls were shown to lead the changes. Herndobler (1977, 1993) also investigated gender differences among her speakers. Her data on the raising of (æ) are consistent with Eckert's and showed women ahead of men by a substantial margin in all three generations.[18] With regard to the fronting of (ɑ), however, Herndobler's data seem to contradict the pattern reported by Eckert, as Herndobler found men in the lead (155). This discrepancy may reflect generational differences, since Eckert's speakers were much younger than most of Herndobler's, or it may indicate a geographic difference between Chicago and Detroit. Whatever the explanation, these contradictory findings suggest that gender is a relevant factor in shaping the NCS variation and certainly merits further attention.

Another speaker variable commonly examined in sociolinguistic studies is social class. Socioeconomic status as determined by factors like income, profession, and education is frequently found to correlate with linguistic behavior, and language-change situations are no exception. Among studies of the NCS, the influence of social class has been addressed only by Herndobler and Eckert, and on this issue, too, there have been contradictory findings. Herndobler (1977, 145, 155) compares two groups which she labels "lower middle class" and "middle class," and finds the latter leading in both the raising of (æ) and the fronting of (ɑ).[19] Eckert (1988, 199), on the other hand, claims that elements of the shift "are currently spreading outward to the suburbs from the urban center" and seems to support the interpretation of the NCS as a "change from below" (in the sense of Labov 1994, 78). Eckert approaches the class variable indirectly through the study of the two opposing social groups, the Jocks and the Burnouts, who are oriented to the middle and working classes, respectively (see §5.2.2). Eckert's (1989a, 262) data show significant differences between these groups for the variables (ɔ), (ʌ) and (ɛ), with the Burnouts leading in each case. Again, then, Herndobler's and Eckert's findings reveal an apparent discrepancy on an issue of the social distribution of the NCS variables.

One final speaker variable to be discussed is ethnicity. Like age, gender, and class, ethnicity is a criterion by which people can be grouped, and the groups thus delimited may employ linguistic means to mark their status. In American sociolinguistics, perhaps the most commonly investigated ethnic distinction is that separating European and African Americans. Labov (1987) made the controversial suggestion that the varieties of English used by blacks and whites are diverging, a proposal that, according to Wolfram and Schilling-Estes (1998, 180), is supported by the NCS data: "There is also little evidence that the Northern Cities Vowel shift . . . is spreading to AAVE speakers in significant numbers in the metropolitan areas affected by the shift." However, it should be noted that there is little evidence that the NCS is NOT spreading to AAVE speakers. As with many aspects of the shift, this issue has not been thoroughly investigated. One study that considered African American speakers, Deser (1991), did indicate some participation in the NCS, at least in the raising of (æ), though the interpretation of these results is not entirely clear. In a recent study designed to investigate this issue, I found no indications of African American participation in the NCS except for some minimal raising of (æ) (Gordon 2000). The phonological patterning of the raising (i.e., the fact that it was largely restricted to prenasal vowels) suggested, however, that this variation was not related to the NCS. Still, these findings were based on a small sample of speakers in a single geographic area. This is an important issue that merits further study.

As for other aspects of ethnicity, both Knack (1991) and Herndobler (1977) discussed the influence of Jewishness on speakers' participation in the NCS. In the lowering and fronting of (ɔ), Knack found non-Jews, both men and women, to be leading over Jews, especially Jewish women. Herndobler did not directly compare Jewish and non-Jewish speakers. However, she suggested that the raised forms of (æ) may have their origin in the neighboring community of South Shore, which until the 1960s had a relatively high proportion of Jewish residents (1977, 148–49). It is interesting to note that Herndobler's findings once again raise the possibility of a contradiction, for they identify an element of the NCS as a feature of Jewish speech, while Knack's study found NCS activity to be typically avoided by Jewish speakers. Discrepancies such as these and the others identified in this section may have bearing on questions related to the broader interpretation of the NCS, particularly about whether the individual changes are indeed properly viewed as part of a single phenomenon. Such questions are addressed below in the discussion of the chain shift issue (chap. 6).

1.4.4. HISTORICAL EVIDENCE OF THE NCS. As a final step in reviewing what is known about the NCS, we turn to a consideration of issues related to the history of the changes. The discussion will center on two main questions: (1) When did the NCS changes get their start? and (2) In what order did the individual changes appear?

1.4.4.1. *The Time Depth of the NCS.* Fixing the origin of a sound change in time is a notoriously difficult task in historical linguistics. Orthoepic texts can offer evidence that a variant pronunciation was prevalent at a certain date, but they cannot tell us how long that pronunciation was around before it caught the critical ear of the orthoepists. Similarly, we may also look to spelling variants for evidence of innovation, but the conservative nature of orthography often conceals changes in pronunciation. With more recent changes, like the NCS, the situation is somewhat improved by greater availability of data; however, we are still very far from being able to identify the starting point of such changes with any great precision.

By almost all accounts, the pattern of change known as the NCS is a recent phenomenon. As noted above, the changes involving the lower three vowels (/æ/, /ɑ/, and /ɔ/) were first identified in Detroit by Fasold (1969), and the broader geographic influence of these changes was not widely known until the report of Labov, Yaeger, and Steiner (1972). Presumably, the shift was fairly well established by the time it gained their attention, but it is important to note that the shift had gone unnoticed in several earlier studies. Even as late as 1965, Pederson does not report any systematic evidence of the shift in Chicago, despite the fact that his sample included 136 speakers, covering an unusually broad range of the city in terms of age, ethnicity, neighborhood, and social class.[20] As Labov (1994, 185) notes, however, the absence of the NCS pattern in Pederson's study is most likely "a product of the methodology as well as the impressionistic notation, both of the most conservative type." Pederson's methods were essentially those of traditional dialectology, in which data are solicited using predesigned worksheets rather than being taken from free conversation, where innovative pronunciations might be assumed to take hold earlier.[21]

We can get some idea of the time depth of the NCS by considering the older speakers in studies like those by Labov, Yaeger, and Steiner (1972) and Herndobler (1977). The oldest Northern Cities speaker in the Labov, Yaeger, and Steiner study was a Detroit woman who was born in 1876.[22] This woman shows clear evidence of /æ/-raising and some degree of both /ɑ/-fronting and /ɔ/-lowering (see Labov, Yaeger, and Steiner 1972, fig. 3-11). Raising of /æ/ and fronting of /ɑ/ were also found among the two oldest speakers from western New York, a Chili man born in 1889 and a Buffalo woman born in 1894 (see Labov, Yaeger, and Steiner 1972, figs. 16 and 3-15). The lowering of /ɪ/ and /ɛ/ were identified by Labov, Yaeger, and Steiner (1972, 121) as a tendency among "some of the older speakers in Detroit and Buffalo" and are shown quite clearly in the speech of a Detroit woman born in 1901 (see their fig. 14) and a Detroit man born in 1910 (see their fig. 11).

While the oldest Chicago speaker in Labov, Yaeger, and Steiner (1972) was born in 1946, Herndobler's study offers a much deeper chronological sample of this city. Herndobler's oldest speaker was born in 1880;[23] however, this woman showed no evidence of either /æ/-raising or /ɑ/-fronting. Out of 24 speakers born in or before 1915, only 3 had raised tokens of /æ/, and they were women born in 1900, 1903, and 1908. These women also showed fronting of /ɑ/, as did 5 older men, 3 born in 1894, 1899, and 1905 and 2 in 1915.

One possible interpretation of this evidence is that the NCS, or at least elements of it, may have been in operation for over a century. This is, in fact, the claim made by Frazer (1993, 15), though based on other evidence.[24] While this may certainly be the case, it is important to recognize the assumptions that underlie such "apparent-time" reasoning, including, as was discussed above (§1.1), the claim that speech patterns are not significantly altered throughout one's life. Empirical results, such as those of Herndobler's (1977) study, where middle-aged adults were found to have greater levels of shifting than younger speakers, may raise questions about this assumption. Similar results are reported for the present study, and this issue is addressed below (§5.2.3).

One of the ways of preventing misinterpretation of apparent-time data is to establish an anchor in real time using reports from earlier research. Somewhat surprisingly, none of the major studies of the NCS has reported on such evidence.[25] In the present case, such an anchor can be sought in various sources of data from the region currently affected by the NCS. Fasold (1969) was apparently the first linguist to recognize NCS as a coordinated movement, but there were various earlier reports of "shifted" pronunciations in the relevant area, and these may serve as early evidence of the NCS in operation.

As a caveat to the discussion of this real-time evidence, it should be noted that the individual changes constituting the NCS are, for the most part, quite common in the history of the language. Although no other current or former variety of English gives indications of having experienced all of the six NCS changes at the same time, there is an abundance of evidence to suggest that each of the individual vowel shifts has occurred at various times and in various places throughout the history of English.[26] For example, the raising of /æ/ now heard in the Northern Cities has precedents dating as far back as the Old English period where *æ* was raised to *e* in the Mercian and Kentish dialects (Wyld 1927, 77). Similarly, the occasional spellings of *a* for *o* (e.g., *caffin* 'coffin', *stap* 'stop', *faly* 'folly') dating from the fifteenth to the seventeenth centuries (Wyld 1936, 240–42) indicate the operation of a fronting process similar to that affecting /ɑ/ today in the NCS.

The prevalence of such historical precedents is an important fact to bear in mind when evaluating the current state of vocalic affairs. One might, for example, argue that, given the frequency with which changes like these appear, their co-occurrence in the NCS is rather more coincidental than reflective of any coordinated series of movements. Such an argument is, of course, highly relevant to the interpretation of the NCS as a chain shift (see chap. 6). Of more immediate concern is the fact that the commonplace nature of changes like those involved in the NCS complicates any attempt to establish the time depth of the shift, muddying the waters of the historical record and raising questions about which changes are directly connected to the present situation and which are simply look-alikes. For this reason, the following discussion proceeds cautiously—as should readers as they weigh the evidence for themselves.

In seeking real-time evidence concerning the NCS (or any ongoing changes in American English), an obvious place to start is with the data from the linguistic atlas projects. Most relevant in this case are the report by Kurath and McDavid (1961), which covers the eastern United States and the data from the Linguistic Atlas of the North Central States (LANCS), which covers Michigan as well as Wisconsin, Illinois, Indiana, Ohio, Kentucky, and Ontario. What one finds in consulting these works is that, while they do offer evidence of pronunciations like those associated with the NCS, they give no indications that any systematic shift was in operation when the data were recorded.[27] As an example we can consider the situation with regard to the raising of /æ/. Kurath and McDavid reported a slight degree of raising in the speech of their Speaker 56, a woman from Buffalo born in 1876 (54). This speaker showed raised variants, transcribed as [æ^], in three of the five /æ/-items (raised in *ashes, bag,* and *half,* unraised in *glass* and *aunt*).[28] Raised /æ/ was also heard in the speech of their Speaker 53, a Rochester woman born in 1884 (53), though only in the word *bag.* In the LANCS data, all 5 Detroit speakers show raising of /æ/ in at least one of the items *January, Saturday,* and *afternoon,* as do 6 of the 17 Chicago speakers and 6 of the 10 speakers from northern Ohio (including Toledo and Cleveland).

While we may be tempted to interpret these data as an early indication of the NCS, at least of the (æ) component, it is important to recall the prevalence of such pronunciations in American English, indeed throughout the English-speaking world.[29] In Kurath and McDavid's work, NCS-like variants were not unique to the

Northern Cities area or even to the North. For example, raised forms of /æ/ are found in 17 of the 70 vowel synopses, including those of speakers from Georgia, South Carolina, Virginia, Pennsylvania, and Maine. Similarly, the LANCS data reveal that, in Michigan alone, raised variants of /æ/ are recorded for 43 of the 58 speakers outside of Detroit, including speakers from the Upper Peninsula.

The situation is the same for many of the other vocalic variables of the NCS: the atlas data show shifted variants occurring in the areas currently affected by the NCS, but there is no clear indication that such pronunciations were any more characteristic of these areas than of others. Of course, the fact that NCS-like variants may be common in areas lying outside the influence of the NCS does not mean that we should dismiss all such evidence even if it comes from the relevant locations, but it does make the job of establishing connections to the current changes more difficult. It seems very likely that the linguistic atlas data from the Northern Cities do contain some early indications of the NCS; however, any systematic pattern remains obscured.

In addition to the linguistic atlases, there are scattered accounts of NCS-like pronunciations in various other works. While for the most part these accounts deal with a specific city or state within the Northern dialect region, there are some that offer a more general view of the region. Interestingly, one tendency that is described in several of these general reports is the fronting of /ɑ/. Thomas (1958, 117) noted the allophonic use of [a] for /ɑ/ in various short-*o* words "in upstate New York and westward through the Great Lakes basin." This tendency was also observed by Kurath and McDavid (1961, 104), who found that /ɑ/ was "not infrequently fronted in the North." Pilch (1955, 76–77) also discussed this fronting, which he described as a "compensatory" strategy, presumably designed to enhance the qualitative difference between /ɑ/ and /ɔ/ in "Western New England and the Mid-West."

Pilch's explanation receives some support from studies conducted by Marckwardt (1941, 1942) on the development of Middle English ŏ and *wa-* in the Great Lakes area. Whereas in most British and many American dialects the reflexes of these ME items are rounded vowels, [ɒ] or [ɔ], Marckwardt found a greater preference for unrounding in Michigan and the northern sections of Illinois, Indiana, and Ohio. Furthermore, even when rounded vowels do appear in these areas, as for example before voiceless fricatives (*frost, off, moth*, etc.), they tend to be "lower and more open," thus [ɒ] rather than [ɔ] (Marckwardt 1941, 565). This tendency appears, from the geographic descriptions, to be coexistent with and perhaps connected to the /ɑ/-fronting discussed in the previous paragraph. The relative ordering of these tendencies is not clear, but if Pilch's (1955) claim of a "compensatory" movement is correct, then this would seem to describe a push chain, where /ɑ/ is fronted to evade the intruding /ɔ/. Such a coordinated movement would, at the very least, represent a significant parallel to the current changes and could possibly be directly related to the NCS.

Turning to descriptions of more specific locations, we find confirmation of the suggestion that /ɑ/-fronting and /ɔ/-lowering coexisted in the same area. DeCamp (1940) noted both tendencies in the dialect of Scranton, Pennsylvania, located in the northeast corner of the state. In /ɔ/ items, such as *off, lost, all, thought, fall*, and *caught*, DeCamp (1940, 369) recorded a lowered [ɒ] and even an unrounded [ɑ].[30] That this tendency applied not just to ME *ŏ* words strengthens the parallel to the behavior of /ɔ/ in the NCS. For /ɑ/, DeCamp (1940, 368) transcribed variants with [a], commenting, "I have never heard such an advanced vowel in these words elsewhere." Interestingly, DeCamp observed no pattern of /æ/-raising in Scranton. He did, however, note the occurrence of a lowered variant in words like *can, adapt*, and *last*. This lowering may be related to tensing, which Labov, Yaeger, and Steiner (1972, 48) suggest is a precursor to raising, but there is insufficient information to be certain.

One of the earliest dialect studies of a Northern city was Emerson's (1891) work on Ithaca, New York. There is some evidence of raised /æ/ in this study, but it seems to be restricted to a few scattered lexical items and cannot be seen as necessarily indicating a general trend. Many of the items have long been commonly pronounced with [ɛ] in various parts of America and Britain (e.g., *catch, axle, gather, January*). Emerson does speak of a length-ened /æ:/ in "broad-*a*" words (e.g., *fast, ask, path, half*), and length-ening is often indicative of tensing, which is felt to be a precursor to raising (Labov, Yaeger, and Steiner 1972), but the phonetic value of this sound is uncertain. It seems likely that the recognition of this phoneme class was an aspect of Emerson's analysis that was simply borrowed from the influential British linguist Henry Sweet and therefore does not represent a significant phonetic difference in this dialect.

Emerson (1891) also observed lowering of /ɪ/ and /ɛ/ to [ɛ] and [æ], respectively, but once again this seems to occur only in a small set of words, many of which are familiar from the dialectological literature. Thus, [ɛ] appeared in *been, since, Indian, engine, inside, Bingham, incline, rid, fit,* and *width* (128), and [æ] was heard in *yellow, yes, well, relative, Elmira, errand, vendue,* and *Schenectady* (122). There is no indication of any /ɑ/-fronting in Emerson's study and the only "unusual" variants of /ʌ/ are fronted, not backed (e.g., [ɛ] in *shut, just, judge;* 147). With regard to /ɔ/, the only hint of an NCS-like pronunciation is found in Emerson's statement that "ɔ is usual in '*dog*,' '*hog*,' '*frog*,' '*log*,' '*fog*,' but â [= ɑː] sometimes occurs" (142). In general, then, it seems there is little, if any, indication that a systematic shift of these vowels was under way in Ithaca at that time, despite Frazer's (1993, 15) belief that Emerson's study supports his claim that the NCS has been operating for over a century.

Half a decade after Emerson's Ithaca report, Monroe (1896) conducted a study investigating 141 speakers from all over the state of New York. Unlike Emerson, Monroe reported actual counts for variant pronunciations; unfortunately, however, his data were rather limited. Monroe did provide a clearer sense of the variability of short-*o* words, and his findings (450) seem to contradict Emerson's statement above. While [ɔ] was the usual vowel in *dog* and *log,* the unrounded [ɑ] was overwhelmingly favored (being used by 94–98% of the speakers) in *fog, hog, bog, grog, jog,* and *frog.* The unrounded vowel was the one prescribed in schools, and many of Monroe's informants considered [dɑg] to be a "learned pronun-ciation." Among other variable words in Monroe's study we find [ɑ] was favored in *swamp, swath, wash, gospel,* and *wasp,* while [ɔ] was more frequent in *daunt, haunt, coffin, coffee, office, long,* and *foster* (451). Not surprisingly, Monroe found no variation with *hot* and *not,* as both consistently appeared with [ɑ] (1896, 456).

While Monroe (1896) offers no better evidence of the NCS than did Emerson, a later study of upstate New York, Thomas (1935–37), suggests a much stronger connection to the current changes. For example, with regard to /æ/-raising, Thomas noted the usual miscellaneous occurrences of [ɛ] in *catch, gather,* and *radish,* but he also described what appears to be a more general type of raising:

In upstate New York, [æ] is usually high and close to [ɛ]. It is often a bit higher still before [n] in such words as *candid, hand, land, man, manners,* and *mechanics,* in which it may also be lengthened and nasalized. A more striking variation results from a raising and tensing of the tongue position, usually without nasalizing, before voiced back consonants, in such words as *anchor, brag, crags, dragged,* and *draggled.* [10: 294]

Thomas transcribes this first variant as a raised low vowel, [æ^], and the more extreme one as a lowered mid vowel, [eᵛ], but he notes that all of the items that show raising also appear with the ordinary [æ] (10: 294). In a further parallel to the NCS, Thomas also observed centralization and lowering of /ɪ/ and /ɛ/. The principal variant of /ɪ/ (after [ɪ]) was the centralized [ɪ᾽], but Thomas also recorded lowered tokens like [ɪᵛ] and the mid central [ɜ]. Both centralized and lowered variants of /ɛ/ were common, with a few of the former tokens being transcribed as [ɜ]. For both /ɪ/ and /ɛ/, Thomas provided data on the variation in over 50 different lexical items, and as with /æ/, he seemed to be describing quite general tendencies of movement. As regards /ɑ/ and /ɔ/, Thomas observed the usual fluctuations in class membership, but he also described a fronted variant of /ɑ/ which was recorded in several short-*o* words with following voiceless stops (e.g., *not, popular, knock*). He also noted a tendency for /ɑ/ to be fronted before /r/, which he found to be more prevalent in the western part of the state. In fact, he speculated that "the 'focus' of this sound seems to be in the neighborhood of Rochester" (11: 69). In various respects, then, Thomas's description bears a strong resemblance to the current NCS pattern, and if the variation he detailed is indeed connected to the current changes, then his study appears to stand as the earliest reliable indication of the shift.

The tendencies Thomas (1935–37) observed, assuming they are historically related to the NCS, can be of great importance in determining the time depth of the shift. Thomas does not provide data on the ages of the speakers he sampled, but he does indicate that many of them were Cornell students. We can assume, then, that a number of his speakers were born around 1915. Even though this date is quite a bit later than the one calculated from the oldest speakers investigated by Labov, Yaeger, and Steiner (1972) and Herndobler (1977), Thomas's study is still a valuable source for dating the NCS since it seems to offer real-time evidence of what appear to be many components of the shift in action in 1935.

The matter of tracing the NCS back in time is complicated by the presence of a similar tendency in several cities along the Atlantic seaboard, including New York and Philadelphia. That tendency is the well-known tensing and raising of /æ/, first detailed by Trager (1930). The fact that the phonetic realizations of this process are virtually identical to those associated with (æ) in the NCS and the observation that both seem to be characteristic of urban speech have led some researchers to conclude that these processes are part of the same sound change (e.g., Bailey 1973). There is, however, one key difference between the behavior of /æ/ in the Middle Atlantic states and its behavior in the Northern Cities, and that is that in the former area the vowel is tensed and raised only in restricted phonological contexts,[31] while in the latter, all /æ/ items are subject to raising (though to varying degrees). In some of his early work, Labov (1971) seems to agree with Bailey (1973) in considering the Northern Cities and Middle Atlantic patterns of /æ/-raising to be different manifestations of a single phenomenon, but more recently he has stated his belief that they are in fact historically unrelated processes (1994, 537). As Ferguson (1975) pointed out and Labov (1994, 535) reiterates, the rule that tenses and raises /æ/ seems to be connected to the change that led to the "broad-*a*" class in RP and other dialects, and, therefore, has deeper roots in the history of the language. By comparison, raising in the Northern Cities appears to be a relatively recent phenomenon and the dialects participating were, in large part, unaffected by the "broad-*a*" pattern.

Although the two types of /æ/-raising seem to be unrelated historically, they do apparently overlap geographically. In such instances it seems to be the case that the NCS-type is innovative and the Middle Atlantic type is more established. Thus, after discussing the raising of /æ/ before nasals and other voiced consonants as a common pattern in the Northeast, Pilch (1955, 83) remarked, "In Waterbury, Conn., I have heard [ɛə] for /æ/ used by teenagers consistently in all environments, even before voiceless consonants." If Pilch was indeed observing the NCS, as his description seems to indicate, then this report is valuable not only in establishing the time depth of the shift but also in determining its geographic spread, as Waterbury is farther east than other locations investigated in early studies.

Also potentially important in delimiting the eastern spread of the NCS is Laferriere's (1977) study of Boston. The situation with regard to short-*a* is complicated in Boston by the presence of a small class of "broad-*a*" words. Laferriere reports that the older backing rule that leads to [a] in items like *half, ask,* and *can't* is giving ground to an incoming raising rule. This raising rule appears for most speakers to be that of the Middle Atlantic states and, in fact, Laferriere makes that connection in her discussion. Among her youngest speakers, however, Laferriere found that raising occurred even before voiceless stops (/t/ and /k/), a pattern that is found with the NCS-type raising and usually not in the Middle Atlantic. Laferriere was apparently unfamiliar with the NCS data, as she commented, "Raising is not recorded by other investigators in these environments" (104–5). If Laferriere's findings on /æ/-raising are connected to the NCS pattern, then they would seem to indicate that the shift has spread further east than Labov claims.

1.4.4.2. *Chronology of the Changes.* An issue closely related to the matter of dating the NCS is the chronological order of appearance of the individual changes constituting the shift. The most explicit discussion of this question is that offered by Labov (1994, 195), who posited the following order of changes:

1. raising of /æ/
2. fronting of /ɑ/
3. centralization and fronting of /ɔ/
4. lowering of /ɪ/ and /ɛ/
5. backing of /ɛ/
6. backing of /ʌ/

The first change is described as "nearing completion," the second and third are "midrange changes," and the others are "new and vigorous changes" (Labov 1994, 195). This chronology is essentially the same as that of Eckert (1989a) and seems to represent the current view of the situation; nevertheless, there are serious questions to be raised about it. These questions are considered in some detail in the discussion of the chain-shift issue in chapter 6, and so are treated more briefly here.

Despite its acceptance by leading researchers such as Labov and Eckert, this ordering is based on rather limited data. As Labov (1994, 195) indicates, most of the support for his chronology comes from apparent-time evidence, with which it is assumed that older speakers will show only older linguistic changes while younger speakers will show recent changes as well as more advanced stages of older changes. The potential pitfalls of apparent-time reasoning have already been mentioned (§1.1), but there is one other problematic issue that is of particular relevance here: the assumption in such an argument that all changes proceed at the same rate. Numerous factors intervene to promote and retard language change, and it is certainly possible that a newer, faster-moving change could overtake an older change and become more widely distributed both within the language (in terms of phonological environments) and within the community (in terms of speakers). In such a case, an apparent-time snapshot would suggest a relative ordering of these changes that was in direct opposition to the historical facts. As with other such dangers associated with the use of apparent-time evidence, the best guard against this problem is to seek real-time support for conclusions drawn from such data.

In many ways it seems the chronology outlined above is based more on the order in which the changes were recognized by linguists than on their synchronic and diachronic distributions. The "oldest" change, /æ/-raising, was well documented in New York City, Philadelphia, and elsewhere before the NCS was postulated, and, as seen above, this Mid-Atlantic change was initially felt to be related to the Northern Cities phenomenon. Fasold (1969) discussed /æ/-raising as well as the movements of /ɑ/ and /ɔ/. Labov, Yaeger, and Steiner (1972) added to the picture the lowering of /ɪ/ and /ɛ/, and the final two stages, the backing of /ɛ/ and /ʌ/, were provided by Eckert (e.g., 1988). While the order in which the changes were observed by analysts is quite clear, the actual evidence, in both apparent and real time, does not present such a tidy picture.

Recalling the earlier discussion of the older speakers from the study by Labov, Yaeger, and Steiner (1972), we do indeed find evidence of /æ/-raising among these people, as we would expect of the oldest change. However, these speakers also show evidence of the fronting of /ɑ/ and /ɔ/ and of the lowering of /ɪ/ and /ɛ/. Similarly, Herndobler (1977) observed both /æ/-raising and /ɑ/-fronting (the only two changes she investigated) in her oldest group of speakers. In fact, in Herndobler's study, more of the older speakers participated in fronting than in raising, a finding that might suggest that /ɑ/ had been shifting longer than /æ/.

The real-time data are equally problematic. It was noted above that some degree of /ɑ/-fronting and of /ɔ/-lowering and unrounding has apparently been quite common throughout the Northern region for some time (see, e.g., Marckwardt 1941, 1942; Thomas 1958). Both of these tendencies were observed in Scranton by DeCamp (1940), who, interestingly, did not report any incidence of /æ/-raising. These studies, therefore, suggest that /ɑ/ and /ɔ/ began to shift before /æ/. Thomas's (1935–37) study, however, seems to contradict, in part, such a claim, as he did find /æ/-raising, some /ɑ/-fronting, and good indications of the centralization and lowering of /ɪ/ and /ɛ/, yet the evidence for lowered and unrounded forms of /ɔ/ is not clear. In sum, then, it seems the issue of chronology is far from resolved and certainly merits more careful consideration. Some steps in this direction are taken below in chapter 6.

1.5. CONCLUSIONS

The purpose of this discussion has been to provide an orientation to some of the central issues raised by this work and to some of the previous scholarship on the particular phenomenon under investigation. A recurrent theme throughout the review of previous research on the NCS has been the observation of vast areas of *terra incognita* in the present state of knowledge about the shift. While a fair amount of solid work has been done, most of our information about the NCS comes from studies that have been somehow restricted in their focus, often examining only certain of the NCS variables and/or only certain aspects of either their social or linguistic patterning. Of course, the focus of the present study has its own restrictions. No one study can hope to fill all the gaps in our knowledge about a change such as the NCS. The lesson to be drawn from the preceding discussion is that, even though a number of researchers (including very prominent scholars) have investigated the NCS, much remains to be done. It is hoped that the questions raised here may, in addition to laying a foundation for the present study, also serve to highlight areas for future research.

NOTES

1. Labov, Yaeger, and Steiner (1972) referred to the changes as "the Northern Shift," though Labov (1994) uses the term "the Northern Cities Shift."

2. Although it may be argued that traditional dialectologists have long recognized the essential nature of variation, their methods reveal that they were concerned largely only with variation in a single dimension, the geographic, and, for the most part, they did not give equal treatment to intraspeaker variation (e.g., stylistic differences) or interspeaker variation occurring within a single location.

3. The qualitative evidence discussed below in chapter 5 strengthens this point.

4. Although this description may suggest a kind of purposefulness is involved in the process (driven either by the concerns of speakers or of language structure), such motivations are not a necessary component of the definition, and other, less functionalist, accounts have

been offered (see, e.g., discussion of Labov's 1994 proposal on pp. 11–13).

5. Labov presents five additional principles governing chain shifting, but these deal with changes across subsystems and for the most part are not relevant to this discussion (for details see Labov 1994, 280–91).

6. Labov (1994, 159–60) defines phonological space in acoustic terms, using measures of the frequencies of the first and second formants (F1 and F2).

7. Labov's account seems to rely on a proposal that /ɑ/ undergoes tensing as part of its shifting, presumably following the Lower Exit Principle (1994, 280), which would bring the two vowels into the same subsystem, but this proposal is an empirical issue that remains to be tested.

8. Acoustically, this question might be approached by comparing the frequencies of the first formant (F1) for each vowel, since F1 is often used as a correlate of vowel height. Peterson and Barney's (1954) data show /ʌ/ has a higher average F1 than both /ɛ/ and /ɔ/, suggesting that it is more open than both these vowels. The average F1 values for male speakers were 530 Hz for /ɛ/, 640 Hz for /ʌ/, and 570 Hz for /ɔ/.

9. These categories are discussed in more detail below (§5.2.2).

10. For a fuller review of the literature see Gordon (1997, 20–37).

11. Parentheses will be used throughout this report to denote sociolinguistic variables.

12. Eckert (1991, 220–22) claimed that Labov, Yaeger, and Steiner (1972) found (ɛ) "to be backing in the speech of Detroiters of all ages," while among Chicagoans they found lowering. However, I could find no mention of the Detroit backing in their report, and the vowel charts for the Detroiters (figs. 11–15) give no indication of backing.

13. A possible example of the latter is the fronting of /u/, which is demonstrated by some of Labov's recent Chicago speakers (see 1994, 191–92). This tendency is dismissed by Labov as one "affecting most western and northern dialects," but it seems possible that such a change could interact with elements of the NCS (e.g., with centralized /ɪ/).

14. Contradicting this finding were Labov, Yaeger, and Steiner's (1972, 77–78) data from Chili, New York, a small town outside Rochester. The two older speakers from Chili were found to be relatively more advanced in terms of their /æ/-raising than speakers from Rochester and Buffalo. Even more surprising, given the usual findings on sex-

based differences (see pp. 21–22), was the fact that both Chili speakers were males and six of the seven urban speakers were females.

15. The only exception to this is the group of adolescents for which there were 13 speakers under age 19 (Labov, Yaeger, and Steiner 1972, 78).

16. Instead of an age difference, this may be indicative of a rural/urban distinction, suggesting, contrary to the usual scenario, that the change began with rural speakers and later spread into the cities.

17. This general tendency was cited by Callary (1975, 158) as a justification for his decision to sample only female speakers.

18. Judgments on Herndobler's results are based on impressionistic comparisons of percentages of use, as she presents no evidence of statistical probability testing.

19. This middle-class lead is shown in Herndobler's conversational data for both (æ) and (ɑ). The lead holds for (æ) in the reading-style data, though the lower middle class is shown to have a very slight lead in the reading style data for (ɑ).

20. Pederson (1965) did record relevant variants of each vowel involved in the NCS but gave no indication that these variants functioned in any patterned way. For example, among the "free variants" of /æ/ we see both raised and fronted forms, but we also find forms that are lowered and/or backed (1965, 30).

21. Much of Pederson's work was used in the Linguistic Atlas of the North Central States.

22. The speaker's age was given as 89 by Labov, Yaeger, and Steiner (1972, 84), but this was presumably her age at the time of recording in 1965. The calculations of birth dates given below for other speakers are also made in this way.

23. Speakers' birth dates were calculated from the ages given by Herndobler on the assumption that her interviews were conducted in 1975, as was indicated in the Linguistic Atlas of the North Central States.

24. To support his claim, Frazer (1993) cites Emerson (1891), a study which is discussed below.

25. In introducing his proposed chronology of the NCS changes, Labov (1994, 195) states that it is based on "apparent-time data and the limited evidence from real-time differences," but he does not elaborate or cite any sources for this statement.

26. A fuller discussion of historical and dialectological precedents of the NCS changes is offered in Gordon (1997, 38–63).

27. Much of the fieldwork for the data from Kurath and McDavid (1961) was carried out in the 1930s. The LANCS project began in 1938, and fieldwork continued into the 1970s.

28. This count excludes items with following /r/, an environment in which many vowels show special developments. In fact, /æ/ appears as raised before /r/ in many American dialects (Bronstein 1960, 154).

29. See Gordon (1997, 39–47) for examples.

30. In certain contexts (e.g., final position), /ɔ/ surfaces as [ɔ], so it seems fairly certain that the lowering tendency in this dialect is not a consequence of the "*cot ~ caught*" merger that affects many areas in Pennsylvania. Besides this fact, /ɑ/ shows no tendency toward backing.

31. The conditioning factors vary by location. For example, in New York City, raising takes place regularly before front nasals, voiceless fricatives, voiced stops, and variably before /v/ and /z/; while in Philadelphia, raising is found regularly only before front nasals, some voiceless fricatives (/f, s, θ/), and variably before /d/ (Labov 1971, 427).

2. METHODOLOGY

THIS RESEARCH OPERATES within the general sociolinguistic para-digm first developed by William Labov and later refined by James Milroy, Lesley Milroy, and others. A central tenet of this paradigm is the insistence that variation is a normal, even necessary, aspect of natural language, and furthermore that this variation is not simply random but rather can often be shown to be highly structured (Weinreich, Labov, and Herzog 1968). It has been a fundamental goal of much of the sociolinguistic research conducted in the last few decades to uncover the order behind the apparent chaos of heterogeneous language data. In the present case, pursuing this goal will involve an examination of which speakers participate in the Northern Cities Shift and how their speech is affected by that participation. Such an investigation requires both attention to linguistic and social detail and a means of drawing links between the two. This chapter describes the methods adopted in this study to examine these matters.

2.1. SAMPLE

In order to explore the question of which speakers participate in the shift, I constructed a sample which allows for comparisons across three social parameters: location, sex, and age. The sample includes a total of 32 speakers, distributed evenly between two Michigan communities (Chelsea and Paw Paw), both sexes, and two age groups (16–18 years and 39–51 years). The sample design is summarized in table 2.1, which also gives the ages and initials of each research subject (throughout this study, speakers are identified by their initials to protect their anonymity).

The towns being investigated were selected to explore the issue of the geographic diffusion of the NCS by providing some sense of how far the shift is spread in Michigan. Because Paw Paw is roughly 30 miles from the western edge of the state and Chelsea is some 50 miles from the eastern edge, the two communities pro-

TABLE 2.1

Participant List

(N = 32; individuals indicated by initials followed by their age)

	Paw Paw				Chelsea			
	Male		Female		Male		Female	
Adolescents	JA	18	MN	18	PF	17	EC	16
	BH	16	TN	18	TH	16	CH	18
	BM	17	CR	17	MM	17	JH	16
	KM	17	SS	17	JS	18	LT	16
Adults	MC	45	RG	42	JF	51	TE	43
	DM	43	KH	42	KF	48	JE	47
	RM	39	DL	43	WP	51	BG	44
	SR	40	TM	41	RR	51	JR	50

vide some sense of the geographic extent of the NCS. Furthermore, both towns are situated along Interstate 94, the main highway linking Detroit and Chicago. Given their locations, we might expect that speakers from Chelsea would have more contact with and be more influenced by Detroit than Chicago, while speakers from Paw Paw might show the opposite tendency.[1] These differences in orientation might be reflected linguistically in some of the subtle phonetic and phonological differences between the Detroit and Chicago versions of the NCS as described above, for example, the backing (Detroit) versus lowering (Chicago) or /ɛ/.[2]

As was discussed above (see §1.2), location is not the only factor involved in determining a community's participation in an innovation. The size of the community may also play a role, particularly when the innovation follows a pattern of hierarchical diffusion (Bailey et al. 1993), as the NCS apparently does. According to this pattern of diffusion, small communities are predicted to be affected later or to a lesser degree than large cities. In the case of the NCS, most of the previous studies have been focused only on major cities like Chicago, Detroit, and Buffalo, and we know very little about the status of the intervening small towns. The towns studied in this project were chosen partially to fill that research gap. With populations under 4,000, according to the 1990 U.S. Census (Chelsea 3,772; Paw Paw 3,169), these communities certainly qualify as small towns. Also, it should be noted that, although these towns are quite small, they are not located in remote, isolated areas. Not only do they have easy access to a major interstate highway, but also both are located within 20 miles of an urban center (Chelsea is west of Ann Arbor, pop. 109,592; Paw Paw is west of Kalamazoo, pop. 80,277). Influence from and contact with these small cities is also considered here as a potential factor affecting participation in the NCS (see §5.2.1).

In addition to location, this study also examines the influence of gender and age. Consideration of these variables is critical because the NCS is reported to be a change in progress. In the case of gender, linguistic differences between men and women have consistently been shown to play a central role in our understanding of patterns of variation and change (Labov 1990). In this study, as in most, gender is approached quantitatively through the variable of sex of speaker. Also offered is a more qualitative discussion of gender issues as they relate to individual speakers (see §5.2.2).

Age, also, is an important variable because differences between older and younger speakers can be used to make diachronic inferences about the course of the NCS. The speakers in this study are taken from two plainly separated age groups, rather than from a broad range of ages, in order to examine more clearly the generational differences expected of a change in progress. Furthermore, the age groups targeted here, while not maximally separated chronologically, may be expected to contrast greatly in terms of their speech behavior because of differences in their social situations. While adolescents are claimed to provide the best access to the uncorrected vernacular, middle-aged adults, who typically have contact with a geographically and socially broader range of people, tend to use a variety more in line with supraregional standards in contexts like the sociolinguistic interview (Labov 1972, 257–58).

One final sampling issue is the matter of how participants in this study were recruited. The basic approach involved the "friend-of-a-friend" technique described by Milroy (1987). An initial contact was made with someone from each town, and from these community insiders, I requested the names of several local people who might be willing to participate. Then, when I approached these others, I mentioned that they had been recommended to me by the insider. At the end of the interviews, I solicited the names of other potential participants, in this way continuing to build my sample until the quotas were reached. This procedure was successful in locating most of the adult and several of the adolescent participants. However, many of the adolescents were contacted through the channel of the local high schools.[3]

Interviews were conducted with many more than the 32 speakers appearing in the sample. Several of the interviewees excluded from this study did not fit within the age groups examined. Others, though relatively few, were not included owing to qualities of the interview which were judged to affect adversely the amount or reliability of the speech data collected. In some of these cases the participant was clearly uncomfortable and offered only minimal responses to questions. In other cases, participants were interviewed in groups of two or three; while these conversations were often very animated, they generally did not produce sufficient amounts of data from any individual speaker to be used in the sample.[4] One final selection criterion was related to the length of time participants had spent in the town: to reduce the possibility of dialect mixing, I hoped to include only speakers who had been born and raised in the town and whose parents were also from the town. In practice this objective proved very difficult to meet. While all participants either were born in the towns being investigated or came there at a young age,[5] many of their parents were from elsewhere. In most cases, however, the parents came from other locations in Michigan, so any influence due to dialect mixing to that extent was minimal.

One of the advantages of the recruitment techniques employed here is that they generally work well in keeping constant certain speaker variables that are not being directly investigated because individuals' social networks tend to comprise others of a comparable status and lifestyle. Such was found to be the case in the present study. For example, as regards ethnicity, the sample was quite uniform. All participants were European Americans (at least third-generation immigrants), and those who expressed a religious preference were either Catholic or Protestant. Similarly, in terms of social class, sample speakers were largely from the center of the socioeconomic continuum, though no formal measure of social class was employed. Most of the adults sampled worked in small family-owned businesses and had at most a bachelor's degree. The class background of the adolescents was somewhat more varied, with some of their parents having advanced degrees and others working factory jobs.[6] All the adolescents planned to pursue postsecondary education of some kind though not all at four-year colleges.

2.2. DATA COLLECTION

Two types of speech data were collected from participants. Samples of free conversational speech were gained through sociolinguistic interviews, and data from reading styles were gathered with the use of a word list.

The conversational data collected through interviews are of paramount importance to this research and constitute the principal input to the quantitative analysis. All speakers included in the sample were interviewed individually by the author. At the beginning of the interviews, participants were briefed in general terms about the nature of the research. They were informed that this is a study of small towns and how such towns are influenced by social changes, particularly how changes originating in large cities affect them. Language was occasionally mentioned as one of the features under investigation, but it was not presented as the focus of the study, for to do so might have caused participants to be unduly self-conscious about their language and could have resulted in less natural speech. Furthermore, such an emphasis was felt likely to compromise subjects' willingness to provide the fairly extensive demographic information required by the project.

The interviews were relatively unstructured (cf. use of "conversational modules" in Labov 1981). There was a prepared list of questions and topics, but they were not approached in any set order, and not every topic from the list was raised with every interviewee. The overarching objective of this approach was to let the conversation flow as freely as possible. Generally, the first part of the interview was devoted to gathering basic demographic information regarding the participant's age, family, employment, education, and the like. Next, the questions usually turned to the topic of life in the town. The adults were asked about what the town was like when they were growing up and how it has changed since then. With the adolescents, the focus was more on what their lives are like now (including questions about school, friends, and activities) and what plans they have for the future. Speakers were also asked about their connectedness to cities, both nearby (Ann Arbor, Kalamazoo) and more distant (Detroit, Chicago). The questions sought both factual responses (e.g., "How long has your family been here?") and attitudinal responses (e.g., "Why is this a good place to grow up?"). The length of the interviews varied between 45 and 90 minutes, though most lasted approximately one hour.

Speakers were asked toward the end of the interview to read a prepared list of words. The word list was intended to complement the main body of data, primarily by examining the phonological conditioning of the NCS. The 242 words on the list illustrate the six vowels at issue in a variety of phonological contexts. These items were chosen to examine the influence of both preceding and following contexts on the NCS vowels, including the effects of place and manner differences among consonants, of single consonants versus clusters, and of mono- versus polysyllabic words. Once the items for the word list had been selected, their order was randomized by computer. An alphabetized version of the list has been included below as appendix A.

The word-list data were useful in the initial stages of the analysis as a means of outlining general patterns. These data were not, however, formally incorporated into the quantitative analysis presented below (chaps. 3 and 4). One of the reasons for their exclusion pertained to questions of comparability. While some speakers (especially the adolescents) read the list at a pace similar to (or even faster than) that used in their normal conversation, others approached the list more cautiously, using a delivery that was slower and more deliberate than they did during the interview.

This variability is certainly interesting and may provide insight into the status of the NCS features in these communities, though these questions will not be pursued in this book.

All interviews, including readings of the word list, were recorded on audio tape. The recordings were made using standard (analog) cassette tapes in a portable, high-fidelity recorder (Marantz PMD222), usually with an external condenser microphone (Sony ECM-44B) pinned to the speaker's lapel. As this procedure implies, all recording was done with the full consent of the participants and the guarantee that the interviews will remain confidential.

2.3. DATA ANALYSIS

A variety of techniques for data analysis were employed, though most took as their starting point the auditory coding of the conversational speech recorded during the interviews. Various quantitative analytic procedures were implemented, and, in addition, instrumental acoustic measures were utilized to address certain phonetic questions and corroborate findings produced by other techniques.

2.3.1. CODING PROCEDURES. The primary data, those upon which virtually all the analysis is based, are those produced by the auditory coding of conversational speech tokens from the interviews. Listening to the taped interviews, coders judged vowel tokens according to their quality (see p. 49 below). The level of detail involved in the coding was determined by the ability to reliably distinguish variants. Distinctions among variants were drawn primarily along the phonetic dimensions of vowel height and backness; in addition, lip rounding was used to distinguish some variants of (ʌ) and (ɔ). As is described below (chaps. 3 and 4), some of the NCS vowels undergo shifting in different directions. For example, (ɛ) is often backed but is also sometimes lowered. Depending on the vowel, the coding system distinguishes up to three degrees of movement in any one direction. To illustrate these differences, the coding schemes for (ɑ) and (æ) are given in table 2.2. The variants

TABLE 2.2
Coded Variants of (ɑ) and (æ)

	0	*1*	*2*	*3*
(ɑ)	[ɑ]	[ɑ<]	[a>]	[a]
(æ)	[æ]	[æ^]	[ɛˇ]	[ɛ]

distinguished for the other vowels are listed in chapters 3 and 4, where the results for each variable are presented.

The number of tokens coded varied by vowel and by speaker. The goal was to code at least 40 tokens of each of the six vowel variables for each speaker. In most cases the number far exceeded that goal. For example, in the case of (ı) the smallest number of tokens from a speaker was 62, while the most was 106, and the average across all speakers was 88.3. Similarly, for (ɛ) the number ranged from 63 to 117 with an overall average of 90.2. With (ɔ) and (ɑ), however, the numbers tended to be much lower, owing to the relative infrequency with which these vowels occur. On average, 52.1 tokens of (ɔ) and 53 of (ɑ) were coded for each speaker. The 40-token minimum was met for all speakers with (ɑ) and for all but two speakers with (ɔ). Even these two cases did not fall short by much, and the numbers (38 tokens from one speaker and 39 from the other) are certainly comparable with those from the rest of the sample.

In accordance with the principle of accountability (Labov 1972, 72; Milroy 1987, 113), a point in the interview was selected and coding began there, taking the first 40 or more tokens of each vowel that appeared after that point. The starting point was usually 15 minutes into the interview, though in the case of shorter interviews (those closer to 45 minutes in length) the coding was started earlier in the interview, either 5 or 10 minutes from the beginning of the tape, depending on the length of the interview. The decision to begin coding after some time had elapsed within each conversation was motivated by the initial discomfort that many speakers exhibited in the early stages of the interview, discomfort that might have resulted in a style of speech that was less natural (typically more formal) than their usual conversational usage. Also, with many of the interviews, the first few minutes were devoted to gathering basic background information and involved questions to which speakers often offered only brief answers, rather than the more extensive responses that appeared later in the conversation.

The determination of which items were potential tokens of each vowel was generally a straightforward matter based on phonemic word classes. Essentially, if a word contained one of the six vowel phonemes investigated, it was considered a token to be coded. However, in order to increase the audibility of the tokens, only those vowels appearing in stressed syllables were coded. Furthermore, it was felt that including unstressed vowels might introduce problems for interpretation, since the acoustic effects of vowel reduction are similar to those involved in the NCS. In addition, vowels occurring in the phonological environment of a following /r/ are not considered because the acoustic effects of this context often lead to special vocalic developments. Furthermore, certain individual words were excluded from analysis because they participate in variation that appears to be unrelated to the NCS. For example, the variant pronunciation of the vowel in *since* as something near [ɛ] is well attested in the older dialectological literature and was recorded in this study even from speakers who show no lowering of (ɪ) in other items. To reduce the potential skewing effect of such variation, these items were not considered in the present analysis. A complete list of the excluded items appears as appendix B.

A number of tokens were not audible enough to be reliably coded, and these had to be excluded from analysis as well. Among these were (1) items appearing in rapid speech where the vowel was judged to be too short for identification, (2) vowels that were reduced because of their unstressed position in an utterance (e.g., *it* in a phrase like *look in it*), (3) items that were pronounced very quietly, and (4) items that were inaudible due to competing noise (e.g., school bells, overlap with interviewer's speech, laughing).

The coding procedures incorporated several measures designed to improve the consistency of the results. The data for each speaker were coded twice (on two separate occasions). After the second coding, the transcripts were compared and any discrepancies were noted. These discrepancies were resolved by reviewing the tapes a third time to make a final determination. In addition, many of the speakers were analyzed by a second coder employed as a check on the judgment of the author. Actually, two people served in this role of second coder, one handling the coding of the (ɪ), (ɛ), and (ʌ) variables, while the other coded (æ), (ɑ), and (ɔ). Both of these individuals were linguists trained in phonetics and familiar with the issues being investigated. The data from all 32 speakers in the sample were coded by the author, and a subsample of these speakers was selected to be analyzed by a second coder. This subsample was socially stratified in a manner similar to the main sample (i.e., by age, sex, and town), and its members were those speakers judged to be most active in their use of the NCS variables since their data were the most challenging to code. For (ɪ), (ɛ), and (ʌ), the subsample analyzed by a second coder contained 16 speakers, while for (æ), (ɑ), and (ɔ), 8 speakers were included. The second coders followed the same procedures as the author, making two separate coding passes through the data and resolving any discrepancies between them on a third pass. Naturally there were some discrepancies between the judgments of these coders and the author, and these were resolved by the author during another review of the recordings.

2.3.2. QUANTITATIVE ANALYSIS. The general objective of quantitative analysis is to uncover robust patterns in the data by exploring correlations both within the language system and between the linguistic and speaker variables. A variety of statistical techniques were applied to achieve this goal. Procedures followed in the application of standard techniques (e.g., *t*-tests, chi-squares) along with their results are described in chapters 3 and 4. Described here are procedures related to a method that is particular to this study, the vowel usage indices.

For each speaker, six indices were constructed (one for each vowel) to characterize that speaker's usage of the linguistic variables, that is, to provide a measure of the speaker's tendency to shift the NCS vowels. The first step in preparing these indices is to assign numeric values to the phonetic codes based on the degree of shifting they represent. Each variant is labeled 0, 1, 2, or 3, with 0 indicating no shifting and 3 the maximum degree of shifting (see table 2.2 for examples). The index for a vowel is calculated simply by taking the average code across all tokens of that vowel produced by a speaker. These indices incorporate information about the degree as well as the frequency of shifting, and thus they provide a measure of how far and how often a speaker shifts a particular vowel. An index near 0 indicates a speaker with very little shifting, while an index near 3 indicates one who consistently produces extremely shifted variants.

For the most part, all the tokens coded according to the procedures described above were taken as input in calculating the vowel indices. There was, however, one important exception involving items excluded on textual frequency grounds. A decision was made to place a limit on the number of times a given morpheme could be represented in a speaker's data set. The general rule was to include only the first three tokens of a morpheme. Thus, if a speaker produced four tokens of *call*, two tokens of *called*, and five tokens of *calls*, only the first three occurrences (whether instances of *call*, *called*, or *calls*) were counted. Exceptions to this rule were made when the morpheme appeared in words differing in number of syllables. For example, if a speaker produced three tokens of *call* and three tokens of *calling*, all six of these would figure into that speaker's index of (ɔ)-shifting. The three-token limit was designed to reduce the potential of any one lexical item biasing the results. In addition, because it leads to a more diverse selection of words being analyzed, this policy often has the effect of widening the sample of phonological contexts considered for each speaker. Thus, it serves to reduce potential bias from phonological sources as well and helps ensure that the data analyzed from a speaker are representative of his/her usage.

2.3.3. ACOUSTIC ANALYSIS. As a supplement to the picture drawn by the auditory coding of speech tokens, some analysis of acoustic data was also conducted. This analysis involved the instrumental measurement of particular spectral characteristics of the NCS vowels. The most important of these characteristics were frequencies of the first and second formants, since these formants are important correlates of the articulatory positioning of a vowel.

Frequency measures were obtained using the spectral analysis routines available in SoundScope (a computer application from GW Instruments). The speech tokens to be analyzed were first digitized from the original audiotapes at a sampling rate of 11.025 kHz. For all vowels that were judged (on the basis of their spectrograms) to be monophthongal, formant values were measured from vowel mid-point, so as to avoid transitions into and out of surrounding consonants. In the case of diphthongal variants, measurements were taken at the midpoints of both the nucleus and the glide, though the determination of the midpoints was necessarily less precise in these cases, given the difficulty of determining where the nucleus ends and the glide begins. Formant frequency data were generally obtained from Linear Predictive Coding spectra, with 14 coefficients (16 for some female speakers) and a window of 25.6 ms, though in some cases measures were based on Fast Fourier Transfer (FFT) spectra.

Because the acoustic analysis is designed as a supplementary rather than primary investigative tool, it considers a much narrower range of data. Measurements were not taken for every vowel token nor for every speaker. Instead, the findings of the auditorily based analysis were used to identify speakers and tokens for which an acoustic analysis would be most revealing. It is important to keep in mind, therefore, that the acoustic results presented below are intended only to be illustrative and not necessarily representative.

NOTES

1. The latter expectation appears not to have been met as the interview questioning revealed that the Paw Paw participants generally have very little contact with Chicago.

2. This assumes, of course, that such differences are in fact geographically based, an issue that remains unresolved.

3. In Paw Paw, my recruitment efforts were aided by a teacher at the Vocational and Technical Center, who introduced me to several of his

students during a visit I made to the school. Three Paw Paw teens in the sample (BH, SS, and CR) were contacted in this way. In Chelsea, I was allowed to solicit participants by addressing a meeting of the student council at the high school. I recruited six participants (TH, JS, MM, PF, JH, and EC) in this way.

4. Using data from these conversations might also introduce questions of comparability with the data from one-on-one interviews.

5. The latter cases consisted of CR who moved to Paw Paw at age 3, DL who moved to Paw Paw at age 10, and MM who moved to Chelsea at age 7.

6. To some extent these differences patterned with the different locations so that the adolescents in Chelsea tended to be more affluent than those in Paw Paw. This issue is considered below in the interpretation of the results (§5.2.1).

3. RESULTS: (ε), (ɪ), AND (ʌ)

Previous discussions of the Northern Cities Shift (e.g., Labov 1994) have suggested that the variables (æ), (ɑ), and (ɔ), which for convenience are referred to here as the LOWER elements of the NCS, form one chain shift while the other variables, (ε), (ɪ), and (ʌ), which are termed here the UPPER elements, form another. While the validity of this claim is debatable (see chap. 6), there are similarities in the variation displayed by the upper elements that are not found with the lower elements, and vice versa. For example, each of the variables (ε), (ɪ), and (ʌ) shows shifting along multiple trajectories, in fact the same trajectories for each vowel, whereas such multidirectionality is generally not found with (æ), (ɑ), and (ɔ). These types of similarities suggest a primary division of the Northern Cities variables into two groups, and accordingly I will treat the UPPER elements in this chapter and the LOWER elements in chapter 4.

In brief, the vowels in the Northern Cities Shift are clearly being shifted, and this shifting appears to be influenced by various linguistic and social factors. For each variable, the presentation in these two chapters begins with a brief phonetic account of the shifting which describes the variant pronunciations in impressionistic and acoustic terms. After establishing the presence of phonetic variation, the discussion moves to explore the factors that condition it, looking first at language-internal influences (especially at elements of the phonological environment) and then at social factors. Interpretation of the results and discussion of their significance will then be given in later chapters of this book.

3.1. THE VARIABLE (ε)

3.1.1. PHONETIC DESCRIPTION OF THE VARIATION. Previous accounts of the NCS (e.g., Eckert 1991; Labov 1994) have suggested that (ε) stands apart from the other shifting vowels as uniquely variable. According to these accounts, it is the only vowel to demonstrate significant shifting in more than one direction.[1] My study confirms the previously reported multidirectionality of the (ε)-shifting; however, as will be discussed below, it is clear that this feature is not unique to (ε).

Two main directions of movement are involved in the variation associated with (ε). In some cases the vowel is backed, leaving its mid-front home for more centralized climes in the neighborhood of schwa. In other cases it heads downward, lowering to assume a more [æ]-like quality. Occasionally these two tendencies combine, resulting in a variant that is both backed and lowered to approach the quality of low central [a]. These variant trajectories appear to be subject to both social and linguistic conditioning, the details of which are described below.

The coding system used to describe the (ε) data was sensitive to the directional differences demonstrated by the shifting vowel. Three degrees of shifting were distinguished for variants that were either backed or lowered, and two degrees were distinguished for those variants heard as both backed and lowered.[2] Approximate phonetic representations of the variants are listed in table 3.1.

An additional pattern of variation in which (ε) was raised toward [ɪ] was found among a few (three or four) speakers.[3] This raising (often called the *pin/pen* merger) occurred only before nasals and, thus, resembles a pattern that is familiar elsewhere in American English, particularly in the South, in which /ɛ/ and /ɪ/ are merged in this context (see Labov 1996). Speakers illustrating this pattern did so variably, that is, not all prenasal tokens of (ε) were raised, and those that were raised generally remained distinct from /ɪ/. Thus, these speakers do not show a complete merger. Because this raising is apparently not related to the NCS shifting, the raised tokens were coded as unshifted for the purposes of this analysis.

TABLE 3.1
Coded Variants of (ε)

	0	1	2	3
Backed	[ɛ]	[ɛ>]	[ʌ<]	[ʌ]
Lowered	[ɛ]	[ɛˇ]	[æ^]	[æ]
Backed-plus-lowered	[ɛ]	[ɛˇ]	[aˇ]	

As for the NCS pattern of (ε)-shifting, another way of describing the multidirectionality reflected in the coding scheme (table
3.1) is through the use of acoustic data, as illustrated by figure 3.1.
This graph plots formant-frequency data for tokens of (ε) from
speaker TM (PP, f, 41).[4] This speaker was one of the most active in
her use of this variable, shifting frequently and in different directions.

In constructing figure 3.1 and similar graphs for other vowels
(e.g., figs. 3.4 and 3.7), the tokens are taken from conversational
data (as opposed to word-list reading). Of course, not all tokens
produced by the speaker being represented are included in these
figures. Reliable spectral measures are not always possible with
conversational speech, and many tokens were abandoned because
of this. Also, some of the tokens that were measured have been
omitted from the graphs to improve their clarity. In some cases,
tokens were omitted because they offered redundant information

FIGURE 3.1

F1 and F2 Frequencies for Tokens of (ε) Produced by TM (PP, f, 41)

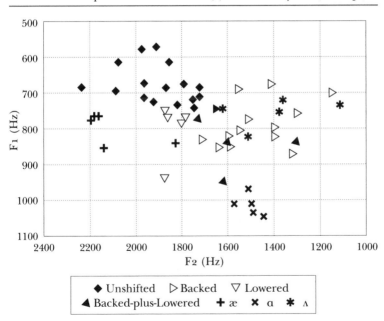

(i.e., their measurements were similar to those of other tokens). In other cases it was felt that, had the omitted tokens been included, they would have unnecessarily confused the picture of the general tendencies. A perfect match between auditory coding and the instrumental measurement of the data is practically unattainable, given the limitations of both means of analysis, and some of the tokens reflected such difficulties.

The horizontal axis in figure 3.1 represents the frequency of the second formant (F2) and the vertical axis the frequency of the first formant (F1). F2 can serve as an acoustic correlate of vowel backness, with higher values corresponding to more fronted articulations, while F1 serves as a correlate of vowel height, with higher values indicative of lower articulations (Borden and Harris 1984, 109).[5] Using these guidelines, we see that (ε) does indeed travel different paths away from its original mid-front position. In the upper-left region of the figure there is a loose group of (ε) tokens that were coded as unshifted. Spreading rightward and downward from this region are items that were coded as backed and lowered, respectively. Also shown are tokens that were heard as both backed and lowered. To provide points of reference, the graph also contains data on three other vowels: /æ/, /ɑ/, and /ʌ/. For these vowels, tokens that were judged to be conservative were selected, with some of the examples coming from the word list.

The acoustic evidence in figure 3.1 serves to corroborate the impressionistically based description of the multidirectionality in the (ε) variation. However, it is evident from figure 3.1 that the different trajectories taken by (ε) are not clearly separated; that is, there do not seem to be distinct paths along which the variants fall. Rather, there is a continuum from more or less straight-backed to more or less straight-lowered variants, with many shifted tokens displaying elements of both (e.g., F2 values under 1,700 Hz and F1 values over 750 Hz). Some of these items are coded as both backed and lowered, though even they are widely dispersed across acoustic space. Given the inherent variability of speech, the largely continuous distribution of the data in figure 3.1 is not surprising. It has been noted here as a way of laying a foundation for the quantitative analysis in the following sections. It serves as a cautionary preface to the later discussion of the sociolinguistic conditioning of the different (ε) variants (e.g., backed vs. lowered), but it also helps to motivate elements of the analysis in which the directional differences among the variants are disregarded.

3.1.2. PHONOLOGICAL CONDITIONING OF (ε). Having described the variable realizations of (ε), we turn now to an examination of factors that work to shape the variation associated with this vowel. The discussion below (§3.1.3) will investigate aspects of the social distribution of (ε), while here we are concerned with the influence of linguistic factors. Because the variation being examined involves a sound change, the linguistic factors most likely to have a significant impact are phonological, and it is on such factors that this discussion is focused.

The question of phonological conditioning is approached in two stages. The first investigates factors influencing the shifting of (ε) in general and does not consider the directional differences involved in this shifting. This simplification is helpful in identifying the conditions that figure most prominently in the choice of shifted-versus-unshifted variants. Once the general patterns are clarified, however, the directional differences are treated in the second stage of the analysis, and a more detailed picture of the phonological conditioning is drawn.

3.1.2.1. *General Conditioning of* (ε). The conditioning of the (ε) variation was investigated by examining various aspects of the phonological environment in which the vowel occurs. Basically, three types of factors were explored: features of the consonant that precedes the vowel, features of the consonant that follows the vowel, and features of the entire word containing the vowel.

As regards the preceding consonant, differences related to voicing and place and manner of articulation were examined. For voicing, a two-way distinction was made, comparing voiceless and voiced segments. In this comparison only obstruents were considered, since voicing is not contrastive for English sonorants. To investigate the effects of place of articulation, six categories were distinguished: labial (including the labiodentals /f/ and /v/ and the labiovelar /w/), interdental, alveolar (including /l/ and /r/),[6] palatal (including alveopalatals), velar, and glottal (used exclusively for /h/). Six types were also distinguished as manners of articulation: stops (including affricates), fricatives, nasals, glides (/j/ and /w/), /l/, and /r/. In addition, the absence of a preceding consonant was also examined in connection with the manner differences.

To examine effects related to following consonants, again, distinctions involving voicing, place, and manner were considered. Voicing differences were approached in the same way, comparing voiceless and voiced obstruents. For place of articulation, five categories were distinguished: labial (including labiodental), inter-dental, alveolar (including /l/), palatal (including alveopalatals), and velar.[7] With manner of articulation, a four-way distinction was made, contrasting stops (including affricates), fricatives, nasals, and /l/. Unlike with the preceding environment, the absence of a consonant was not an option in this analysis because /ɛ/ never occurs in word-final position. Finally, an additional factor was examined in relation to the following environment: the presence of a consonant cluster within the same syllable as the vowel. This factor was coded binarily for presence-versus-absence of such a cluster.

Two types of word-level effects were also investigated. One was based on the number of syllables in the word and distinguished items of one, two, three, and four or more syllables. The other involved the position of the syllable containing the (ɛ) token, indicating whether it was initial, medial, or final.[8] This factor was, of course, only relevant for words of at least two syllables, and monosyllabic items were excluded from this part of the analysis.

This information on the phonological factors investigated and the categories distinguished within them is summarized in table 3.2.

The possible conditioning effects of all these phonological factors were tested using data from a subsample of the speakers. The speakers selected were those found to be most active in the shifting of (ɛ) as measured by the usage indices (see §2.3.2). Though in theory the highest possible index was 3.000, in practice these indices were found to range from zero (indicating no shift-ing) to a high of just 0.667. The subsample included all those

TABLE 3.2
Phonological Factors Investigated

Factors	*Categories*
Preceding	
Voicing	Voiceless, voiced
Place	Labial, alveolar, interdental, palatal, velar, glottal
Manner	Stop, fricative, nasal, glide, /l/, /r/, #__ (initial position)
Following	
Voicing	Voiceless, voiced
Place	Labial, alveolar, interdental, palatal, velar
Manner	Stop, fricative, nasal, /l/
Cluster	Cluster, no cluster
Word level	
Number of syllables	1, 2, 3, 4+
Syllable postition	Initial, medial, final

speakers with an (ɛ) index of at least 0.200, as well as speaker JH (C, f, 16), who produced a sizable number of shifted tokens (12) but had an index score of only 0.142 due to the large total number of tokens recorded for her. In all, data from 11 speakers were considered. The decision to use only a subsample of the speakers was motivated by a concern that data from speakers with minimal (ɛ)-shifting might obscure patterns related to the phonological conditioning of this variable. The clearest picture should be found where the phonological conditioning has taken the best hold, that is, in the variation shown by the most active speakers.

The data from all speakers in the subsample were pooled together and sorted according to the phonological categories detailed above. An index of (ɛ)-shifting was calculated for each category by taking the average code of all the tokens that fit the phonological criterion. Thus, these indices measure the rate of shifting under particular phonological circumstances (e.g., following a labial consonant, preceding a nasal, in a disyllabic word). For this stage of the analysis, directional differences among the shifted items are not considered, and all tokens, whether backed lowered or both, are counted together. The question of the phonological conditioning of alternative trajectories is addressed below (§3.1.2.2).

Unlike for the general indices (see §2.3.2), the input data for this phonological analysis were all coded tokens; that is, the restriction of including only the first three occurrences of an item was not applied here. Underlying this decision was the goal of including as much relevant information as possible in the analysis. Because the shifting of (ε) is a fairly rare phenomenon, occurring at a rate of just 11.2% across the entire sample, information about the conditions promoting it is already in short supply. Discarding tokens simply because they were not among the initial three occurrences of a morpheme would reduce that supply even further. Suppose, for example, that a speaker produced ten tokens of the word *never* and that two of these tokens had a shifted vowel. The three-token restriction, if applied, would seriously skew the results here. If the two shifted tokens appeared among the first three, then the shifting rate for this particular item would be overestimated at about 67%. If the shifted tokens were not among the first three, then the shifting rate would be underestimated at 0%. More importantly in the latter case (which is statistically more likely to occur), two examples of (ε)-shifting would be omitted from the analysis and with them the information they provide about the phonological conditioning of the shift. The danger in lifting the three-token restriction is the same one that motivated its imposition in calculating the general indices, namely, the possibility of introducing lexical bias. However, the objective of this analysis is to uncover the linguistic factors conditioning the (ε) variation, and occurrence in a context that is defined lexically is as much a linguistic factor as occurrence in a context that is defined phonologically. Evidence of lexical bias would, therefore, be highly relevant and might, for example, suggest that the change is being spread by lexical diffusion.[9] For this reason, no limit was placed on the number of tokens included in the calculation of the phonologically separated indices.

The possibility of lexical effects being reflected in the data indicates that the phonological indices need to be approached with some caution. The following analysis is framed in terms of the phonological classification outlined above (table 3.2), thus, it uses the indices to describe the rates of vowel shifting found in particular phonological contexts. However, in some cases, the input data to the indices are more limited than their category labels suggest. For example, one of the categories distinguished with regard to place of articulation of preceding consonants was interdentals. In the case of (ɛ), the index for this category was calculated on the basis of 147 tokens; however, only two lexical items, *them* and *then*, were represented among these tokens. While it is possible that the index score for this category is indicative of a phonological effect (i.e., an effect of preceding interdentals), it is also possible that the effect is one characteristic of these particular lexical items. In addition, because the only interdental consonants in English are fricatives, it is also possible that the effect is related to this manner category. A wider variety of data will be needed to sort out these possibilities. For now, such alternative interpretations should be borne in mind when approaching the phonological analysis in this and the following chapter. Indices deriving from limited data sets are noted here, and their implications are discussed in more detail in chapter 5.

Turning now to the results, an overview of the patterns related to possible phonological conditioning of (ɛ) is provided in tables 3.3–5. The indices indicate the relative degree of shifting found for each of phonological categories analyzed and were calculated by pooling the data from all 11 of the speakers analyzed. Higher values correspond to increased amounts of shifting and, thus, are indicative of categories promoting the change. An overall index score measuring the rate of (ɛ)-shifting across all phonological environments was also calculated (at 0.317) and is included as a point of reference.

Many of the phonological categories compared in tables 3.3–5 seem to have little if any effect on the shifting of (ɛ). For example, the data in table 3.5 show almost no differentiation according to word length, with roughly the same amount of shifting found in words of one, two, or three syllables—and only slightly less found in words of four or more syllables. Similarly, the data on voicing of the following consonant (table 3.4) suggest that this feature does not play much of a conditioning role.

TABLE 3.3

Effects of Preceding Phonological Factors on (ε)-Shifting:
General Indices, Frequency of Shifting, and Chi-Square Results

	Index	Unshifted	Shifted	Total
Voicing ($\chi^2 = 12.01$; $p = .001$)				
Voiceless	0.313	272 (77.3%)	80 (22.7%)	352
Voiced	0.189	264 (87.7%)	37 (12.3%)	301
Place ($\chi^2 = 37.21$; $p < .0005$)				
Labial	0.352	247 (74.8%)	83 (25.2%)	330
Alveolar	0.338	399 (77.0%)	119 (23.0%)	518
Interdental	0.190	131 (89.1%)	16 (10.9%)	147
Palatal	0.122	37 (90.2%)	4 (9.8%)	41
Velar	0.143	54 (85.7%)	9 (14.3%)	63
Glottal	0.833	10 (41.7%)	14 (58.3%)	24
Manner ($\chi^2 = 19.55$; $p = .003$)				
Stop	0.250	252 (81.8%)	56 (18.2%)	308
Fricative	0.261	284 (82.3%)	61 (17.7%)	345
Nasal	0.289	101 (78.9%)	27 (21.1%)	128
Glide	0.416	110 (71.4%)	44 (28.6%)	154
/l/	0.622	23 (62.2%)	14 (37.8%)	37
/r/	0.411	108 (71.5%)	43 (28.5%)	151
#__	0.335	143 (78.6%)	39 (21.4%)	182
OVERALL	0.317			

On the other hand, such a role is evident in the findings for other phonological contexts. Thus, a good deal of variation is apparent among the data on place of articulation of the preceding consonant (table 3.3). Here, in the index of 0.833 associated with preceding glottals (i.e., /h/), we find the highest index score for any phonological category, while nearby we find the two lowest scores, the 0.122 associated with preceding palatals and the 0.143 of preceding velars. Similar, though less dramatic, differences are seen in the data on place and manner features of the following consonant (table 3.4). Environments such as following interdentals and /l/ have above-average index scores, while following palatals and nasals score below average.

The significance of the patterns suggested in tables 3.3–5 was assessed through a series of chi-square tests. This procedure tests

TABLE 3.4

Effects of Following Phonological Factors on (ɛ)-Shifting:
General Indices, Frequency of Shifting, and Chi-Square Results

	Index	*Unshifted*	*Shifted*	*Total*
Voicing ($\chi^2 = 0.17$; $p = .679$)				
Voiceless	0.315	305 (78.2%)	85 (21.8%)	390
Voiced	0.335	243 (76.9%)	73 (23.1%)	316
Place ($\chi^2 = 3.80$; $p = .434$)				
Labial	0.330	245 (77.8%)	70 (22.2%)	315
Alveolar	0.324	636 (77.8%)	182 (22.2%)	818
Interdental	0.444	12 (66.7%)	6 (33.3%)	18
Palatal	0.152	28 (84.8%)	5 (15.2%)	33
Velar	0.264	100 (82.6%)	21 (17.4%)	121
Manner ($\chi^2 = 27.46$; $p < .0005$)				
Stop	0.323	211 (78.4%)	58 (21.6%)	269
Fricative	0.325	337 (77.1%)	100 (22.9%)	437
Nasal	0.240	405 (83.2%)	82 (16.8%)	487
/l/	0.607	68 (60.7%)	44 (39.3%)	112
Cluster ($\chi^2 = 7.02$; $p = .008$)				
Cluster	0.387	212 (72.6%)	80 (27.4%)	292
No cluster	0.297	809 (79.9%)	204 (20.1%)	1,013
OVERALL	0.317			

TABLE 3.5

Effects of Word-Level Factors on (ɛ)-Shifting:
General Indices, Frequency of Shifting, and Chi-Square Results

	Index	*Unshifted*	*Shifted*	*Total*
Number of syllables ($\chi^2 = 0.72$; $p = .869$)				
1	0.322	478 (78.1%)	134 (21.9%)	612
2	0.325	276 (78.0%)	78 (22.0%)	354
3	0.320	207 (77.8%)	59 (22.2%)	266
4+	0.233	60 (82.2%)	13 (17.8%)	73
Syllable position ($\chi^2 = 4.73$; $p = .094$)				
Initial	0.356	352 (76.0%)	111 (24.0%)	463
Medial	0.216	136 (84.0%)	26 (16.0%)	162
Final	0.250	55 (80.9%)	13 (19.1%)	68
OVERALL	0.317			

for dependency between variables by comparing the frequencies with which each combination of variables was observed in the data with the frequencies that would be expected if the variables were independent.[10] In the present case, the tests examined the distribution of shifted tokens within each of the nine phonological factors investigated (voicing, place, and manner of preceding consonant; voicing, place, and manner of following consonant; following tautosyllabic cluster; number of syllables; and position of the token in the word). Thus, a significant chi-square result for a phonological factor indicates that the differences in the amount of shifting associated with the categories of that factor are greater than would be expected by chance. Statistical significance is defined here by an alpha level of .05, so that all p-values below this level are judged significant.

The data for the chi-square tests were the pooled results from the eleven speakers selected for the phonological analysis.[11] The number of tokens coded as shifted and the number coded as unshifted were calculated for each category within a phonological factor. Differences in the degree of shifting (i.e., whether the shifted token was coded as 1, 2, or 3) were ignored for the purposes of these tests in order to simplify the interpretation of results. If such differences were considered, this would introduce the possibility that a finding of statistical significance was due to an unexpected distribution among the shifted tokens rather than between the shifted and unshifted tokens. Tables 3.3–5 include the distributions of shifted and unshifted tokens and the results of the chi-square analysis.

As the data in table 3.3 indicate, the preceding consonant plays a key role in the conditioning of (ɛ)-shifting. Each of the three preceding factors (voicing, place, and manner of articulation) was shown to have a significant effect, a finding that confirms impressions of the variation suggested by the index data. Shifting is certainly favored by some phonological categories and disfavored by others, though it should be noted that the probability testing employed here does not evaluate the significance of individual categories. Nevertheless, in the case of the place factor, it seems clear that a preceding glottal /h/ favors shifting, while a preceding interdental, palatal, or velar disfavors it, and preceding labials and alveolars seem to have little effect either way.[12] Similar effects are evident in the data for the manner factor, where shifting is strongly favored by a preceding /l/, more weakly favored by a preceding glide or /r/, and slightly disfavored by preceding stops, fricatives and nasals, while almost no effect is shown by the absence of a preceding consonant.[13] Finally, in the case of the voicing factor, a preceding voiced obstruent appears to disfavor shifting significantly, while a voiceless one seems to have no effect (i.e., it neither favors nor disfavors shifting).

Among the factors associated with the following consonantal environment (see table 3.4), only the manner differences and those associated with the presence-versus-absence of a tautosyllabic cluster were shown to be significant. In the former case, it seems that a following /l/ strongly favors shifting, while a following nasal has the opposite effect, and stops and fricatives show little influence of either kind. In the case of the cluster factor, shifting appears to be promoted when such a cluster occurs, and slightly dispreferred when it is absent. Like those pertaining to the preceding factors, these results, too, were largely predictable from the index data, as was the finding that the voicing status of the following consonant has no significant effect on (ε)-shifting. More surprising were the results on place of articulation of the following consonant, as the differences for this factor turned out not to be significant. The reason for this result apparently lies with the small number of tokens available for the interdental ($N = 18$) and palatal ($N = 33$) categories, a fact which increases the probability of any observed differences being due to chance.

Neither of the word-level factors (table 3.5) was found to have a significant conditioning effect. Here again, the results were expected on the basis of the index data, which show almost no differentiation according to the number of syllables and very little according to the position of the vowel in the word.

The results on the phonological conditioning of (ε)-shifting are summarized in table 3.6. This table simply lists those phonological categories that have been judged to favor or disfavor shifting.

3.1.2.2. *Phonological Conditioning of Variant Trajectories of* (ε). In the preceding analysis, the multidirectionality in the (ε) variation was ignored, and all shifted variants (whether backed, lowered, or both) were treated together. This allowed for a relatively straightforward examination of the factors influencing (ε)-shifting. Still, the analysis would remain incomplete without consideration of the directional differences involved in the shifting. While some phonological contexts seem to promote all types of shifting, others may favor shifting in one direction and disfavor shifting in another. Such distinctions can provide important information about how the (ε) variation is conditioned.

As described above (§3.1.1), the shifting of (ε) involves two principal paths of movement, one leading to backing and the other to lowering. The coding scheme employed in this study distinguished variants along these paths as well as variants that seemed to fall between them, combining backing and lowering. As the results of this coding make clear, however, these directional differences are not equally represented in the data. By far the most common direction of shifting is backing, which accounted for roughly 73.7% of all shifted tokens of (ε), while just 20.1% were heard as lowered and 6.2% as both lowered and backed.[14] This

TABLE 3.6

Phonological Conditioning of (ε)-Shifting: Summary of Effects

Favor Shifting	Disfavor Shifting
PRECEDING GLOTTAL*	Preceding voiced
Preceding glide*	Preceding interdental*
PRECEDING /l/	PRECEDING PALATAL
Preceding /r/	PRECEDING VELAR
FOLLOWING /l/	Following nasal
Following cluster	

NOTE: Categories shown in small capitals strongly favored or disfavored shifting (i.e., their phonological index scores were greater than one standard deviation above or below the overall score). Those marked with asterisks are represented by a limited data set (see discussion in text here and in §5.1.2).

imbalance presents an analytic dilemma. While the less-common tendencies are clearly a key component of the (ε) variation and one apparently conditioned by both linguistic and social factors, the small number of tokens by which they are represented makes their quantitative analysis difficult. Nevertheless, some such analysis is possible, despite limitations, and can add important definition to the picture being drawn of the (ε) variation.

The conditioning of the different directions of (ε)-shifting was investigated using the same phonological factors as in the previous analysis (see table 3.2). Also as above, the data considered came from a subset of the speakers, the same subsample analyzed in the earlier discussion. Using these data, indices were calculated to measure the amount of shifting in each direction across the various phonological categories; that is, three separate indices (for backing, lowering, and combined backing-plus-lowering) were constructed for each category. These directional indices are shown in tables 3.7–9. As before, overall index scores were also calculated for each direction of shifting (backed = 0.215; lowered = 0.069; backed-plus-lowered = 0.028), and these are included as points of reference. Each index is followed by either a plus, minus, or equal sign, which indicates whether that score is higher, lower, or equal to the overall index.

An initial approach to these data can be made by considering the factors that seem to have the greatest influence (positive or negative) on each direction of shifting (i.e., those categories that generated directional indices lying outside of one standard deviation from the overall index for that direction).

We begin with backing, which is confirmed by these data to be the most common direction taken by the shifting (ε). As table 3.7 indicates, backing of this vowel is affected by several elements of its preceding context. A preceding glide (which here most often means /w/), /l/, or /r/ strongly favors backing, while a preceding palatal, velar, or stop has the opposite effect. The following environment (table 3.8) seems to exert less of an influence on backing, as only the favorable impact of following /l/ and the disfavoring impact of following velars are noteworthy. For the word-level factors, table 3.9 shows a bit more variability among the directional

TABLE 3.7
Effects of Preceding Phonological Factors on (ε)-Shifting:
General and Directional Indices

	General	Backed	Lowered	Backed-plus-Lowered
Voicing				
Voiceless	0.313 −	0.173 −	0.097 +	0.040 +
Voiced	0.189 −	0.130 −	0.043 −	0.010 −
Place				
Labial	0.352 +	0.248 +	0.076 +	0.024 −
Alveolar	0.338 +	0.245 +	0.071 +	0.017 −
Interdental	0.190 −	0.156 −	0.020 −	0.000 −
Palatal	0.122 −	0.122 −	0.000 −	0.000 −
Velar	0.143 −	0.016 −	0.079 +	0.048 +
Glottal	0.833 +	0.292 +	0.250 +	0.292 +
Manner				
Stop	0.250 −	0.127 −	0.101 +	0.019 −
Fricative	0.261 −	0.177 −	0.046 −	0.032 +
Nasal	0.289 −	0.133 −	0.156 +	0.000 −
Glide	0.416 +	0.364 +	0.006 −	0.039 +
/l/	0.622 +	0.459 +	0.108 +	0.054 +
/r/	0.411 +	0.364 +	0.026 −	0.013 −
#__	0.335 +	0.198 −	0.077 +	0.055 +
OVERALL	0.317	0.215	0.069	0.028

indices than was seen among the general indices (table 3.5). Backing appears to be disfavored in longer words (those of three or more syllables) and in medial and final syllables. Still, the indices associated with these effects are within a standard deviation of the overall score, suggesting that any conditioning role they play is relatively minor.

The lowering of (ε) is favored when a glottal (/h/) or a nasal appears in its preceding context and is disfavored by a palatal or glide in that same context (table 3.7). The following environment promotes lowering when it is occupied by a velar or an /l/, while palatals and nasals here have the opposite effect (table 3.8). As for the word-level factors (table 3.9), the lowering indices show even

TABLE 3.8
Effects of Following Phonological Factors on (ε)-Shifting:
General and Directional Indices

	General	Backed	Lowered	Backed-plus-Lowered
Voicing				
Voiceless	0.315 −	0.182 −	0.110 +	0.021 −
Voiced	0.335 +	0.228 +	0.066 −	0.041 +
Place				
Labial	0.330 +	0.213 −	0.073 +	0.038 +
Alveolar	0.324 +	0.236 +	0.056 −	0.028 =
Interdental	0.444 +	0.278 +	0.056 −	0.111 +
Palatal	0.152 −	0.152 −	0.000 −	0.000 −
Velar	0.264 −	0.091 −	0.165 +	0.000 −
Manner				
Stop	0.323 +	0.182 −	0.112 +	0.026 −
Fricative	0.325 +	0.215 =	0.078 +	0.032 +
Nasal	0.240 −	0.203 −	0.018 −	0.010 −
/l/	0.607 +	0.348 +	0.152 +	0.098 +
Cluster				
Cluster	0.387 +	0.291 +	0.051 −	0.034 +
No cluster	0.297 −	0.193 −	0.074 +	0.027 −
OVERALL	0.317	0.215	0.069	0.028

TABLE 3.9
Effects of Word-Level Factors on (ε)-Shifting:
General and Directional Indices

	General	Backed	Lowered	Backed-plus-Lowered
Number of syllables				
1	0.322 +	0.227 +	0.054 −	0.033 +
2	0.325 +	0.240 +	0.068 −	0.014 −
3	0.320 +	0.169 −	0.109 +	0.041 +
4+	0.233 −	0.164 −	0.055 −	0.014 −
Syllable position				
Initial	0.356 +	0.240 +	0.091 +	0.024 −
Medial	0.216 −	0.130 −	0.062 −	0.025 −
Final	0.250 −	0.147 −	0.074 +	0.029 +
OVERALL	0.317	0.215	0.069	0.028

less variation than did the backing indices and, thus, give no indication of any conditioning effects.

The indices for the combined backing and lowering tendency reflect the relative infrequency of these variants. Only three categories were found to occasion exceptional indices: preceding glottal, following interdental, and following /l/, all of which promote shifting in this direction. It is more difficult to determine which factors disfavor this type of shifting. Indices of zero are found for many phonological contexts, including preceding interdentals, palatals, and nasals, and following palatals and velars, though even these are within one standard deviation of the overall index of 0.028.

It is clear from this discussion as well as from tables 3.7–9 that, while the effects of some phonological categories are consistent across the three directions of shifting, many categories show variable influences. For example, a preceding glottal was found to promote shifting in all directions. A preceding glide (mostly /w/), on the other hand, is shown to favor shifting in one direction (backing) but disfavor it in another (lowering). The significance of such patterns was investigated using chi-square testing of the distributions of the directional variants across each phonological factor. These distributions and the statistical results are given in tables 3.10–12.

Due to the small input numbers available for many of the cells, a number of adjustments to these tables had to be made in order to achieve reliable test results. The most common strategy was to collapse the directional distinctions from three to two, combining the lowered tokens with the backed-plus-lowered tokens. This grouping seems justified, given that these tendencies are both much less common than backing and that they show similar effects from a number of phonological categories. Also, in testing the significance of the place factors for both the preceding and following consonant it was necessary to combine the tokens for the interdentals and palatals. In the preceding context, these sounds have the same disfavoring effect on shifting, though in the context following the vowel their effects are more variable (see table 3.8). This possible confounding of influences may help explain why the significance level was not as great in the latter case ($p = .022$).

The data in these tables are meant to identify factors that have significantly differential effects on the relationship between backing, lowering, and backing-plus-lowering for (ɛ). They provide an important complement to those offered earlier (tables 3.3–5), which identified factors having a significant impact on shifting in general. By way of concluding the discussion on the conditioning of (ɛ), we will consider both sets of results in a brief examination of each of the factors.

I will begin by considering the effects of voicing. In the preceding context, this factor was found to have a significant effect on shifting in general (table 3.3), with innovative variants disfavored

TABLE 3.10
Effects of Preceding Phonological Factors on Direction of (ɛ)-Shifting

	Backed	*Lowered*	*Backed-plus-Lowered*	*Total Shifted*
Voicing ($\chi^2 = 0.27$; $p = .873$)				
Voiceless	48 (60.0%)	24 (30.0%)	8 (10.0%)	80
Voiced	24 (64.9%)	10 (27.0%)	3 (8.1%)	37
Place ($\chi^2 = 29.36$; $p < .0005$)				
Labial	63 (75.9%)	16 (19.3%)	4 (4.8%)	83
Alveolar	88 (73.9%)	25 (21.0%)	6 (5.0%)	119
Interdental	14 (87.5%)	2 (12.5%)	0 (0.0%)	16
Palatal	4 (100%)	0 (0.0%)	0 (0.0%)	4
Velar	1 (11.1%)	5 (55.6%)	3 (33.3%)	9
Glottal	5 (35.7%)	5 (35.7%)	4 (28.6%)	14
Manner ($\chi^2 = 30.52$; $p < .0005$)				
Stop	29 (51.8%)	22 (39.3%)	5 (8.9%)	56
Fricative	43 (70.5%)	12 (19.7%)	6 (9.8%)	61
Nasal	14 (51.9%)	13 (48.1%)	0 (0.0%)	27
Glide	40 (90.9%)	1 (2.3%)	3 (6.8%)	44
/l/	11 (78.6%)	2 (14.3%)	1 (7.1%)	14
/r/	38 (88.4%)	3 (7.0%)	2 (4.7%)	43
#__	25 (64.1%)	7 (17.9%)	7 (17.9%)	39

NOTE: The lowered and backed-plus-lowered tokens were combined in the test for place and manner. In the test for place, the categories of interdental and palatal were combined.

TABLE 3.11

Effects of Following Phonological Factors on Direction of (ε)-Shifting

	Backed	Lowered	Backed-plus-Lowered	Total Shifted
Voicing ($\chi^2 = 6.90$; $p = .032$)				
Voiceless	51 (60.0%)	29 (34.1%)	5 (5.9%)	85
Voiced	50 (68.5%)	13 (17.8%)	10 (13.7%)	73
Place ($\chi^2 = 9.67$; $p = .022$)				
Labial	47 (67.1%)	15 (21.4%)	8 (11.4%)	70
Alveolar	136 (74.7%)	32 (17.6%)	14 (7.7%)	182
Interdental	3 (50.0%)	1 (16.7%)	2 (33.3%)	6
Palatal	5 (100%)	0 (0.0%)	0 (0.0%)	5
Velar	9 (42.9%)	12 (57.1%)	0 (0.0%)	21
Manner ($\chi^2 = 23.83$; $p = .001$)				
Stop	34 (58.6%)	20 (34.5%)	4 (6.9%)	58
Fricative	67 (67.0%)	22 (22.0%)	11 (11.0%)	100
Nasal	73 (89.0%)	6 (7.3%)	3 (3.7%)	82
/l/	26 (59.1%)	12 (27.3%)	6 (13.6%)	44
Cluster ($\chi^2 = 4.96$; $p = .084$)				
Cluster	64 (80.0%)	11 (13.8%)	5 (6.3%)	80
No cluster	136 (66.7%)	49 (24.0%)	19 (9.3%)	204

NOTE: The lowered and backed-plus-lowered tokens were combined in the test for place, as were the interdental and palatal categories.

by a preceding voiced obstruent. This conservative impact was consistent regardless of the direction of shifting, as all three directional indices were below normal (i.e., the overall scores). The effects of a preceding voiceless obstruent were less consistent, as this context was found to disfavor backing, though it slightly favored the other two directions, which led to a general index (0.313) that nearly matched the overall score (0.317). Still, the directional differences were below the level of statistical significance (table 3.10). The situation was reversed in the results on voicing of the following consonant. Here the general indices showed no significant differences (table 3.4), while the directional distribution was significant (table 3.11). As table 3.8 indicates, the latter finding is due to the effects on lowering, particularly to the fact

TABLE 3.12

Effects of Word-Level Factors on Direction of (ɛ)-Shifting

	Backed	Lowered	Backed-plus-Lowered	Total Shifted
Number of syllables (χ^2 = 6.14; p = .105)				
1	98 (73.1%)	24 (17.9%)	12 (9.0%)	134
2	59 (75.6%)	16 (20.5%)	3 (3.8%)	78
3	34 (57.6%)	17 (28.8%)	8 (13.6%)	59
4+	9 (69.2%)	3 (23.1%)	1 (7.7%)	13
Syllable position (χ^2 = 0.10; p = .950)				
Initial	76 (68.5%)	27 (24.3%)	8 (7.2%)	111
Medial	17 (65.4%)	6 (23.1%)	3 (11.5%)	26
Final	9 (69.2%)	3 (23.1%)	1 (7.7%)	13

NOTE: The lowered and backed-plus-lowered tokens were combined in both tests.

that a following voiceless consonant, promotes lowering while having the opposite effect on the other directions of shifting. Conversely, a following voiced obstruent generally favors shifting except for lowering which is slightly disfavored in this context.

Similar effects are evident in the data on place of articulation of the preceding consonant where the distributions of both the general and directional indices were found to be highly significant. The influence of some categories is consistent across all directions of change. This was most clear in the case of preceding glottals (/h/), which greatly favored shifting of all types. Though less dramatic, the effects of preceding labials and alveolars were also fairly consistently favorable toward shifting (with the minor exception of shifting in the combined backed and lowered direction). On the other hand, consistently unfavorable effects were shown by preceding interdentals and palatals (the latter serving as a very strong demoter of shifting). The remaining category, preceding velar, seems to have variable influences. Its general index (0.143) suggests that it strongly disfavors shifting, but the directional indices reveal that this effect only pertains to backing, as shifting in the other two directions is actually favored (albeit slightly) in this environment.

Some of the most extreme divergences are seen among the indices conditioned by manner of the preceding consonant. The general indices show shifting to be strongly favored following a glide, /l/, and /r/ very slightly favored in initial position and disfavored following a stop, fricative, or nasal. Only in the cases of fricatives, /l/, and initial position, however, do the environments have consistent effects, a fact reflected in the highly significant chi-square result (table 3.10). With stops and especially nasals, for example, the generally conservative tendencies do not hold with regard to lowering. Similarly, the favoring of shifting seen with glides and /r/ seems pretty clearly to apply primarily to backing, as lowering in these contexts is disfavored (strongly so following glides).

The following context appears to have a much less clear effect. With regard to place of articulation of the following consonant, for example, the labial and alveolar categories show a mix of favoring and disfavoring effects across the indices, though all differ only slightly from their respective overall indices. Largely consistent effects are seen with following interdentals and palatals, though the former favors shifting and the latter disfavors it. As was the case in the preceding context, the velar category shows contradictory tendencies: strongly favoring lowering and strongly disfavoring the other directions of shifting. This example highlights the value of considering the conditioning of the different directions. The general index for this category (0.264) was fairly unremarkable, but the directional indices make it clear that this stems from a combination of strong countervailing tendencies.

The results on manner of articulation of the following consonant show great consistency across the indices. There is some variability among the effects of stops and fricatives, but it is relatively minor. Furthermore, the disfavoring effect of following nasals holds for all directions of shifting, as does the favoring effect of following /l/. The latter appears to be highly significant as it resulted in overwhelmingly high indices for each of the three directions.

The data on the influence of a following tautosyllabic cluster are also fairly consistent. For the most part, shifting is favored when such a cluster is present and slightly disfavored otherwise. The lowering data show the opposite patterning, though in both cases (with and without a cluster) the effects are slight.

The word-level factors (as has been noted above and con-firmed by the chi-square results) seem to play little role in the conditioning of (ε). The indices vary, but all remain within one standard deviation of expectations.

The analysis presented here has investigated the phonological conditioning of the (ε) variation. A variety of phonological factors were considered, and their effects on vowel shifting (both in general and in particular directions) were measured and evalu-ated. The results of this analysis represent an important part of the present account of the (ε) variation, though the account would remain incomplete without considering nonlinguistic factors. This task is taken up in §3.1.3.

3.1.3. SOCIAL DISTRIBUTION OF (ε). I examined the extent to which linguistic behavior for the (ε) variants correlates with those social factors for which the sample of speakers was stratified: town (Paw Paw, Chelsea), age (adult, adolescent), and sex (male, female). For the primary quantitative analysis, linguistic behavior is measured by the general indices for (ε), which indicate the degree to which a speaker shifts the vowel in any direction (backed, lowered, backed-plus-lowered); however, the later discussion also considers the social conditioning of the directional differences in (ε)-shifting.

3.1.3.1. *Social Aspects of General* (ε)*-Shifting.* A comparison of speak-ers according to their use of (ε) is provided in figure 3.2. Above each of the eight category labels that appear along the horizontal axis are four dots representing the data points for each of the four speakers who fit that category.[15]

A number of interesting patterns are suggested by the distribu-tion of scores in figure 3.2. The generally downward slope of the points from left to right across the graph indicates differences in each of the three social parameters examined. The clearest separa-tion seems to be along the geographic lines that divide Paw Paw and Chelsea, as innovative use of (ε) appears to be much more common among Paw Paw speakers. It is important to note, how-

FIGURE 3.2

Indices for the Shifting of (ε) across the Sample of Speakers

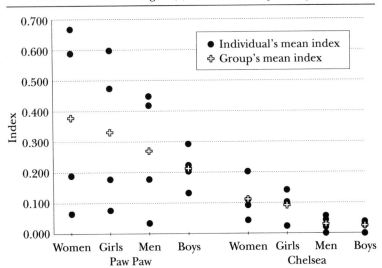

ever, the tremendous dispersal of the Paw Paw data. Except for the boys, each of the Paw Paw groups pairs two exceptionally high indices with two that are closer to average. Still, even these lower scores exceed many of those shown for Chelsea speakers.

Sex-based differences are also apparent, with females generally showing higher indices than males. This distinction is particularly clear among Chelsea speakers, though these scores are overall much lower than those of Paw Paw speakers.

As for differences between the age groups, the situation appears more complicated. A simple comparison of all adults and all adolescents does not reveal much of a distinction. However, when generational differences are considered within the context of the other social factors, the pattern seems quite clear. The indices of adults are generally higher than those of adolescents, as can be seen by pairwise comparisons of the women and girls or the men and boys in each town. This finding comes as a surprise, given that the shifting of (ε) is supposed to be a change in progress and, thus, is expected to be more frequent among younger speakers. The implications of these results are explored below (§5.2.3).

Before investigating these patterns further, it is necessary to establish that they are indeed socially defined. Given the indications that the (ε) variation is conditioned by a number of phonological factors (§3.1.2), it is reasonable to question whether these factors could have played a role in determining the distribution seen here. Perhaps the differences among the indices in figure 3.2 reflect differences in the representation of the key conditioning factors in the words from which the indices are calculated. A speaker whose index is constructed on the basis of an unusually high number of words containing, for example, a following /l/ would naturally score higher than one whose index derived from an unusually high number of words with following palatals. Fortunately, the procedures for calculating the indices incorporated measures to help prevent such bias (see §2.3.1). The large number of tokens coded for each speaker—averaging over 90 for (ε)—combined with the restriction of counting only three occurrences of any lexical item helped ensure that the indices were based on a wide variety of words, and hence upon a wide variety of phonological contexts.

To demonstrate the effectiveness of these measures, a comparison was made of the frequencies with which certain key phonological categories occurred in the data sets of various speakers. The representation of six phonological factors shown above to favor the shifting of (ε) and three factors shown to disfavor shifting was examined for six speakers. The speakers chosen were those with the three highest and the three lowest (ε) indices. The results of this comparison are shown in table 3.13. The data on the individual phonological environments show a good deal of variation, but this variation does not appear to be correlated with the rates of shifting. The same holds for the summary data that indicate the overall frequencies of favoring and disfavoring environments for each speaker. Thus, speaker TM, who had the highest (ε) index in the entire sample, used words containing environments favoring shifting at a rate of 42.9% and words containing disfavoring environments at a rate of 14.3%, while speaker PF, whose (ε) index shows no shifting, used words with favoring environments at a rate of 47.6% and those with disfavoring environments at a rate of

TABLE 3.13

Rates of Occurrence of Phonological Environments That Favor
or Disfavor (ɛ)-Shifting in the Data Sets of Six Speakers

	TM	MN	KH	PF	KF	JF
(ɛ) Index	0.667	0.597	0.589	0.000	0.000	0.020
Favoring Contexts						
Preceding glottal	0.0%	1.4%	3.2%	0.0%	4.1%	2.0%
Preceding glide	20.6%	15.3%	13.7%	12.4%	16.3%	13.7%
Preceding /l/	5.0%	1.0%	6.0%	10.0%	5.0%	5.0%
Preceding /r/	11.0%	10.0%	7.0%	15.0%	7.0%	12.0%
Following interdental	3.2%	1.4%	5.3%	0.0%	0.0%	4.9%
Following /l/	7.9%	13.9%	11.6%	10.5%	10.2%	14.7%
ALL FAVORING	42.9%	37.5%	41.1%	47.6%	36.7%	48.0%
Disfavoring Contexts						
Preceding palatal	7.9%	1.4%	5.3%	5.7%	9.2%	7.8%
Preceding velar	6.3%	4.2%	3.3%	4.8%	3.1%	2.9%
Following palatal	0.0%	1.4%	4.2%	2.9%	1.0%	1.0%
ALL DISFAVORING	14.3%	6.9%	14.7%	13.3%	13.3%	11.8%

NOTE: Percentages include all tokens counted for each speaker.

13.3%. These results suggest very strongly that the general indices are unlikely to reflect any bias from phonological conditioning.

Having effectively ruled out the possibility that linguistic factors can account for the distribution shown in figure 3.2, we return to a consideration of social influences. The patterns that were sketched above are examined further with the data in figure 3.3. This graph compares mean index scores for the three social factors investigated. For each factor, a pairwise comparison of the means across the entire sample is shown (i.e., Paw Paw vs. Chelsea, adults vs. adolescents, females vs. males). It is clear, however, that the most dramatic difference is between the two towns, and so the age and sex data are subdivided to allow for separate comparisons within each town.

These mean data confirm the observations made on the basis of the individually plotted scores (fig. 3.2). Thus, generally speaking, Paw Paw speakers show a much greater degree of shifting than Chelsea speakers, adults show more than adolescents, and females

FIGURE 3.3
Mean (ɛ) Indices Comparing Social Factors: Town, Age, and Sex

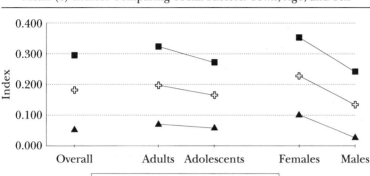

show more than males. Importantly, these generalizations hold regardless of how the data are subdivided. In each town, for example, older speakers lead younger speakers and females lead males.

The significance of these tendencies was investigated statistically through a multiway analysis of variance (ANOVA). This test examines the variation in the dependent variable—the (ɛ) indices—to determine the influence of independent variables—the speaker factors—acting individually or in combination. The results of this analysis are given in table 3.14. The only factor identified as

TABLE 3.14
Multiway ANOVA Results for Social Factors in (ɛ) Variation

Factor	F	df	p-value
Town	17.56	1, 24	<.0005
Age	0.34	1, 24	.565
Sex	2.82	1, 24	.106
Town × Age	0.13	1, 24	.726
Town × Sex	0.13	1, 24	.726
Sex × Age	0.00	1, 24	.988
Town × Age × Sex	0.01	1, 24	.906

Multiple r = .683; multiple r^2 = .466.

significant (and very highly so with $p < .0005$) by this analysis is town, which confirms the overwhelming separation of the Paw Paw and Chelsea indices. In addition, the result for the sex factor ($p = .106$), while not statistically significant, is suggestive of a trend and supports the suggestion that the female lead over males is a characteristic of the (ε) distribution.

The failure to produce statistically significant results may seem surprising, given the clear differences associated with the factors as illustrated in figure 3.3. However, it should be noted that procedures like ANOVA are very sensitive to sample size. Because the sample of speakers in this study is, by statistical standards, small, any differences conditioned by a factor need to be rather dramatic to achieve significance. For this reason, the negative results in table 3.14 should not be interpreted as disproving the possibility that use of (ε) is related to such factors as age and sex. Rather, they should be taken as indicating a need for more data to verify the patterns suggested by the distributions of the individual and mean indices (figs. 3.2 and 3.3).

3.1.3.2. *Social Distribution of Variant Trajectories of* (ε). The preceding analysis has explored the social aspects of (ε)-shifting in general without considering the different directions taken by the shifting vowel. However, as was demonstrated during the investigation of phonological factors, examination of these differences can add definition to the picture being drawn of the (ε) variation, and, so, I turn now to such an examination.

A view of the social distribution of the directional variants of (ε) is provided by table 3.15. This table details the use of the three directions of shifting by each of eight categories of speakers. The figures next to each category label indicate how many of the shifted tokens used by those speakers were backed, lowered, or both. Shown are the number of tokens and the percentage they represent of the total number of shifted tokens for those speakers.[16] Also given are summary data, which combine Paw Paw and Chelsea speakers to allow for a four-way comparison of women, men, girls, and boys.

Not surprisingly, these data largely reflect the same asymmetries discussed above, namely, Paw Paw leading Chelsea, females

TABLE 3.15
Distribution of Directional Variants of (ε) by Social Factors

	Backed	*Lowered*	*Backed-plus-Lowered*	*Total Shifted*
Females				
Adults				
Paw Paw	63 (74.1%)	13 (15.3%)	9 (10.6%)	85
Chelsea	18 (64.3%)	10 (35.7%)	0 (0.0%)	28
TOTAL	81 (71.7%)	23 (20.4%)	9 (8.0%)	113
Adolescents				
Paw Paw	29 (45.3%)	28 (43.8%)	7 (10.9%)	64
Chelsea	15 (60.0%)	9 (36.0%)	1 (4.0%)	25
TOTAL	44 (49.4%)	37 (41.6%)	8 (9.0%)	89
TOTAL	125 (61.9%)	60 (29.7%)	17 (8.4%)	202
Males				
Adults				
Paw Paw	62 (98.4%)	1 (1.6%)	0 (0.0%)	63
Chelsea	8 (100%)	0 (0.0%)	0 (0.0%)	8
TOTAL	70 (98.6%)	1 (1.4%)	0 (0.0%)	71
Adolescents				
Paw Paw	36 (85.7%)	3 (7.1%)	3 (7.1%)	42
Chelsea	7 (87.5%)	1 (12.5%)	0 (0.0%)	8
TOTAL	43 (86.0%)	4 (8.0%)	3 (6.0%)	50
TOTAL	113 (93.4%)	5 (4.1%)	3 (2.5%)	121

leading males, adults leading adolescents. However, they also show a new dimension to these asymmetries, suggesting the use of variant trajectories is related to social factors. The most obvious example of this is seen in the sex-based differences. Comparing the two halves of table 3.15, it is clear that, while males overwhelming prefer backing to the other directions of change, females tend to employ a broader range of variants. In fact, of the 85 lowered and backed-plus-lowered tokens, only 8 were produced by male speakers.

Given this imbalance, we may question the generality of the previously described female lead in (ε)-shifting. Indeed, it instead appears to be the case that males and females show roughly the same amount of backing of this vowel, and it is only the dramatic differentiation in the use of the other directions that results in the overall female lead. A comparison of the amount of backing shown by each sex can be made by recalculating data from table 3.15 as percentages of the total number of all tokens, not just of the shifted tokens (these totals are not shown in the table). Thus, the backed tokens produced by women constitute 11.5% (81/706) of all items coded for this group, and those produced by men constitute 9.3% (70/754) of their items. Similarly, the backed tokens produced by girls represent 6.3% (44/697) of their total, and those produced by boys represent 5.9% (43/730) of all their items. If we combine these data across age groups, we see that backing was found among females at a rate of 8.9% while the rate for males was 7.6%. Thus, whether males and females are compared within generations or across the entire sample, they show roughly equivalent amounts of backing of (ε). Therefore, any sex-based difference in the use of this variable appears to be due primarily to female-led shifting in the other directions.

The data in table 3.15 also elaborate the pattern noted earlier regarding the age factor. Whereas the distribution of the general indices (fig. 3.2) suggested (ε)-shifting was slightly more common among adults than adolescents, this appears to hold only for backing of the vowel. The other directions of shifting are utilized more frequently in the repertoires of the younger speakers. Lowering, for example, accounts for nearly 41.6% of the shifted tokens used by girls but only 20.3% of those used by women. The pattern is the same among males, though the numbers are much smaller (8.0% for boys, 1.4% for men). Moreover, this generational difference holds in the absolute rates of use of the directional variants. While the backing rates given in the preceding paragraph show adults leading adolescents (11.5% for women, 6.3% for girls; 9.3% for men, 5.9% for boys), the rates for the other directions indicate the opposite tendency. Thus, excluding the backed variants, women shifted at a rate of 4.5% (32/706), but girls shifted at a rate of 6.5% (45/697). The boys shifted (ε) in directions other than backing in only 1.0% of their tokens (7/730); still, this was much more than the men, who, except for a lone token of lowered (ε), made no use of other directions (1/754 = 0.1%). When the male and female data are combined, adults are found to use lowered or combined backed-plus-lowered variants at a rate of 2.3% (33/1,460), while adolescents use these forms at a rate of 3.6% (52/1,427). Though the differences are small, they are important to note because they run counter to the general tendency.

As was the case in the analysis of phonological factors, consideration of the differing distributions of the variant trajectories of (ε) has provided a new perspective on the social dimensions of the variation. These issues will be taken up again in chapter 5, which considers the results discussed here for (ε) along with those for the other vowels, which are presented in the remainder of this chapter and in the next. The presentation for these other variables will follow the pattern established for (ε).

3.2. THE VARIABLE (ɪ)

3.2.1. PHONETIC DESCRIPTION OF THE VARIATION. As noted earlier (§1.4.1), most of the previous research on the NCS has described the movement of (ɪ) as one of lowering toward [ε] (Labov, Yaeger, and Steiner 1972; Labov 1994). In recent work, however, Labov has modified his description, indicating that the lowering is often accompanied by centralization as well (Labov 1997). This combined lowering-plus-backing results in schwa-like pronunciations. I find evidence for both of these directional tendencies in the present study, together with indications of a third, in which the vowel is backed (centralized) without significant lowering and results in a vowel near [ɨ]. With these directional variants the (ɪ) pattern of shifting shows a remarkable parallel to that of (ε).

In coding the (ɪ) data, differences in the degree and trajectory of shifting were noted. The coding scheme distinguished two degrees of shifting in each of the three directions. Approximate phonetic representations of the variants coded are provided in table 3.16.

An acoustic representation of the (ɪ) variation is offered in figure 3.4. This diagram plots tokens of (ɪ) in a vowel space defined by the first and second formants. The tokens were produced by

TABLE 3.16

Coded Variants of (ɪ)

	0	1	2
Backed	[ɪ]	[ɪ˃]	[ɨ˂]
Lowered	[ɪ]	[ɪᵛ]	[ɛ^]
Backed-plus-lowered	[ɪ]	[ɪ˅]	[ʌ²]

FIGURE 3.4

F1 and F2 Frequencies for Tokens of (ɪ) Produced by TM (PP, f, 41)

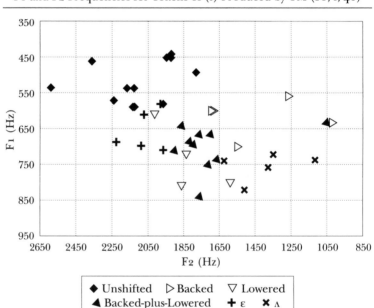

speaker TM (PP, f, 41), the same subject whose data were represented in figure 3.1. As was the case for (ɛ), TM was found to be among the most active of all speakers in her shifting of (ɪ) and demonstrated use of all three variant trajectories. The tokens of (ɪ) represented in figure 3.4 occurred in conversational (unscripted) speech. Also shown, to serve as reference points, are conservative tokens of /ɛ/ and /ʌ/, some of which are taken from TM's reading of the word list.

The instrumentally derived picture of the (i) variation largely confirms the auditory-based description given above. There is a loosely defined group of conservative tokens in the upper left portion of the diagram, and radiating out from this group in a generally diagonal direction are the shifted tokens. Even among the conservative tokens, there is only a short acoustic distance between /ı/ and /ɛ/ (at least in terms of F1 and F2), and lowering brings (i) well within the neighborhood of [ɛ], just as the combined lowering and backing brings (i) to the doorstep of [ʌ]. It should be noted again here, as it was in the case of (ε), that there are no clear boundaries separating the three directions of shifting; rather, the tokens fan out in a continuum from backed to lowered.

3.2.2. PHONOLOGICAL CONDITIONING OF (i). The issue of phonological conditioning is again approached in two stages. The first considers the influence of phonological factors on (i)-shifting in general, while the second explores the conditioning of the variant directions of shifting.

3.2.2.1. *General Conditioning of* (i). Evidence of phonological conditioning in the shifting of (i) was investigated using the procedures outlined above (§3.1.2.1). The same phonological categories (see table 3.2) were tested using data from a subsample of the most active users of this variable. Ten speakers were selected for this analysis. Five of these speakers had also served in the subsample for the (ε) analysis.

General indices of (i)-shifting were calculated for each of the phonological categories by pooling the data from the subsample of speakers. These indices are shown in tables 3.17–19, where, once again, index scores are give for the influence of preceding factors (table 3.17), following factors (table 3.18), and word-level factors (table 3.19). Also shown in each figure is the overall index (0.149) which indicates the degree of shifting across all phonological contexts.

One of the first things to note about the shifting of (i) is its relative infrequency compared with (ε)-shifting. The overall index of 0.149 is less than half the 0.317 found for (ε). Low numbers of shifted tokens presented difficulties in the analysis of (ε), and such

TABLE 3.17
Effects of Preceding Phonological Factors on (1)-Shifting:
General Indices, Frequency of Shifting, and Chi-Square Results

	Index	Unshifted	Shifted	Total
Voicing ($\chi^2 = 0.90$; $p = .334$)				
Voiceless	0.212	279 (84.5%)	51 (15.5%)	330
Voiced	0.174	316 (87.1%)	47 (12.9%)	363
Place ($\chi^2 = 24.06$; $p < .0005$)				
Labial	0.179	262 (85.6%)	44 (14.4%)	306
Alveolar	0.238	385 (84.4%)	71 (15.6%)	456
Interdental	0.073	39 (95.1%)	2 (4.9%)	41
Palatal	0.423	16 (61.5%)	10 (38.5%)	26
Velar	0.303	78 (78.8%)	21 (21.2%)	99
Glottal	0.049	59 (96.7%)	2 (3.3%)	61
Manner ($\chi^2 = 123.93$; $p < .0005$)				
Stop	0.223	391 (83.2%)	79 (16.8%)	470
Fricative	0.126	204 (91.5%)	19 (8.5%)	223
Nasal	0.239	39 (84.8%)	7 (15.2%)	46
Glide	0.084	91 (95.8%)	4 (4.2%)	95
/l/	0.489	60 (65.2%)	32 (35.8%)	92
/r/	0.222	54 (85.7%)	9 (14.3%)	63
#__	0.024	496 (98.2%)	9 (1.8%)	505
OVERALL	0.149			

difficulties can be expected again in the present case. Nevertheless, there are robust patterns in the data as suggested by these figures.

From the data in table 3.17 the conditioning influence of a number of preceding contexts is evident. For the place factor, shifting is strongly favored by a preceding palatal or velar and strongly disfavored by a preceding glottal (/h/). However, it should be noted that the index for each of these categories is based on a rather limited range of lexical items. Most (75/99) of the velar examples were found in the item *kid(s)*, while many (11/26) of the palatal tokens were in *children*, and most of the glottal cases (56/61) occurred in either *him* or *his*. A better lexical mix contributed to the index for preceding alveolars, which were also found to favor

TABLE 3.18
Effects of Following Phonological Factors on (ɪ)-Shifting:
General Indices, Frequency of Shifting, and Chi-Square Results

	Index	*Unshifted*	*Shifted*	*Total*
Voicing (χ^2 = 1.74; p = .188)				
Voiceless	0.157	585 (88.9%)	73 (11.1%)	658
Voiced	0.196	383 (86.3%)	61 (13.7%)	444
Place (χ^2 = 14.45; p = .006)				
Labial	0.233	156 (82.5%)	33 (17.5%)	189
Alveolar	0.140	972 (90.3%)	105 (9.7%)	1,077
Interdental	0.038	51 (98.1%)	1 (1.9%)	52
Palatal	0.122	43 (87.8%)	6 (12.2%)	49
Velar	0.157	113 (89.0%)	14 (11.0%)	127
Manner (χ^2 = 23.81; p < .0005)				
Stop	0.195	574 (86.8%)	87 (13.2%)	661
Fricative	0.138	394 (89.3%)	47 (10.7%)	441
Nasal	0.045	297 (96.4%)	11 (3.6%)	308
/l/	0.226	70 (83.3%)	14 (16.7%)	84
Cluster (χ^2 = 23.08; p < .0005)				
Cluster	0.298	149 (79.3%)	39 (20.7%)	188
No cluster	0.128	1,186 (90.8%)	120 (9.2%)	1,306
OVERALL	0.149			

TABLE 3.19
Effects of Word-Level Factors on (ɪ)-Shifting:
General Indices, Frequency of Shifting, and Chi-Square Results

	Index	*Unshifted*	*Shifted*	*Total*
Number of syllables (χ^2 = 16.66; p = .001)				
1	0.122	882 (91.8%)	79 (8.2%)	961
2	0.205	360 (84.9%)	64 (15.1%)	424
3	0.188	68 (85.0%)	12 (15.0%)	80
4+	0.138	25 (86.2%)	4 (13.8%)	29
Syllable position (χ^2 = 8.77; p = .012)				
Initial	0.181	386 (86.2%)	62 (13.8%)	448
Medial	0.221	63 (81.8%)	14 (18.2%)	77
Final	1.000	4 (50.0%)	4 (50.0%)	8
OVERALL	0.149			

shifting, though less strongly than the velar and palatal categories. Finally, preceding interdentals are seen to disfavor shifting, though, again, this effect may be lexical, as all 41 items contributing to the index were tokens of *this*.

For the manner factor, the most dramatic effects are seen when (1) is preceded by an /l/, which promotes shifting, and when it occurs in initial position (i.e., #__), which disfavors shifting.[17] A preceding stop, nasal, or /r/ seems to have a mildly positive influence on shifting, while a preceding fricative or glide (here represented solely by /w/) has a slightly disfavoring influence. The voicing status of the preceding obstruent does not appear to have much of an impact on shifting. Shifting is slightly more common following a voiceless segment, though even the shifting following a voiced obstruent is higher than usual.

The factors of the context following the vowel (table 3.18) show less extreme differences across categories. For the place factor, following alveolars, palatals, and velars appear to have little effect. Following labials favor shifting, but the only really strong influence seems to be the one found with following interdentals, which disfavor shifting, yet this result is based solely on tokens of the item *with(in)*. Another strongly disfavoring context is seen with following nasals, while among the other manner categories, shifting is slightly favored by a following stop or /l/, and a following fricative has little effect.[18] As in the preceding context, voicing does not appear to play a significant role, though with what minor difference there is, it is the voiced obstruents that show the lead over voiceless. Finally, shifting is clearly favored by a following tautosyllabic cluster, though the absence of such a cluster does not have a comparable negative effect on shifting.

With one obvious exception, the word-level categories do not show much differentiation. The number of syllables in a word appears to have only a minor influence on shifting, favoring in the case of two- and three-syllable words and very slightly disfavoring in the other two categories. For the position factor, all three choices seem to favor shifting, though the index for the final syllable category dwarfs the others. This apparent difference may, however, not be reliable, as the index is based on only eight tokens.

The statistical significance of the patterns suggested was examined using chi-square testing. As before, the tests were used to evaluate the distribution of the shifted-versus-unshifted tokens within each of the nine phonological factors. These distributions and the chi-square results are also provided in tables 3.17–19.

These statistical results largely confirm the observations suggested by the indices. All but the two voicing factors showed significant differentiation among their categories. The only real surprise is the significance of the word-level factors, particularly the syllable-number factor. The position factor turned out to be significant, despite the fact that the index was based on very few tokens.

Suggestions about which categories contributed to the significance of each factor have already been discussed. This discussion is summarized in table 3.20, which lists the factors that favor and disfavor shifting.

TABLE 3.20
Phonological Conditioning of (ı)-Shifting: Summary of Effects

Favor Shifting	*Disfavor Shifting*
Preceding alveolar	Preceding interdental
PRECEDING PALATAL*	PRECEDING GLOTTAL*
PRECEDING VELAR*	INITIAL POSITION*
PRECEDING /l/	Preceding glide*
Preceding stop	Following interdental*
Preceding nasal	FOLLOWING NASAL*
Preceding /r/	
Following labial	
Following /l/	
FOLLOWING CLUSTER	
FINAL POSITION*	

NOTE: Categories shown in small capitals strongly favored or disfavored shifting (i.e., their phonological index scores were greater than one standard deviation above or below the overall score). Those marked with asterisks are represented by a limited data set (see discussion in text here and in §5.1.2).

3.2.2.2. Phonological Conditioning of Variant Trajectories of (ɪ). In this second stage of the phonological analysis we consider the conditioning of the different directions of shifting. As was found with (ɛ), the three directional variants do not appear with equal frequency. As before, backing is by far the most common, accounting for 58.0% of the shifted tokens produced by the entire sample of speakers. Unlike with (ɛ), however, the combined lowering-plus-backing ranks second, with 25.5% of the (ɪ)-shifting, while straight lowering was heard in only 16.6% of the cases.

To investigate how these variants are conditioned, directional indices were calculated for each of the usual phonological categories. As before, these indices are calculated from the pooled data of the subsample of the most active speakers, and they represent the amount of backing, lowering, or combined backing and lowering found in each phonological context. These indices are shown in tables 3.21–23. Also shown are the overall indices for each direction, which indicate the amount of shifting across all phonological categories (backing = 0.082; lowering = 0.024, backing-plus-lowering = 0.043).

A number of these phonological categories result in directional indices that are either exceptionally high or exceptionally low (i.e., their indices lie outside of one standard deviation from the overall index for each direction of shifting).

With the backing indices, shifting is strongly favored by a preceding palatal, alveolar, or /l/, or by a following labial. When (ɪ) appears in a final syllable, backing appears to be strongly disfavored; however, as noted earlier, this result is based on a suspiciously small number of tokens.

Lowering of (ɪ) is promoted by a preceding velar or nasal. It is also promoted when the vowel appears in words of three syllables or when it appears in either a medial or final syllable (though the same caveat applies to this latter result). Given the low overall index for lowering, even scores of zero are within one standard deviation, and so it is difficult to identify disfavoring factors. Still, among the likely candidates (all of which had lowering indices at zero) are preceding interdentals, glottals, and glides; following interdentals; and words of four or more syllables.

TABLE 3.21

Effects of Preceding Phonological Factors on (ɪ)-Shifting:
General and Directional Indices

	General	*Backed*	*Lowered*	*Backed-plus-Lowered*
Voicing				
Voiceless	0.212 +	0.094 +	0.033 +	0.085 +
Voiced	0.174 +	0.099 +	0.019 −	0.055 +
Place				
Labial	0.179 +	0.085 +	0.046 +	0.042 −
Alveolar	0.238 +	0.162 +	0.020 −	0.061 +
Interdental	0.073 −	0.024 −	0.000 −	0.049 +
Palatal	0.423 +	0.192 +	0.038 +	0.192 +
Velar	0.303 +	0.111 +	0.061 +	0.131 +
Glottal	0.049 −	0.033 −	0.000 −	0.016 −
Manner				
Stop	0.223 +	0.115 +	0.032 +	0.077 +
Fricative	0.126 −	0.058 −	0.013 −	0.054 +
Nasal	0.239 +	0.065 −	0.174 +	0.000 −
Glide	0.084 −	0.063 −	0.000 −	0.021 −
/l/	0.489 +	0.457 +	0.011 −	0.022 −
/r/	0.222 +	0.016 −	0.048 +	0.159 +
#__	0.024 −	0.008 −	0.012 −	0.004 −
OVERALL	0.149	0.082	0.024	0.043

Shifting in the combined backed-plus-lowered direction is favored by preceding a palatal, velar, or /r/; by a following tautosyllabic cluster; or (perhaps) by appearing in a final syllable. No cases of shifting in this direction were found in the context of preceding nasals, following interdentals, or in words of four or more syllables; however, the zero indices associated with these categories are still technically within one standard deviation of the overall index of 0.043.

From the data in tables 3.21–23, it is clear that many phonological contexts do not have consistent effects across the three directions of shifting. They may favor one direction but disfavor the others. The significance of such differing effects was investi-

TABLE 3.22
Effects of Following Phonological Factors on (ɪ)-Shifting:
General and Directional Indices

	General	Backed	Lowered	Backed-plus-Lowered
Voicing				
Voiceless	0.157 +	0.094 +	0.021 −	0.041 −
Voiced	0.196 +	0.113 +	0.023 −	0.061 +
Place				
Labial	0.233 +	0.175 +	0.005 −	0.053 +
Alveolar	0.140 −	0.069 −	0.030 +	0.042 −
Interdental	0.038 −	0.038 −	0.000 −	0.000 −
Palatal	0.122 −	0.082 =	0.020 −	0.020 −
Velar	0.157 +	0.079 −	0.016 −	0.063 +
Manner				
Stop	0.195 +	0.094 +	0.033 +	0.068 +
Fricative	0.138 −	0.113 +	0.005 −	0.020 −
Nasal	0.045 −	0.006 −	0.026 +	0.013 −
/l/	0.226 +	0.107 +	0.048 +	0.071 +
Cluster				
Cluster	0.298 +	0.149 +	0.037 +	0.112 +
No cluster	0.128 −	0.073 −	0.022 −	0.033 −
OVERALL	0.149	0.082	0.024	0.043

TABLE 3.23
Effects of Word-Level Factors on (ɪ)-Shifting:
General and Directional Indices

	General	Backed	Lowered	Backed-plus-Lowered
Number of syllables				
1	0.122 −	0.058 −	0.024 =	0.040 −
2	0.205 +	0.137 +	0.009 −	0.059 +
3	0.188 +	0.063 −	0.113 +	0.013 −
4+	0.138 −	0.138 +	0.000 −	0.000 −
Syllable position				
Initial	0.181 +	0.132 +	0.007 −	0.042 −
Medial	0.221 +	0.104 +	0.104 +	0.013 −
Final	1.000 +	0.000 −	0.250 +	0.750 +
OVERALL	0.149	0.082	0.024	0.043

gated through a series of chi-square tests on the distributions of the shifted tokens of each type across the categories of each phonological factor. These data are given in tables 3.24–26.

As a result of the small numbers of shifted tokens, many categories had to be collapsed to allow for reliable probability testing. Among the directional differences, the lowered tokens were often combined with those that were both lowered and backed so that these less common tendencies could be compared to the more common backing. This combination was necessary in the testing of all factors except for the two voicing factors (preceding

TABLE 3.24

Effects of Preceding Phonological Factors on Direction of (ε)-Shifting

	Backed	Lowered	Backed-plus-Lowered	Total Shifted
Voicing (χ^2 = 1.22; p = .544)				
Voiceless	26 (51.0%)	6 (11.8%)	19 (37.3%)	51
Voiced	29 (61.7%)	5 (10.6%)	13 (27.7%)	47
Place (χ^2 = 4.88; p = .087)				
Labial	28 (63.6%)	8 (18.2%)	8 (18.2%)	44
Alveolar	48 (67.6%)	6 (8.5%)	17 (23.9%)	71
Interdental	1 (50.0%)	0 (0.0%)	1 (50.0%)	2
Palatal	4 (40.0%)	1 (10.0%)	5 (50.0%)	10
Velar	10 (47.6%)	3 (14.3%)	8 (38.1%)	21
Glottal	1 (50.0%)	0 (0.0%)	1 (50.0%)	2
Manner (χ^2 = 25.07; p < .0005)				
Stop	45 (57.0%)	9 (11.4%)	25 (31.6%)	79
Fricative	10 (52.6%)	2 (10.5%)	7 (36.8%)	19
Nasal	3 (42.9%)	4 (57.1%)	0 (0.0%)	7
Glide	3 (75.0%)	0 (0.0%)	1 (25.0%)	4
/l/	30 (93.8%)	1 (3.1%)	1 (3.1%)	32
/r/	1 (11.1%)	2 (22.2%)	6 (66.7%)	9
#__	3 (33.3%)	5 (55.6%)	1 (11.1%)	9

NOTE: The lowered and backed-plus-lowered tokens were combined in the test for place and manner. In the test for place, the interdental, palatal, velar, and glottal categories were combined, and in the test for manner, the nasal and /r/ categories and those of glide and initial position were combined.

TABLE 3.25

Effects of Following Phonological Factors on Direction of (ı)-Shifting

	Backed	Lowered	Backed-plus-Lowered	Total Shifted
Voicing ($\chi^2 = 0.38$; $p = .828$)				
Voiceless	48 (65.8%)	8 (11.0%)	17 (23.3%)	73
Voiced	38 (62.3%)	6 (9.8%)	17 (27.9%)	61
Place ($\chi^2 = 5.21$; $p = .074$)				
Labial	25 (75.8%)	1 (3.0%)	7 (21.2%)	33
Alveolar	57 (54.3%)	20 (19.0%)	28 (26.7%)	105
Interdental	1 (100%)	0 (0.0%)	0 (0.0%)	1
Palatal	4 (66.7%)	1 (16.7%)	1 (16.7%)	6
Velar	8 (57.1%)	1 (7.1%)	5 (35.7%)	14
Manner ($\chi^2 = 15.92$; $p = .001$)				
Stop	49 (56.3%)	12 (13.8%)	26 (29.9%)	87
Fricative	37 (78.7%)	2 (4.3%)	8 (17.0%)	47
Nasal	2 (18.2%)	7 (63.6%)	2 (18.2%)	11
/l/	7 (50.0%)	2 (14.3%)	5 (35.7%)	14
Cluster ($\chi^2 = 1.87$; $p = .392$)				
Cluster	22 (56.4%)	4 (10.3%)	13 (33.3%)	39
No cluster	73 (60.8%)	19 (15.8%)	28 (23.3%)	120

NOTE: The lowered and backed-plus-lowered tokens were combined in the tests for place and manner. In the test for place, the labial, interdental, and palatal categories were combined.

and following) and the tautosyllabic cluster factor. Other cases for which categories were combined are noted in the tables.

The results in these tables need to be considered in the context of the earlier discussions of the general and directional indices (tables 3.21–23). These data illustrate the variety of effects that each of the nine phonological factors has in shaping the (ı) variation.

The conditioning effects from the voicing factors are not great. In neither the preceding nor the following context did the voicing status of the adjacent obstruent have a significant influence on the shifting of (ı). Both voiced and voiceless obstruents have a positive effect on shifting, though there is an interesting reversal between the categories: before the vowel the greater degree of

TABLE 3.26
Effects of Word-Level Factors on Direction of (ɪ)-Shifting

	Backed	*Lowered*	*Backed-plus-Lowered*	*Total Shifted*
Syllables ($\chi^2 = 6.38$; $p = .041$)				
1	42 (53.2%)	14 (17.7%)	23 (29.1%)	79
2	44 (68.8%)	3 (4.7%)	17 (26.6%)	64
3	5 (41.7%)	6 (50.0%)	1 (8.3%)	12
4+	4 (100%)	0 (0.0%)	0 (0.0%)	4
Position ($\chi^2 = 4.94$; $p = .026$)				
Initial	45 (72.6%)	3 (4.8%)	14 (22.6%)	62
Medial	8 (57.1%)	5 (35.7%)	1 (7.1%)	14
Final	0 (0.0%)	1 (25.0%)	3 (75.0%)	4

NOTE: The lowered and backed-plus-lowered tokens were combined in both tests. In the test for syllable number, the 2 and 4+ categories were combined.

shifting is found with voiceless obstruents; after the vowel increased shifting is heard with voiced obstruents. These patterns hold fairly consistently across the different directions of shifting, as indicated by the insignificant results of the chi-square testing (tables 3.24 and 3.25).

A similar consistency is seen in the data for place of articulation of the preceding consonant. The differences reflected in the general indices for the place categories are significant, particularly the favorable influence of preceding palatals and velars and the unfavorable influence of glottals and interdentals. The directional differences (table 3.24) are not significant, however, as is suggested by the individual indices for the variant trajectories, which for the most part show the same effects as the general indices.

A more complicated picture is seen in the data on the manner factor for the preceding consonant. The general indices show significant differentiation and suggest that shifting is favored by a preceding stop, nasal, /l/, or /r/, and disfavored in initial position and by a preceding fricative or glide. However, not all of these effects hold across the different directions of shifting. Preceding nasals, for example, strongly promote lowering but have the opposite effect on the other directions of change. Similarly, it seems clear that the strongly favorable influence of preceding /l/ applies only to backing, as the other directional indices are much lower than usual for this category. The reverse is found with preceding /r/, however, which promotes both lowering and the combined lowering-plus-backing but disfavors straight backing. The chi-square results (table 3.24) confirm the significance of these directional differences.

As was also seen in the (ɛ) variation, the factors of the following context condition less extreme differences in (ɪ)-shifting. Among the place categories, the only notable general indices were the exceptionally high one for following labials and the exceptionally low one for following interdentals. Still, these differences were apparently enough to achieve statistical significance (table 3.18). This was not the case, however, for the directional differences (table 3.25). The directional indices pattern fairly consistently with the general indices, particularly in the case of interdentals, which clearly disfavor all types of shifting. Nevertheless, the effects of following labials are not as consistent, with backing strongly favored, combined backing-plus-lowering mildly favored, and lowering clearly not favored.

For the manner factor, the general indices show a fairly high degree of shifting for a following stop or /l/ and a very low degree for a following nasal. The directional indices show these tendencies to be consistent in the former two cases. In the case of following nasal, however, the consistency is disrupted by the lowering index, which, rather than indicating a strongly disfavoring effect, shows a very slight positive effect. These differences combined with those conditioned by following fricatives (which favor backing and disfavor shifting in the other directions) are apparently what led to the significant chi-square results reported in table 3.25.

The tautosyllabic cluster factor shows very consistent results. Shifting in all directions is favored by the presence of such a cluster and slightly disfavored when it is absent. The insignificant results on the directional data confirm this consistency.

The word-level factors appear to play a more influential role in conditioning the (ɪ) variation than they did for (ɛ). The chi-square results on both the general (table 3.19) and directional data (table 3.26) were significant for both the syllable number and position factors. In the case of syllable number, no exceptional general indices were seen with any category despite the overall significance of the distribution. With the directional indices, however, the situation is quite messy. The disfavoring effects of monosyllables are consistent across the different directions, but the effects of the other categories are more variable. Two-syllable words favor lowering and lowering-plus-backing, but they disfavor straight lowering. The reverse is seen with three-syllable words, which favor lowering but disfavor the other two directions. Finally, backing was the only type of shifting heard in four-syllable words (only four shifted tokens were recorded in this context).

Concerns about low numbers of tokens have already been mentioned in discussing the data for the position factor. The exceptionally high index for the final-syllable category was calculated on the basis of only eight tokens, four of which were shifted. Thus, the directional indices associated with this category are necessarily unusual (exceptionally low in the case of backing and exceptionally high in the other two cases). With the other categories, initial position appears to have a slightly favorable effect on shifting, but the directional indices suggest that this only applies to backing. Similarly, the overall favorable influence of position in a medial syllable does not hold for backing-plus-lowering, which is strongly disfavored in this context.

Possible explanations for these patterns and the others associated with phonological conditioning are explored below (chap. 5).

3.2.3. SOCIAL DISTRIBUTION OF (ɪ)

3.2.3.1. *Social Aspects of General* (ɪ)-*Shifting.* Social differences in the use of (ɪ) are illustrated in figure 3.5, which plots the general (ɪ) indices for all speakers sampled. The distribution of the (ɪ) indices resembles in many ways that of the (ε) indices, though the (ɪ) scores are overall much lower. The downward-sloping pattern seen earlier is repeated here, but with some exceptions. Again we find generally higher scores (1) in Paw Paw than in Chelsea, (2) in females than in males, and (3) in adults than in adolescents.

FIGURE 3.5
Indices for the Shifting of (ɪ) across the Sample of Speakers

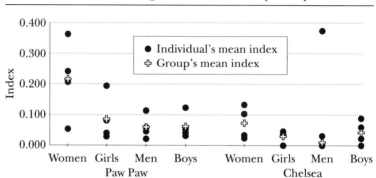

Among the exceptions to these general tendencies, the most obvious is the unusually high index of one Chelsea man (RR). Whereas little or no shifting was found with the other three Chelsea men, this speaker's index of 0.373 was the highest in the entire sample. The reason for this exceptional usage is not clear. It is possible that this speaker is an early adopter of the change (in the sense of Milroy and Milroy 1985), but he did not show unusual indices for the other NCS variables. It is also possible that his usage represents a pattern not related to the NCS, perhaps a relic pattern, though his usage seems to be similarly conditioned phonologically (e.g., shifting is favored by adjacent /l/). This outlier case thus remains a mystery, and for now it seems best to omit it from the analysis because of its potential to obscure the general patterning.

The other major exception is seen with the boys' indices. In both towns, the boys show slightly higher degrees of shifting than the men (excluding the exceptional speaker RR), a finding that runs counter to the pattern seen earlier of adults leading adolescents. Also, in Chelsea the boys' indices are generally higher than the girls', which contradicts the usual gender pattern, as seen before with (ε) as well as here with the other groups.

The possibility that the patterns in figure 3.5 are affected by phonological as well as social factors is, of course, an important consideration for (ɪ) as it was for (ε). However, for the same reasons raised earlier, this possibility seems remote. The large number of tokens counted for each speaker (88 on average for (ɪ)) and the three-token limit on lexical items result in a wide variety of phonological contexts being sampled for each speaker. As was shown above, this variety produces a fairly even distribution of contexts favorable and unfavorable to shifting across speakers.

Accepting that the patterning described here is indeed socially (rather than linguistically) defined, we can investigate further the (ɪ) variation by considering the group data shown in figure 3.6. The categories of the social factors town, age, and sex are compared using the mean indices for the entire sample (e.g., all Paw Paw speakers vs. all Chelsea speakers). In addition, the data for the age and sex factors are further broken down by town.

These data corroborate the patterns suggested by the individual scores in figure 3.5. Higher degrees of shifting are found in Paw Paw over Chelsea, adults over adolescents, and females over males. Furthermore, the age and sex patterns hold consistently in both towns, though the distinctions are less dramatic in Chelsea, given the overall lower levels of shifting found there.

To evaluate the statistical strength of these patterns the data were subjected to a multiway ANOVA (omitting the index of the exceptional Chelsea man). The results of this procedure are given in table 3.27.

The ANOVA results identify both town ($p = .007$) and sex ($p = .018$) as significant factors. The age factor was not found to be

FIGURE 3.6

Mean (ɪ) Shifting across Social Factors: Town, Age, and Sex

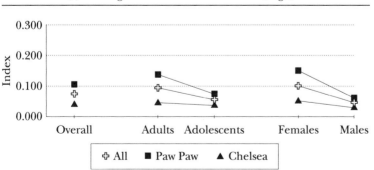

TABLE 3.27
Multiway ANOVA Results for Social Factors in (1) Variation

Factor	F	df	p-value
Town	8.81	1, 23	.007
Age	2.32	1, 23	.141
Sex	6.46	1, 23	.018
Town × Age	1.69	1, 23	.206
Town × Sex	2.06	1, 23	.165
Sex × Age	5.25	1, 23	.031
Town × Age × Sex	0.40	1, 23	.533

Multiple r = .735; multiple r^2 = .541.

significant on its own; however, the analysis indicates a significant interactional effect of age and sex (p = .031). This result suggests that the age differences illustrated in figure 3.6 are not indicative of a general pattern but rather one that is sex-specific. Hints of such age/sex interactions were seen above in discussing the apparently exceptional indices of boys. Whereas women's indices are generally higher than girls' in each town, men's are generally lower than boys'. Across both towns, the mean index for women was 0.144 as compared to 0.058 for girls. For men, however, the mean index was 0.039, while the boys' mean was 0.053.[19] Thus, the pattern of adults leading adolescents holds only for female speakers.

3.2.3.2. *Social Distribution of Variant Trajectories of* (1). Social patterns in the use of the different directions of shifting are investigated by examining the distribution of these directional variants across groups of speakers. These data are shown in table 3.28 (see n. 17). As was the case with (ε), the distribution of the directional variants elaborates the patterns indicated by the data on general shifting. With the sex factor, for example, again we find differential use of the variants. Males show a clear preference for backing.[20] Females, however, tend to divide their usage more evenly among the variants, particularly between backing and backing-plus-lowering; thus they tend to be phonetically more variable. This raises the same question as it did for (ε) as to whether the overall female lead in

TABLE 3.28
Distribution of Directional Variants of (ɪ) by Social Factors

	Backed	*Lowered*	*Backed-plus-Lowered*	*Total Shifted*
Females				
Adults				
Paw Paw	20 (46.5%)	7 (16.3%)	16 (37.2%)	43
Chelsea	8 (44.4%)	7 (38.9%)	3 (16.7%)	18
TOTAL	28 (45.9%)	14 (23.0%)	19 (31.1%)	61
Adolescents				
Paw Paw	7 (36.8%)	3 (15.8%)	9 (47.4%)	19
Chelsea	3 (50.0%)	1 (16.7%)	2 (33.3%)	6
TOTAL	10 (40.0%)	4 (16.0%)	11 (44.0%)	25
TOTAL	38 (44.2%)	18 (20.9%)	30 (34.9%)	86
Males				
Adults				
Paw Paw	8 (57.1%)	4 (28.6%)	2 (14.3%)	14
Chelsea	2 (100%)	0 (0.0%)	0 (0.0%)	2
TOTAL	10 (62.5%)	4 (25.0%)	2 (12.5%)	16
Adolescents				
Paw Paw	11 (68.8%)	3 (18.8%)	2 (12.5%)	16
Chelsea	6 (66.7%)	1 (11.1%)	2 (22.2%)	9
TOTAL	17 (68.0%)	4 (16.0%)	4 (16.0%)	25
TOTAL	27 (65.9%)	8 (19.2%)	6 (14.6%)	41

the innovative use of (ɪ) is related to their utilization of alternatives to straight backing. Comparing the overall rates of backing for males and females, we see very little difference. The 38 backed tokens produced by females (28 from women, 10 from girls) represent 2.8% of their total number of (ɪ) items coded ($N = 1,370$). Males, by comparison, produced 27 backed tokens (10 from men, 17 from boys), which accounted for 2.0% of their total (ɪ) usage ($N = 1,353$). It appears, then, that males and females are roughly equivalent in their participation in backing, and it is only through the use of the other directions (especially lowering-plus-backing) that females achieve their overall advantage in (ɪ)-shifting.

Such asymmetrical usage of the variant trajectories is not found with the other social factors. In the case of the town factor, for

example, the relative frequencies of the variants fluctuate somewhat, but there do not appear to be consistent differences between
comparable Paw Paw and Chelsea speakers (e.g., the percentage of
backed tokens for women is 46.5% in Paw Paw and 44.4% in
Chelsea). The same can be said for the age factor, though it is
interesting to note in the distribution of the girls' tokens a hint of
a pattern mentioned above with regard to (ɛ). In that case it was
observed that the tendency to use a more even mix of directional
variants was greater among the adolescents, and in table 3.28 we
see that girls are the only group to use one of the other directions
of shifting in nearly equal amounts that nearly equal their use of
backing.

   This is an intriguing finding and one that we will return to in
chapter 5.

3.3. THE VARIABLE (ʌ)

3.3.1. PHONETIC DESCRIPTION OF THE VARIATION. The variation
found with the mid-central vowel (ʌ) demonstrates many of the
same tendencies seen with the other variables discussed in this
chapter. In agreement with the standard picture of the NCS (Labov
1994), shifting of (ʌ) most commonly involves backing and rounding to something like [ɔ]. Not to be outdone by its neighbors,
however, the vowel also shifts along different paths. At times,
variants lowered to near [a] are heard, as are variants that are both
lowered and backed—closer to [ɑ] or [ɒ]. In addition, (ʌ) occasionally shows a trajectory not found with the other vowels: raising,
sometimes accompanied by rounding, which results in variants
near [ɨ] or [ʊ].

   The coding scheme for (ʌ), therefore, made a four-way distinction in the directions of shifting. For each direction, two degrees of
shifting were recorded. Approximate phonetic representations of
the coded variants are shown in table 3.29.

   An acoustic portrayal of the variation in (ʌ) is given in figure
3.7. The (ʌ) tokens were produced in conversational speech and
were directionally coded as indicated in the figure.[21] Also shown as

TABLE 3.29
Coded Variants of (ʌ)

	0	1	2
Backed	[ʌ]	[ʌ⁾]	[ɔ˂]
Lowered	[ʌ]	[ʌˇ]	[aˆ]
Backed-plus-lowered	[ʌ]	[ʌˀ]	[ɑˀ]
Raised	[ʌ]	[ʌˇ]	[ɨˇ]

FIGURE 3.7
F1 and F2 Frequencies for Tokens of (ʌ) Produced by TN (PP, f, 18)

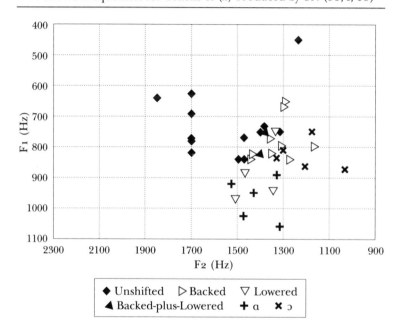

points of reference are tokens of /ɔ/ and /ɑ/ that were judged to be conservative.

The acoustic picture of the (ʌ) variation is similar to those seen with (ε) and (ɪ). The unshifted tokens appear in the upper left portion of the diagram, while the shifted ones fan out downward and rightward. There is a clearly separated group of unshifted tokens with F2 frequencies around 1,700 Hz, but many of the tokens coded as unshifted are found in the more crowded center area of figure 3.7. In this crowd we also find tokens heard as backed, lowered, and both, and not too far from these are /ɔ/ and /ɑ/ items. This diagram shows a greater degree of overlap among the ranges occupied by the coded variants of (ʌ) than was found with other vowels. The tighter clustering suggests that this vowel undergoes less extreme shifting than the others. Impressionistically, this appears to be the case, as the distinctions among the variants were not as great; that is, the contrasts between unshifted and shifted forms of (ʌ) as well as those among the directional variants of shifted (ʌ) seem to be more subtle than they are for (ɛ) or (ɪ). However, it should be noted that small F2 frequency differences in this back region of acoustic space (where F2 is lower) are generally more perceptually distinct than they would be for front vowels (Johnson 1997, 55). Thus, the perceived differences among the variants may be greater than the plot in figure 3.7 suggests.

3.3.2. PHONOLOGICAL CONDITIONING OF (ʌ).
3.3.2.1. *General Conditioning of* (ʌ). The conditioning of (ʌ) was approached following the model established for the other vowels. The distribution of data from a subsample of speakers was analyzed using the same phonological classification as before. This subsample contained ten speakers—those with the highest (ʌ) indices. All but one of these speakers had also been used in either the (ɪ) or (ɛ) subsamples.

The data from these speakers were pooled, and from this pool indices were calculated to measure the amount of shifting found in each phonological category. These indices are presented in tables 3.30–32. The overall index for (ʌ)-shifting in these data was 0.114, and it is shown in each figure as a reference point. As this low overall index indicates, shifting of (ʌ) was rare, even in the speech of the most active shifters. This infrequency merits a cautionary note, because, as before, it presents certain analytic challenges and limits the firmness of the conclusions that can be drawn. Still, despite their rarity, the data do reveal patterns in their distribution.

As table 3.30 indicates, several preceding contexts seem to play a conditioning role in (ʌ)-shifting. For the place factor, a

TABLE 3.30
Effects of Preceding Phonological Factors on (ʌ)-Shifting:
General Indices, Frequency of Shifting, and Chi-Square Results

	Index	Unshifted	Shifted	Total
Voicing (χ^2 = 2.63; p = .105)				
Voiceless	0.122	381 (91.4%)	36 (8.6%)	417
Voiced	0.156	247 (87.6%)	35 (12.4%)	282
Place (χ^2 = 11.67; p = .020)				
Labial	0.125	543 (90.7%)	56 (9.3%)	599
Alveolar	0.080	516 (94.2%)	32 (5.8%)	548
Palatal	0.000	31 (100%)	0 (0.0%)	31
Velar	0.186	84 (86.6%)	13 (13.4%)	97
Glottal	0.150	18 (90.0%)	2 (10.0%)	20
Manner (χ^2 = 37.79; p < .0005)				
Stop	0.166	396 (87.4%)	57 (12.6%)	453
Fricative	0.081	232 (94.3%)	14 (5.7%)	246
Nasal	0.154	115 (88.5%)	15 (11.5%)	130
Glide	0.023	297 (98.3%)	5 (1.7%)	302
/l/	0.196	44 (86.3%)	7 (13.7%)	51
/r/	0.071	108 (95.6%)	5 (4.4%)	113
#__	0.163	149 (89.8%)	17 (10.2%)	166
OVERALL	0.114			

preceding velar clearly promotes shifting, while a preceding palatal has the opposite effect. In fact, not a single shifted token was found in the latter environment. The interdental category is absent from the place data in table 3.30, because no applicable items (e.g., *thus, thumb*) occurred. Within the manner factor, there is a good deal of intercategory differentiation. The most dramatic examples are seen with preceding /l/, which favors shifting, and with preceding glides, which disfavor shifting. The index for the latter category, however, may reflect a lexical bias, as the data set on which it is based is dominated by occurrences of *was(n't)* and *one*, which together account for 85.8% of the 302 tokens (see §5.1.2.1).[22] The voicing factor does not show such extreme differences. Shifting is more common following a voiced obstruent, though it is not particularly disfavored by a voiceless one.

TABLE 3.31

Effects of Following Phonological Factors on (ʌ)-Shifting:
General Indices, Frequency of Shifting, and Chi-Square Results

	Index	Unshifted	Shifted	Total
Voicing (χ^2 = 22.10; p < .0005)				
Voiceless	0.181	446 (86.9%)	67 (13.1%)	513
Voiced	0.050	328 (96.5%)	12 (3.5%)	340
Place (χ^2 = 4.74; p = .316)				
Labial	0.095	479 (93.0%)	36 (7.0%)	515
Alveolar	0.120	652 (91.3%)	62 (8.7%)	714
Interdental	0.089	85 (94.4%)	5 (5.6%)	90
Palatal	0.179	59 (88.1%)	8 (11.9%)	67
Velar	0.160	66 (88.0%)	9 (12.0%)	75
Manner (χ^2 = 20.06; p < .0005)				
Stop	0.187	372 (86.9%)	56 (13.1%)	428
Fricative	0.071	402 (94.6%)	23 (5.4%)	425
Nasal	0.091	565 (93.4%)	40 (6.6%)	605
/l/	0.667	2 (66.7%)	1 (33.3%)	3
Cluster (χ^2 = 12.71; p < .0005)				
Cluster	0.276	71 (81.6%)	16 (18.4%)	87
No cluster	0.104	1,270 (92.4%)	104 (7.6%)	1,374
OVERALL	0.114			

NOTE: Because there were too few tokens of /l/ for reliable chi-square testing, this category was omitted in the test for manner.

The results for the factors of the following context (table 3.31) identify a number of other categories that appear to have a favorable influence on shifting. With the place factor we see that following velars and especially palatals promote shifting.[23] For manner, it seems that following /l/ overwhelmingly favors shifting, though this index may not be reliable, having been calculated from only three tokens. The data for following stops, however, are more reliable and suggest that this context also favors shifting. We find similarly favorable contexts for the voicing and cluster factors when the (ʌ) is followed by a voiceless obstruent or a tautosyllabic cluster. As for following contexts that disfavor shifting, labials, interdentals, fricatives, and nasals all appear to qualify, though the

TABLE 3.32
Effects of Word-Level Factors on (ʌ)-Shifting:
General Indices, Frequency of Shifting, and Chi-Square Results

	Index	Unshifted	Shifted	Total
Number of syllables (χ^2 = 8.23; p = .016)				
1	0.131	887 (90.4%)	94 (9.6%)	981
2	0.081	398 (94.5%)	23 (5.5%)	421
3	0.055	53 (96.4%)	2 (3.6%)	55
4+	0.250	3 (75.0%)	1 (25.0%)	4
Syllable position				
Initial	0.076	414 (95.0%)	22 (5.0%)	436
Medial	0.158	17 (89.5%)	2 (10.5%)	19
Final	0.080	23 (92.0%)	2 (8.0%)	25
OVERALL	0.114			

NOTE: Because there were too few tokens for 4+ syllables for reliable chi-square testing, this category was omitted in the test for syllable number. No test was possible for position because of the low number of shifted token for the medial and final categories.

most extremely conservative index in table 3.31 is found with following voiced obstruents.

The word-level factors in table 3.32 demonstrate somewhat less extreme differences. Within the syllable-number factor, there appears to be a major distinction between words of three syllables (which disfavor shifting) and those of four or more syllables (which favor shifting). The result for trisyllabics is reliable, but that for four or more syllables is not because it is based on only four tokens. For the position factor, shifting is somewhat less frequent in initial and final syllables, but the data do not suggest that these categories have great conditioning effects.

The distributions reflected in these tables were subjected to chi-square testing in order to assess their significance. Many of the patterns noted in the index data are confirmed by these statistical results. Thus, among the factors related to preceding context, both place and manner showed strongly favorable and strongly disfavorable categories, are found to be significant, while voicing, which showed only minor differences, is not. With the factors related to following context, only place fails to achieve significance, a result that may have been predicted from table 3.31, where little separation is seen among the place categories. A more surprising result is that for the syllable number factor, which turns out to be significant despite the minor differences suggested by table 3.32 (excluding the data for the Syl4+ category, which were omitted from the chi-square test).

The particulars of which phonological categories play a significant role in conditioning (ʌ)-shifting are summarized in table 3.33.

3.3.2.2. Phonological Conditioning of Variant Trajectories of (ʌ). As the analysis of the other vowels has shown, consideration of directional variants adds an important new dimension to the account of phonological conditioning. For (ʌ), we find, once again, an uneven use of those variants. Backing holds its usual rank as the most frequent direction of shifting, accounting for 54.9% of the shifted tokens recorded from the complete sample of speakers. Another 33.0% were coded as lowered, making this the next most common direction. By comparison, raising and the combination of backing-plus-lowering were quite rarely heard, representing only 8.9% and

TABLE 3.33
Phonological Conditioning of (ʌ)-Shifting: Summary of Effects

Favor Shifting	Disfavor Shifting
PRECEDING VELAR	PRECEDING PALATAL
Preceding stop	PRECEDING GLIDE*
PRECEDING /l/	Preceding /r/
Initial position	FOLLOWING VOICED
FOLLOWING VOICELESS	Following fricative
FOLLOWING STOP	3-SYLLABLE WORDS
Following cluster	

NOTE: Categories shown in small capitals strongly favored or disfavored shifting (i.e., their phonological index scores were greater than one standard deviation above or below the overall score). Those marked with asterisks are represented by a limited data set (see discussion in text here and in §5.1.2).

3.3%, respectively, of all cases of shifting. In fact, only 10 raised tokens and 6 backed-plus-lowered tokens occurred in the data set examined for the phonological analysis. Given these small numbers, the usual directional indices will not be presented for these variants, and the issue of their conditioning is addressed separately below.

To examine possible conditioning factors for the two most common variant trajectories, directional indices were constructed for the usual phonological categories. The input data for these indices were the same as for the general indices, that is, the pooled data from the 10-speaker subsample. The directional indices are presented in tables 3.34–36, which also show the overall indices for each direction (backing = 0.069, lowering = 0.028).

These figures suggest that backing of (ʌ) is influenced by a number of phonological factors. Among those preceding catego-

TABLE 3.34
Effects of Preceding Phonological Factors on (ʌ)-Shifting:
General and Directional Indices

	General	*Backed*	*Lowered*
Voicing			
Voiceless	0.122 +	0.060 –	0.048 +
Voiced	0.156 +	0.124 +	0.014 –
Place			
Labial	0.125 +	0.083 +	0.023 –
Alveolar	0.080 –	0.029 –	0.035 +
Palatal	0.000 –	0.000 –	0.000 –
Velar	0.186 +	0.134 +	0.031 +
Glottal	0.150 +	0.050 –	0.100 +
Manner			
Stop	0.166 +	0.117 +	0.031 +
Fricative	0.081 –	0.028 –	0.041 +
Nasal	0.154 +	0.100 +	0.031 +
Glide	0.023 –	0.007 –	0.010 –
/l/	0.196 +	0.059 –	0.020 –
/r/	0.071 –	0.018 –	0.053 +
#__	0.163 +	0.127 +	0.018 –
OVERALL	0.114	0.069	0.028

TABLE 3.35
Effects of Following Phonological Factors on (ʌ)-Shifting:
General and Directional Indices

	General	Backed	Lowered
Voicing			
Voiceless	0.181 +	0.133 +	0.027 −
Voiced	0.050 −	0.029 −	0.015 −
Place			
Labial	0.095 −	0.058 −	0.027 −
Alveolar	0.120 +	0.069 =	0.028 =
Interdental	0.089 −	0.033 −	0.033 +
Palatal	0.179 +	0.164 +	0.015 −
Velar	0.160 +	0.107 +	0.040 +
Manner			
Stop	0.187 +	0.152 +	0.019 −
Fricative	0.071 −	0.031 −	0.026 −
Nasal	0.091 −	0.035 −	0.036 +
/l/	0.667 +	0.667 +	0.000 −
Cluster			
Cluster	0.276 +	0.138 +	0.080 +
No cluster	0.104 −	0.065 −	0.025 −
OVERALL	0.114	0.069	0.028

TABLE 3.36
Effects of Word-Level Factors on (ɛ)-Shifting:
General and Directional Indices

	General	Backed	Lowered
Number of syllables			
1	0.131 +	0.086 +	0.030 +
2	0.081 −	0.033 −	0.026 −
3	0.055 −	0.055 −	0.000 −
4+	0.250 +	0.000 −	0.250 +
Syllable position			
Initial	0.076 −	0.032 −	0.023 −
Medial	0.158 +	0.105 +	0.053 +
Final	0.080 −	0.040 −	0.040 +
OVERALL	0.114	0.069	0.028

ries producing exceptional backing indices (defined, as before, as falling beyond one standard deviation of the overall score) are preceding voiced obstruents, velars, stops, and initial position, all of which strongly favor shifting. The indices for preceding palatals, glides, and /r/ are also exceptional, though backing is disfavored in all these contexts. For the factors related to following context, there are no exceptionally low backing indices, but following voiceless obstruents, palatals, stops, and clusters are shown to condition exceptionally high degrees of backing. As was mentioned earlier, the extremely high score for following /l/ may be considered unreliable because of the few tokens recorded for this context. Similarly, the only exceptional backing index among the word-level categories was for words of four or more syllables, and this category was suspiciously underrepresented.

There are fewer categories that are shown to condition exceptional indices for lowering. Among the preceding factors, lowering is promoted by a voiceless obstruent, glottal, or /r/, while a preceding palatal has the opposite effect. In the data on following contexts, the only exceptional lowering score (other than the unreliable one for /l/) is the high index conditioned by a following cluster. For the word-level categories, lowering is found to be disfavored in words of three syllables and favored when the vowel appears in a medial syllable. Again, the findings for the category of words of four or more syllables, which show an exceptionally high index for lowering, are highly suspect.

The extent to which these directional tendencies are conditioned by different phonological contexts was examined using chi-square testing; the results are shown in tables 3.37–39.

As before, the small number of tokens for many categories made certain adjustments necessary in order to produce reliable statistical results. In some cases, the data for a category were simply omitted (e.g., preceding glottal), and in others data from different categories were combined (e.g., preceding fricatives, glides, and /r/). In the latter cases, of course, the combinations involved categories that behaved similarly with respect to their directional effects.

TABLE 3.37

Effects of Preceding Phonological Factors on Direction of (ʌ)-Shifting

	Backed	Lowered	Total Shifted
Voicing ($\chi^2 = 9.06$; $p = .003$)			
Voiceless	17 (47.2%)	15 (41.7%)	36
Voiced	28 (80.0%)	4 (11.4%)	35
Place ($\chi^2 = 8.72$; $p = .013$)			
Labial	37 (66.1%)	11 (19.6%)	56
Alveolar	12 (37.5%)	15 (46.9%)	32
Velar	9 (69.2%)	3 (23.1%)	13
Glottal	1 (50.0%)	1 (50.0%)	2
Manner ($\chi^2 = 14.60$; $p = .002$)			
Stop	40 (70.2%)	12 (21.1%)	57
Fricative	5 (35.7%)	7 (50.0%)	14
Nasal	9 (60.0%)	4 (26.7%)	15
Glide	1 (20.0%)	2 (40.0%)	5
/l/	3 (42.9%)	1 (14.3%)	7
/r/	1 (20.0%)	4 (80.0%)	5
#_	13 (76.5%)	2 (11.8%)	17

NOTE: The palatal and glottal categories were omitted in the test for place. In the test for manner, the categories of fricative, glide, and /r/ and those of nasal and /l/ were combined.

Following the pattern established for the other vowels, the results on the directional differences are considered together with those on the conditioning of shifting in general. The general and directional indices are compared in tables 3.34–36. As in the earlier tables of this type, each index is indicated as being either higher (+), lower (–), or equal to (=) to the comparable overall index.

As a factor in the conditioning of (ʌ), the voicing status of an adjacent obstruent operates rather differently depending on the position of the obstruent. In the preceding context, voicing conditions significant directional differences (table 3.37). Backing is disfavored by a preceding voiceless and favored by a preceding voiced, whereas the reverse pattern is found for lowering (see table 3.34). The canceling effects of this opposition are reflected in the general indices, which did not show significant differences (table

TABLE 3.38

Effects of Following Phonological Factors on Direction of (ʌ)-Shifting

	Backed	Lowered	Total Shifted
Voicing			
Voiceless	48 (71.6%)	12 (17.9%)	67
Voiced	8 (66.7%)	3 (25.0%)	12
Place (χ^2 = 2.00; p = .368)			
Labial	21 (58.3%)	12 (33.3%)	36
Alveolar	36 (58.1%)	15 (24.2%)	62
Interdental	2 (40.0%)	2 (40.0%)	5
Palatal	7 (87.5%)	1 (12.5%)	8
Velar	6 (66.7%)	2 (22.2%)	9
Manner (χ^2 = 15.88; p < .0005)			
Stop	45 (80.4%)	7 (12.5%)	56
Fricative	11 (47.8%)	8 (34.8%)	23
Nasal	15 (37.5%)	17 (42.5%)	40
/l/	1 (100%)	0 (0.0%)	1
Cluster			
Cluster	8 (50.0%)	4 (25.0%)	16
No cluster	64 (61.5%)	28 (26.9%)	104

NOTE: In the test for place, the interdental and labial categories were combined, as were the palatal and velar categories. The test for manner omitted the data for the /l/ category. Reliable testing of the voicing and cluster factors was not possible because of an insufficient number of tokens.

3.30). In the context following the vowel, however, voicing was found to condition a significant difference in the general indices, as a following voiceless was identified as strongly promoting shifting and a following voiced as strongly discouraging shifting (table 3.31). These effects appear to be fairly consistent regardless of the direction of shifting (table 3.35), though there were insufficient data for reliable significance testing (table 3.38).

The data on the place factor for the preceding consonant show significant differences for both shifting in general and the directional variants. The general indices identified preceding palatal as a context strongly disfavoring shifting and preceding velar as one strongly favoring shifting (table 3.30). These effects are also seen

TABLE 3.39
Effects of Word-Level Factors on Direction of (ʌ)-Shifting

	Backed	*Lowered*	*Total Shifted*
Number of syllables (χ^2 = 1.95; p = .163)			
1	60 (63.8%)	23 (24.5%)	94
2	10 (43.5%)	8 (34.8%)	23
3	2 (100%)	0 (0.0%)	2
4+	0 (0.0%)	1 (100%)	1
Syllable position			
Initial	10 (45.5%)	7 (31.8%)	22
Medial	1 (50.0%)	1 (50.0%)	2
Final	1 (50.0%)	1 (50.0%)	2

NOTE: The 3 and 4+ categories were omitted in the test for syllable number. Reliable testing of position was not possible because of the insufficient number of tokens.

in the directional indices, though the favorable influence of velars appears to be greater for backing. The directional indices also reveal a pattern not evident in the general data: preceding glottals (/h/) strongly favor lowering but have a mildly discouraging effect on backing.

A similar mixture of effects is evident among the categories of the manner factor. Significant differences were found for general shifting, with preceding fricatives, glides, and /r/ disfavoring shifting, while the other four categories favored shifting. The directional data show that this pattern also applies to backing, with the one exception of preceding /l/, which significantly promotes shifting in general but slightly disfavors backing. Surprisingly, lowering is also disfavored in this context, and, as is discussed below, the high general index for /l/ can be traced to several tokens of (ʌ)-raising in the morpheme *lunch.* Some of the other indices for lowering (e.g., preceding glides) pattern like the backing indices, but this is not the case for preceding fricatives, /r/, or initial position. The disfavoring effects of the former two toward backing are reversed for lowering (as seen in the crossovers in table 3.34), while for the context of initial position, the favorable influence on backing is shown not to apply in the case of lowering.

Among the factors related to following context, place was the only one not to condition significant differences in either the general or directional data. Examining the indices, we see that the only extreme score was the high backing index for the palatal category (see n. 3.23). Interestingly, this context has the opposite effect on lowering and resulted in the lowest lowering index for any of the place categories.

Manner of the following consonant was identified as a significant factor affecting both shifting in general and the different directions of shifting. The general indices show shifting to be promoted by following stops and /l/, though the latter is based on an unreliably small number of tokens. The directional indices indicate that these positive effects apply only to backing, as lowering is disfavored in these contexts. On the other hand, lowering is slightly favored by a following nasal, though this category disfavors backing.

For the cluster factor, the significant differences seen are more consistent. Shifting, whether backing or lowering, is strongly promoted when a tautosyllabic cluster is present, while the absence of such a cluster has a slightly disfavoring effect on both types of shifting.

A similar degree of consistency is seen with the word-level factors. With syllable number, we find shifting to be favored in monosyllabic words and disfavored in words of two and especially three syllables, tendencies that hold for both backing and lowering. The data for four or more syllables indicate this to be a favorable context for lowering and a disfavorable one for backing, but these results are unreliable because of the low number of tokens available for analysis.

Low input numbers also prevented significance testing of the distribution for the position factor. From the indices, however, it seems unlikely that this factor plays a major conditioning role. None of the general indices was exceptional, and only the high score for lowering in the medial category (which also favors backing) was exceptional among the directional indices.

The other two directional variants of (ʌ) have not been considered in the above analysis because they are represented by so few tokens. For the subsample of active (ʌ)-shifters, a total of 10 tokens were coded as raised and 6 tokens were coded as both lowered and backed. These items are listed in table 3.40. It is difficult to identify patterns in such limited data sets. Still, among the examples of raising, the number of items containing following nasals is striking (7 out of the 10), as is the number with preceding labials (again 7 out of 10). It is also possible that some kind of lexical conditioning is at work here as 3 of the raised examples are in *but* and another 3 in the morpheme *lunch*.[24] The possibility of raising being a restricted feature of particular speakers should also be noted, since these 10 examples were produced by just 3 speakers, with 7 of them coming from a single speaker.

For the lowering-plus-backing direction we might logically expect to find conditioning influences similar to those found individually for lowering and backing. To some extent this is the case. Thus, 4 of the 6 examples occurred before voiceless obstruents, a context shown to favor both backing and lowering. On the other hand, following fricatives are also found in 4 of these examples, even though this context was shown earlier to disfavor both backing and lowering. Lexical conditioning seems a less likely possibility here, as the only repetition is seen in the two tokens of *us*. The possibility of this feature being a peculiarity of particular speakers also seems more remote, since these 6 tokens were produced by 4 different speakers.

TABLE 3.40
(ʌ) Items Coded as Raised or Lowered-plus-Backed

Raised	*Lowered-plus-Backed*
but (3)	couple
function	mother
lunch	some
lunches	stuff
lunchtime	us (2)
months	
once	
ones	

It is obvious that more data are needed before definitive patterns can be identified for these less common directional variants, though this must remain a goal for future research.

3.3.3. SOCIAL DISTRIBUTION OF (ʌ)

3.3.3.1. *Social Aspects of General* (ʌ)-*Shifting.* Before discussing the social patterning of these data, a general cautionary note should be made about the overall rarity of (ʌ)-shifting. One of the most striking aspects of the distribution in figure 3.8 is the congregation of scores along the horizontal axis. Out of 32 speakers, 13 showed absolutely no shifting of (ʌ) and another 5 had only a single shifted token—unlike (ɪ), for which 4 speakers had no shifting and 3 had 1 shifted token). With over half the speakers essentially removed from the picture of shifting, social patterns become harder to detect and especially to verify statistically. Acknowledging these difficulties, there are still important observations to be made.

At first glance, the social distribution of the (ʌ) indices appears rather different from those seen with (ε) and (ɪ). The steady downward slope of the earlier graphs is replaced by greater undulation here. Still, traces of the previous pattern are still evident. Most obvious are the differences between the towns, where once again generally higher scores are found in Paw Paw. The previously observed lead of females over males also appears to hold for (ʌ),

FIGURE 3.8
Indices for the Shifting of (ʌ) across the Sample of Speakers

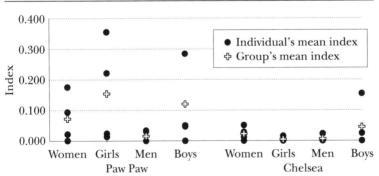

regardless of town. The one exception to this tendency is found with the Chelsea adolescents, where the boys' indices are generally higher than the girls', who show almost no shifting.[25]

The major differences between the (ʌ) distribution and that of the vowels discussed above occurs with the age factor. Whereas shifting of those vowels was found to be more common among adults, for (ʌ) it is the adolescents who show greater shifting, regardless of sex or town, though again, the very low indices of the Chelsea girls make this group exceptional.[26]

These tendencies are examined further by the group data offered in figure 3.9. These mean indices show the patterns observed in the individual scores to be fairly consistent. The town difference is strongest with Paw Paw speakers averaging an (ʌ) index of 0.091, while the Chelsea average is just 0.019. For the age factor, we find the adolescents leading in both locations, though the difference is much more pronounced in Paw Paw. Such consistency is not found, however, with the sex factor, which shows females clearly leading in Paw Paw, while males have a slight lead in Chelsea. The latter result seems to derive from the adolescent pattern noted earlier (i.e., the low scores for Chelsea girls and the high scores for Chelsea boys).

Statistical testing of the tendencies observed here was conducted using a multiway ANOVA. These results are shown in table 3.41.

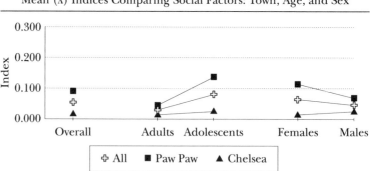

FIGURE 3.9
Mean (ʌ) Indices Comparing Social Factors: Town, Age, and Sex

TABLE 3.41
Multiway ANOVA Results for Social Factors in (ʌ) Variation

Factor	F	df	p-value
Town	4.57	1, 24	.043
Age	2.35	1, 24	.138
Sex	0.25	1, 24	.625
Town × Age	1.51	1, 24	.231
Town × Sex	0.72	1, 24	.404
Sex × Age	0.38	1, 24	.545
Town × Age × Sex	0.07	1, 24	.800

Multiple r = .539; multiple r^2 = .291.

TABLE 3.42
Distribution of Directional Variants of (ʌ) by Social Factors

	Backed	Lowered	Backed-plus-Lowered	Raised	Total Shifted
Females					
Adults					
Paw Paw	3 (18.8%)	13 (81.3%)	0 (0.0%)	0 (0.0%)	16
Chelsea	3 (50.0%)	3 (50.0%)	0 (0.0%)	0 (0.0%)	6
TOTAL	6 (27.3%)	16 (72.7%)	0 (0.0%)	0 (0.0%)	22
Adolescents					
Paw Paw	19 (65.5%)	6 (20.7%)	3 (10.3%)	1 (3.4%)	29
Chelsea	1 (100%)	0 (0.0%)	0 (0.0%)	0 (0.0%)	1
TOTAL	20 (66.7%)	6 (20.0%)	3 (10.0%)	1 (3.3%)	30
TOTAL	26 (50.0%)	22 (42.3%)	3 (5.8%)	1 (1.9%)	52
Males					
Adults					
Paw Paw	3 (60.0%)	1 (20.0%)	0 (0.0%)	1 (20.0%)	5
Chelsea	0 (0.0%)	1 (100%)	0 (0.0%)	0 (0.0%)	1
TOTAL	3 (50.0%)	2 (33.3%)	0 (0.0%)	1 (16.7%)	6
Adolescents					
Paw Paw	17 (81.0%)	2 (9.5%)	0 (0.0%)	2 (9.5%)	21
Chelsea	4 (33.3%)	4 (33.3%)	0 (0.0%)	4 (33.3%)	12
TOTAL	21 (63.6%)	6 (18.2%)	0 (0.0%)	6 (18.2%)	33
TOTAL	24 (61.5%)	8 (20.5%)	0 (0.0%)	7 (17.9%)	39

As was the case for (ε), only the town factor is identified as significant by the ANOVA. Given the high number of extremely low indices, the failure of the other factors to achieve significance is not particularly surprising. Further research will be needed to confirm the patterns observed in figures 3.8 and 3.9.

3.3.3.2. *Social Distribution of Variant Trajectories of* (ʌ). A view of the social differences in the use of the directional variants of (ʌ) is provided in table 3.42 (see n. 16). As was found with the (ε) and (ɪ), these data reveal some interesting asymmetries, though they are not the same asymmetries seen with the other vowels. For example, the clear sex-based differences observed earlier are not evident here. Instead, it seems the clearest distinctions fall along age lines. Whereas adolescents show a strong preference for backed variants, adults are more varied. Among the few tokens from men, backing is slightly more common, but the women's tokens indicate a clear preference for lowering. This raises questions similar to those examined before as to whether the overall lead among adolescents is due to their reliance on backing. To examine this issue, we can compare the rates of backing and lowering for both groups. The 20 tokens of backing produced by girls account for 3.4% of the total number of (ʌ) items coded, and the 6 lowered tokens account for 1.0% of that total ($N = 587$). Remarkably, the boys' rates are identical ($21/615 = 3.4\%$; $6/615 = 1.0\%$). There are too few men's tokens to produce a reliable picture, but for women, the rate of backing was 0.9% ($6/667$), while the lowering rate was 2.4% ($16/667$). Thus, lowering is over twice as common among women than among adolescents, but backing is nearly four times as common among adolescents. These findings indicate, therefore, that the overall adolescent lead in shifting is certainly due to their overwhelming lead in backing, but they also show that this lead is restricted to backing and that the other major direction of change, lowering, is led by women.

While the variation between lowering and backing does not show clear sex differences, this cannot be said for the less common directional variants. The combination of backing-plus-lowering, for example, was heard only from female speakers.[27] On the other hand, raising is found almost exclusively with male speakers. Actually, the raising tendency may be further restricted primarily to young male speakers. These observations, like others made here, will require further research for confirmation.

NOTES

1. Eckert (1988, 1989a, 1991) acknowledges the multidirectionality of many of the NCS vowels, but only in the case of (ɛ) are such variants distinguished in her analysis.
2. A third degree of shifting would have been coded here, but no such extremely lowered and backed tokens appeared in the data.
3. It is difficult to determine precisely which speakers are affected because [ɪ]-like variants may also occur in rapid speech as reduced forms.
4. Here, as throughout this study, individual speakers are denoted by their initials followed by identifying information about their town (Paw Paw = PP or Chelsea = C), their sex (female = f or male = m), and their age.
5. Alternatively, vowel frontness may be represented as the difference between F2 and F1 (Ladefoged 1982).
6. The symbol [r] is used throughout this dissertation to denote the English sound represented by the IPA [ɹ].
7. Recall that items with following /r/ were not included in the analysis of any of the vowels studied (see §2.3.1).
8. Because only tokens of (ɛ) occurring in stressed syllables were analyzed, this factor also denotes the position of the primary word stress.
9. Wang (1969) describes this process of change, which has attracted much debate including the recent discussion by Labov (1994, 421–39).
10. "Variable" is used here in the general statistical sense and not as it is elsewhere in this study to denote sociolinguistic variables such as (ɛ), (ɪ), and (ʌ).
11. An attempt was made to examine the data using an analysis of variance model, a statistical procedure that would consider the data from each individual speaker, but the low numbers of tokens available for many of the phonological categories (e.g., preceding /l/, following interdentals) made this type of analysis unfeasible.

12. Actually, the interpretation of the results with respect to /h/ and interdentals merits caution. Most of the tokens (18/24) containing preceding /h/ also contained an /l/ following the vowel (e.g., *help, health*), a context which is also shown to favor (ɛ)-shifting. This point is considered below (§5.1.2.2). Moreover, as noted above and discussed further below (§5.1.2.1), the index for the category of preceding interdental is based solely on tokens of *them* and *then*.

13. Most (137/154) of the items containing preceding glides had /w/ (e.g., *went, well*).

14. These figures are based on the data used to calculate the (ɛ) indices for each speaker in the sample.

15. In labeling the categories the terms "women," "men," "girls," and "boys" are used as a convenient alternative to more formal locutions such as adult females, adolescent males etc.

16. Readers may note a discrepancy between the number of shifted tokens presented in this table and the number seen in the earlier discussion of phonological conditioning (e.g., table 3.5). The figures in table 3.15 are based on the data used to calculate the index scores for each speaker. They thus reflect the three-token limit employed to reduce lexical bias (see §2.3.2).

17. The latter result may be a lexical effect related to the high number of function words illustrating this category (e.g., *in, it, is, if*; see §5.1.2.1).

18. The index for the nasal category is possibly biased by the great number of tokens of *in* (221/308), and this environment may not be as strongly disfavoring to shifting as suggested by this result (see §5.1.2.3).

19. These results are not represented in figure 3.6.

20. The data for speaker RR, the Chelsea man with the exceptionally high (ɪ) index, are not included in table 3.24, though they would serve to strengthen this point. RR produced 30 tokens of (ɪ), 26 of which were backed.

21. No raised tokens were produced by this speaker, and, thus, only the other three directions are represented here.

22. These items may also have biased the index for the category of preceding labials. From the data in table 3.30, it appears that this category does not play much of a conditioning role, but when these items are omitted from the calculation, the resulting index suggests that this context strongly favors shifting (see §5.1.2.1). Similarly, the category of following nasals may also play a greater role in promoting

(ʌ)-shifting than the index in table 3.31 indicates, as explained below (§5.1.2.1).

23. Many (50/67) of the palatal cases were tokens of *much* and may reflect a lexical effect or one due to the influence of the preceding labial in this item (see §5.1.2.1).

24. As noted earlier, these three *lunch* tokens resulted in a high general index for the category of preceding /l/. Given that these examples occurred in the same morpheme, it is possible that this tendency is conditioned lexically rather than phonologically (i.e., by the context of preceding /l/).

25. The young Chelsea speakers showed a similarly exceptional pattern for (ɪ).

26. It is also possible that there is an interactional effect between age and sex, whereby females lead among adults but males lead among adolescents. Under this scenario it would be the Paw Paw girls whose indices are exceptional (though not by much).

27. In addition to the 3 tokens listed in table 3.42, 3 more examples were identified in the phonological analysis (which did not limit the number of tokens accepted as input). These other 3 also came from female speakers (2 women and 1 girl).

4. RESULTS: (æ), (ɑ), AND (ɔ)

Tʜᴇ ᴘʀᴇꜱᴇɴᴛᴀᴛɪᴏɴ ᴏꜰ ʀᴇꜱᴜʟᴛꜱ from this study of the pattern of vowel changes known as the Northern Cities Shift continues in this chapter with the examination of the lower half of the shift. Described are the findings regarding (æ), (ɑ), and (ɔ). These vowels exhibit a more restricted range of phonetic variation than those discussed in chapter 3, because the shifting they undergo is, for the most part, unidirectional. These variables are also distinguished from the others by the frequency of their shifting. Whereas the shifted variants of (ɛ), (ɪ), and (ʌ) were generally rare, with many speakers making little or no use of them, the shifted variants of (æ), (ɑ), and (ɔ) are quite common, in some cases appearing more frequently than the unshifted variants.

4.1. THE VARIABLE (æ)

4.1.1. ᴘʜᴏɴᴇᴛɪᴄ ᴅᴇꜱᴄʀɪᴘᴛɪᴏɴ ᴏꜰ ᴛʜᴇ ᴠᴀʀɪᴀᴛɪᴏɴ. The principal direction of movement for the low front vowel (æ) involves raising into the traditional range of the mid vowels /e/ and /ɛ/. According to previous accounts of the NCS (e.g., Labov 1994), this raising is preceded by a process of tensing which leads to fronting of the vowel. Also resulting from this tensing (according to Labov 1994) is the development of a schwa-like inglide, which appears when the vowel is raised. These tense, diphthongal variants of raised (æ) were observed in the present study, though not consistently. In some cases the raising produced variants sounding like lax monophthongs very near [ɛ]. Whether these lax variants serve as an alternative (with differing phonological and social distributions) to the tense forms in the same way as do, say, the directional variants of (ɛ), (ɪ), or (ʌ) is an important question but was not pursued in this study.

The coding scheme used for (æ) focused on raising and fronting, as the tense/lax differences (including the presence or absence of the inglide) were judged too difficult to distinguish

consistently. Three degrees of shifting were recorded. Table 4.1
provides approximate phonetic representations of the variants.

An alternative means of representing the variation in the
phonetic realization of (æ) is through the use of acoustic measures, as in figure 4.1. This diagram plots tokens of (æ) according
to their formant frequencies (F1 × F2). The tokens were produced
by speaker MN (PP, f, 18), who, in comparison with other speakers
sampled, showed a high rate of shifting for this vowel. All of the
tokens shown in figure 4.1 occurred in conversational speech.
Most of the shifted variants are monophthongs, but there are a few
diphthongal examples. In the latter cases, the measurements were

TABLE 4.1
Coded Variants of (æ)

0	1	2	3
[æ]	[æ^]	[ɛˇ]	[ɛ]

FIGURE 4.1
F1 and F2 Frequencies for Tokens of (æ) Produced by MN (PP, f, 18)

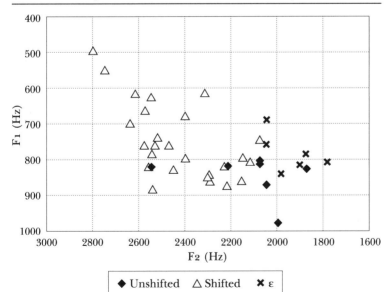

taken from the midpoint of the nucleus. Conservative tokens of (ε) produced by MN are also shown in this figure to provide a point of reference.

One of the most striking aspects of this acoustic picture is how little distance there is between (æ) and (ε). A good deal of intermingling is found even among the conservative variants of these vowels. When shifted, the F1 of (æ) is well within, and in many cases beyond, the range occupied by (ε). The shifted variants of (æ) are, however, pretty clearly distinguished from (ε) in terms of F2, as the raising is accompanied in almost all cases by fronting. In fact, a fair number of the tokens coded as shifted appear to involve little raising at all and instead are primarily fronted. Despite these indications, shifting of (æ) will still be referred to as a raising process in the following discussion because impressionistically this is how the shifted variants are perceived.

4.1.2. PHONOLOGICAL CONDITIONING OF (æ). From a description of how (æ) is shifting, we turn to consider factors that might influence that shifting. As with the vowels discussed earlier, we look first at the roles played by phonological factors before examining social influences in the next section.

The question of phonological conditioning was investigated, as before, by measuring the amount of (æ)-raising found in certain environments. The environments examined were those defined by the now very familiar factors related to the preceding and following consonantal contexts and to the context of the entire word (§3.1.2.1). Again, data from a subsample of the most active users of (æ) were employed in this analysis. Because shifting of this vowel is more common than with those discussed above, the pool of active users from which a subsample could be drawn was greater. The subsample included 16 speakers, representing half of the full sample.

The data from these speakers were pooled and indices were calculated to represent the amount of shifting found in various phonological contexts. These indices are provided in tables 4.2–4. An overall index, representing the amount of (æ)-shifting across all phonological environments, has also been calculated at 0.794 and is included in the tables as a reference point.

TABLE 4.2

Effects of Preceding Phonological Factors on (æ)-Shifting:
General Indices, Frequency of Shifting, and Chi-Square Results

	Index	Unshifted	Shifted	Total
Voicing (χ^2 = 4.59; *p* = .032)				
Voiceless	0.932	260 (39.0%)	406 (61.0%)	666
Voiced	0.804	266 (45.0%)	325 (55.0%)	591
Place (χ^2 = 59.21; *p* < .0001)				
Labial	0.850	191 (41.5%)	269 (58.5%)	460
Alveolar	0.680	332 (51.6%)	312 (48.4%)	644
Interdental	0.798	127 (47.6%)	140 (52.4%)	267
Palatal	0.471	23 (67.6%)	11 (32.4%)	34
Velar	1.217	26 (18.8%)	112 (81.2%)	138
Glottal	0.849	130 (45.8%)	154 (54.2%)	284
Manner (χ^2 = 56.34; *p* < .0001)				
Stop	0.954	204 (35.9%)	365 (64.1%)	569
Fricative	0.804	322 (46.8%)	366 (53.2%)	688
Nasal	0.893	43 (38.4%)	69 (61.6%)	112
Glide	0.889	4 (44.4%)	5 (55.6%)	9
/l/	0.654	131 (53.9%)	112 (46.1%)	243
/r/	0.505	125 (60.7%)	81 (39.3%)	206
#__	0.746	175 (52.9%)	156 (47.1%)	331
OVERALL	0.794			

The high indices in tables 4.2–4 offer a striking contrast to those in comparable tables in chapter 3 and illustrate the much greater frequency of shifting found for (æ). As before, differences in the indices indicate differing influences on (æ)-raising, with some phonological categories serving to promote raising, while others discourage it.

Among the contexts preceding the vowel (table 4.2), shifting is found to be strongly favored by a preceding velar and strongly disfavored by a preceding palatal or /r/. Somewhat weaker influences are seen with preceding stops and voiceless obstruents which promote shifting, and preceding alveolars and /l/ which disfavor shifting. The category of preceding interdentals did not show an exceptional index, though it should be noted that this score was based solely on tokens of the item *that*.

TABLE 4.3

Effects of Following Phonological Factors on (æ)-Shifting:
General Indices, Frequency of Shifting, and Chi-Square Results

	Index	Unshifted	Shifted	Total
Voicing (χ^2 = 7.46; p = .006)				
Voiceless	0.772	562 (49.3%)	579 (50.7%)	1,141
Voiced	0.648	232 (57.1%)	174 (42.9%)	406
Place (χ^2 = 21.13; p < .0001)				
Labial	0.790	200 (48.3%)	214 (51.7%)	414
Alveolar	0.798	637 (45.5%)	764 (54.5%)	1,401
Interdental	1.347	10 (20.4%)	39 (79.6%)	49
Palatal	0.657	16 (45.7%)	19 (54.3%)	35
Velar	0.695	141 (54.4%)	118 (45.6%)	259
Manner (χ^2 = 54.10; p < .0001)				
Stop	0.757	477 (50.1%)	475 (49.9%)	952
Fricative	0.711	317 (53.3%)	278 (46.7%)	595
Nasal	0.891	197 (35.2%)	362 (64.8%)	559
/l/	1.385	13 (25.0%)	39 (75.0%)	52
Cluster (χ^2 = 0.44; p = .508)				
Cluster	0.761	209 (47.9%)	227 (52.1%)	436
No cluster	0.803	795 (46.2%)	927 (53.8%)	1,722
OVERALL	0.794			

TABLE 4.4

Effects of Word-Level Factors on (æ)-Shifting:
General Indices, Frequency of Shifting, and Chi-Square Results

	Index	Unshifted	Shifted	Total
Number of syllables (χ^2 = 17.53; p = .001)				
1	0.781	599 (47.1%)	672 (52.9%)	1,271
2	0.857	227 (42.3%)	310 (57.7%)	537
3	0.824	110 (45.1%)	134 (54.9%)	244
4+	0.566	68 (64.2%)	38 (35.8%)	106
Syllable position (χ^2 = 11.95; p = .003)				
Initial	0.818	348 (45.3%)	421 (54.7%)	769
Medial	0.587	44 (58.7%)	31 (41.3%)	75
Final	1.189	9 (24.3%)	28 (75.7%)	37
OVERALL	0.794			

The most extreme indices among the categories related to the context following the vowel (table 4.3) are those for following interdentals and /l/, both of which strongly favor raising. Following nasals, which have been identified by previous studies (e.g., Labov 1994) as key promoters of (æ)-shifting, do show a favorable influence, though it is not overwhelmingly so. None of the categories of following context appears to have an extremely negative impact on raising, although fairly low indices are found with following voiced obstruents, palatals, velars, and fricatives.

The indices for the word-level categories suggest that raising is strongly favored when the vowel appears in a final syllable and strongly disfavored in a medial syllable. A comparable disfavorable context is found in words of four or more syllables, while little difference is seen among the other word-level categories.

The statistical significance of the differences suggested by the indices was investigated through a series of chi-square tests. These tests examined the distribution of shifted and unshifted tokens across the categories of each phonological factor. As before, differences in the degree of shifting (i.e., whether a token was coded as 1, 2, or 3) were ignored to allow for a straightforward comparison of raised versus unraised tokens. The distributions and the chi-square results are shown in tables 4.2–4.

In all but one case, the statistical testing identifies the differences associated with the phonological factors as significant. The sole exception is the cluster factor where the presence or absence of a tautosyllabic cluster seems to have little effect on (æ)-raising. As regards the other factors, the categories that seem to play key conditioning roles (e.g., preceding velar, following /l/) have already been discussed based on the index data in tables 4.2–4, though it should be reiterated that the chi-square tests evaluate the significance of the whole distribution of shifted and unshifted tokens across the set of categories (e.g., labial, alveolar) under each factor (e.g., preceding place, following manner), rather than the significance of each individual category. By way of concluding this discussion, the results are summarized in table 4.5, which list those categories identified as conditioning the (æ) variation.

TABLE 4.5
Phonological Conditioning of (æ)-Shifting: Summary of Effects

Favor Shifting	*Disfavor Shifting*
Preceding voiceless	Preceding alveolar
PRECEDING VELAR	PRECEDING PALATAL
Preceding stop	Preceding /l/
FOLLOWING INTERDENTAL	PRECEDING /r/
Following nasal	Following voiced
FOLLOWING /l/	Following palatal
FINAL SYLLABLE	Following velar
	Following fricative
	4+ SYLLABLES
	MEDIAL SYLLABLE

NOTE: Categories shown in small capitals strongly favored or disfavored shifting (i.e., their phonological index scores were greater than one standard deviation above or below the overall score).

4.1.3. SOCIAL DISTRIBUTION OF (æ). The variation demonstrated by (æ) is shaped by social as well as phonological factors, and it is to such external influences that the discussion now turns. Differences in the social distribution of (æ) are investigated here in terms of the broad divisions upon which the sample of speakers is structured (town, age, and sex), and usage of (æ) is measured by the individual indices calculated for each speaker in the sample (see §2.3.2).

An overview of social differences in the use of (æ) is provided by figure 4.2. This graph plots the (æ) indices for all 32 speakers sampled. As in similar graphs above, the speakers are grouped according to the factors of town, age, and sex. Group means have been calculated and appear in the graph, marked by a plus sign.

The similarity between the distribution in figure 4.2 and those seen with other vowels, especially (ε) (fig. 3.2), is striking. The downward slope of the points from left to right across the graph is repeated here. Once again there appears to be a substantial difference between the two towns, with Paw Paw speakers generally showing greater degrees of shifting than comparable Chelsea speakers. Also evident are age- and sex-based differences, as adults are

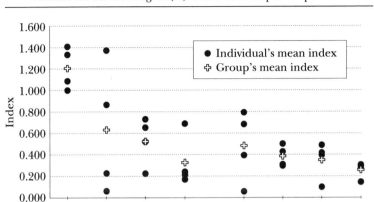

FIGURE 4.2

Indices for the Shifting of (æ) across the Sample of Speakers

seen as generally more advanced than adolescents and females as more advanced than males.

These observations are examined further by comparing the mean indices plotted in figure 4.3. This graph shows the group means for each of the three binary splits in the sample (Paw Paw vs. Chelsea, adults vs. adolescents, females vs. males). The data for the

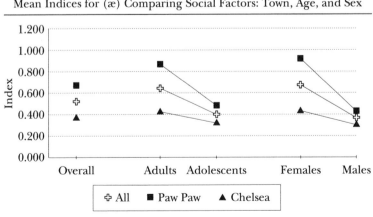

FIGURE 4.3

Mean Indices for (æ) Comparing Social Factors: Town, Age, and Sex latter two factors are further subdivided by town to allow for comparisons within each location.

The patterns suggested by the individual indices are confirmed by these mean data, as the lead in (æ)-shifting is found with Paw Paw speakers over Chelsea speakers, adults over adolescents, and females over males. The mean data also demonstrate the consistency of the age and sex patterns, which hold in both towns, though the differences appear to be much more pronounced in Paw Paw.

To assess the statistical significance of the observed social differences, the index data (the individual scores from each speaker) were subjected to a multiway ANOVA. The results of this analysis are listed in table 4.6.

Each of the three social factors is identified by ANOVA as significant with no significant interactional effects among them. These findings, thus, confirm the observations made throughout this discussion regarding the socially differentiated use of (æ).

The suggestions offered here will be given further consideration and elaboration below in chapter 5. For now, the discussion turns away from (æ) and toward its low, back neighbor, (ɑ).

TABLE 4.6
Multiway ANOVA Results for Social Factors in (æ) Variation

Factor	F	df	p-value
Town	9.04	1, 24	.006
Age	5.64	1, 24	.026
Sex	9.24	1, 24	.006
Town × Age	2.07	1, 24	.163
Town × Sex	3.12	1, 24	.090
Sex × Age	0.86	1, 24	.362
Town × Age × Sex	0.80	1, 24	.379

Multiple $r = .750$; multiple $r^2 = .562$.

4.2 THE VARIABLE (ɑ)

4.2.1. PHONETIC DESCRIPTION OF THE VARIATION. The low, back (ɑ), which is found in words of both the "short *o*" (e.g., *pot*) and "long *a*" (e.g., *father*) classes, undergoes fronting as part of the NCS. While some researchers (Eckert 1989a; Labov 1994) have reported variants as far front as [æ], such extreme forms were not observed in this study. Even the most fronted forms heard here were clearly back of the range of conservative /æ/ and were coded phonetically as central [a]. Phonetic representations of all the coded variants are shown in table 4.7.

While fronting was found to be the primary direction of shifting, there were occasional tokens heard as raised and having a schwa-like quality. Often this raising appeared to be a reduction phenomenon, though in some cases it was found in fully stressed syllables. In a handful of cases, the vowel was heard as both raised and fronted. Raised tokens were not coded as shifted unless they also involved fronting. Given the rarity of raising, the distinction will not be considered in the following analysis.

An acoustic picture of the variation in the realization of (ɑ) is provided in figure 4.4. This graph plots the formant frequencies for several (ɑ) tokens produced by speaker MN (PP, f, 18), whose (æ) data were seen above in figure 4.1. Conservative tokens of (æ) are also shown here for comparison purposes.

These acoustic data corroborate the impressionistic description of (ɑ)-shifting as a fronting process marked by an increase in F_2. However, they also indicate a sizable variation in F_1, suggesting that the fronting is often accompanied by lowering.[1] Interestingly, while fronting produces F_2 frequencies just short of those seen with conservative tokens of (æ), the shifted tokens of (ɑ) are, in most cases, kept well clear of the (æ) range because of the concomitant lowering. This apparent lowering tendency was not dis-

TABLE 4.7
Coded Variants of (ɑ)

0	1	2	3
[ɑ]	[ɑ<]	[a>]	[a]

FIGURE 4.4

F1 and F2 Frequencies for Tokens of (ɑ) Produced by MN (PP, f, 18)

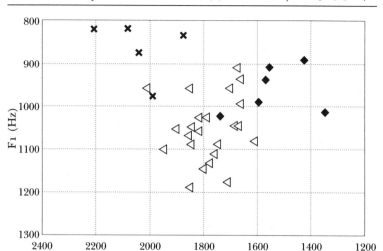

tinguished in the auditory coding done here, though it seems possible that it contributed to the impression that (ɑ) was not "fronted" as far as [æ].

4.2.2. PHONOLOGICAL CONDITIONING OF (ɑ). The investigation of factors conditioning the variation described in the previous section begins by considering possible phonological influences. Such influences were examined using the familiar procedure of calculating indices of (ɑ)-shifting for each of several phonological categories. The data used for this analysis were taken from a subsample of speakers, which, as for (æ), contained the 16 most active users of the (ɑ) variable. The indices from these pooled data are given in tables 4.8–10. Also shown is the overall index of 0.664, which represents the degree of shifting across all phonological contexts.

As in earlier tables, evidence of conditioning influence is seen in the differences across categories. Among the categories of preceding context (table 4.8), high degrees of shifting are found with preceding voiceless obstruents, palatals, glottals (/h/), and nasals.

TABLE 4.8
Effects of Preceding Phonological Factors on (ɑ)-Shifting:
General Indices, Frequency of Shifting, and Chi-Square Results

	Index	*Unshifted*	*Shifted*	*Total*
Voicing (χ^2 = 25.49; p < .0005)				
Voiceless	0.915	125 (42.4%)	170 (57.6%)	295
Voiced	0.566	170 (63.7%)	97 (36.3%)	267
Place (χ^2 = 8.67; p = .070)				
Labial	0.762	110 (54.5%)	92 (45.5%)	202
Alveolar	0.634	414 (58.9%)	289 (41.1%)	703
Palatal	0.853	31 (45.6%)	37 (54.4%)	68
Velar	0.660	169 (58.1%)	122 (41.9%)	291
Glottal	0.833	18 (42.9%)	24 (57.1%)	42
Manner (χ^2 = 66.39; p < .0005)				
Stop	0.760	235 (52.2%)	215 (47.8%)	450
Fricative	0.705	60 (53.6%)	52 (46.4%)	112
Nasal	0.885	127 (44.3%)	160 (55.7%)	287
Glide	0.125	36 (90.0%)	4 (10.0%)	40
/l/	0.508	172 (68.8%)	78 (31.2%)	250
/r/	0.467	112 (67.1%)	55 (32.9%)	167
#__	0.572	124 (63.9%)	70 (36.1%)	194
OVERALL	0.664			

By contrast, preceding /l/, /r/, and glides (which here most involves /w/) are seen as disfavoring shifting.

Among the categories of following context (table 4.9), the highest index is that of following /l/, while the opposite extreme is found with following palatals. The latter result, however, should be approached with caution, as this index is largely based on occurrences of *watch* (20/37 tokens), an item which may be less likely to be shifted because of the context preceding the vowel (see §5.1.2.4). None of the other categories appears to have a overwhelmingly negative effect on shifting, but following interdentals, velars, and tautosyllabic clusters all seem to be fairly strong promoters of the change.

Much less differentiation is evident among the word-level categories. The only notable index is that for two-syllable words, which seem to favor shifting.

TABLE 4.9

Effects of Following Phonological Factors on (ɑ)-Shifting:
General Indices, Frequency of Shifting, and Chi-Square Results

	Index	Unshifted	Shifted	Total
Voicing ($\chi^2 = 0.007$; $p = .935$)				
Voiceless	0.599	508 (60.8%)	327 (39.2%)	835
Voiced	0.628	135 (60.5%)	88 (39.5%)	223
Place ($\chi^2 = 21.59$; $p < .0005$)				
Labial	0.688	189 (55.6%)	151 (44.4%)	340
Alveolar	0.659	590 (58.1%)	426 (41.9%)	1,016
Interdental	0.808	14 (53.8%)	12 (46.2%)	26
Palatal	0.081	34 (91.9%)	3 (8.1%)	37
Velar	0.840	39 (48.1%)	42 (51.9%)	81
Manner ($\chi^2 = 20.55$; $p < .0005$)				
Stop	0.594	610 (61.4%)	384 (38.6%)	994
Fricative	0.781	33 (51.6%)	31 (48.4%)	64
Nasal	0.756	179 (53.3%)	157 (46.7%)	336
/l/	0.962	44 (41.5%)	62 (58.5%)	106
Cluster ($\chi^2 = 3.69$; $p = .055$)				
Cluster	0.841	29 (46.0%)	34 (54.0%)	63
No cluster	0.656	837 (58.2%)	600 (41.8%)	1,437
OVERALL	0.664			

TABLE 4.10

Effects of Word-Level Factors on (ɑ)-Shifting:
General Indices, Frequency of Shifting, and Chi-Square Results

	Index	Unshifted	Shifted	Total
Number of syllables ($\chi^2 = 14.38$; $p = .002$)				
1	0.617	583 (60.9%)	374 (39.1%)	957
2	0.820	149 (48.7%)	157 (51.3%)	306
3	0.656	110 (56.4%)	85 (43.6%)	195
4+	0.643	24 (57.1%)	18 (42.9%)	42
Syllable position ($\chi^2 = 1.01$; $p = .603$)				
Initial	0.764	237 (51.3%)	225 (48.7%)	462
Medial	0.604	31 (58.3%)	22 (41.5%)	53
Final	0.750	15 (53.6%)	13 (46.4%)	28
OVERALL	0.664			

In order to evaluate the statistical strength of these observations, the data were subjected to chi-square testing. As before, these tests examined the distribution of shifted and unshifted tokens within each phonological factor. These distributions and the test results are listed in tables 4.8–10.

The chi-square testing identifies as significant the factors of voicing and manner for the preceding context and place and manner for the following context as well as the word-level factor of syllable number. The results for the factor of preceding place and especially for the factor of following cluster approach significance, though with their *p*-values lying just outside the alpha level of .05, these effects are not strong enough to safely rule out the possibility that these distributions are due to chance.

For the most part, these statistical results reveal no great surprises. Based on the index data (tables 4.8–10), we might have expected to find the voicing and manner differences of the preceding context and the place and manner differences of the following context significant, just as we suspected the voicing differences in the following consonant and those related to the position factor to be insignificant. More unexpected were the findings on the place differences in the preceding context and those for the syllable number factor. In the former case, the index data suggest that preceding palatals and glottals promote shifting, but the number of tokens available for these categories was apparently too low to achieve statistical significance. This also appears to be the case with the cluster factor, where the chi-square results are very close to significant. In the case of the syllable number factor, the opposite situation seems to apply. While the only notable index score was that of the two-syllable category and that was still within a standard deviation of the overall index, the fact that it was based on so many tokens ($N = 306$) probably accounts for its statistical significance.

This discussion of phonological conditioning concludes with a summary list of the results. This list appears in table 4.11.

4.2.3. SOCIAL DISTRIBUTION OF (ɑ). As has been seen with the other elements in the NCS, the variation in (ɑ) involves patterns that are socially, as well as linguistically, defined. Social differences in the use of (ɑ) are examined in figure 4.5, which shows the index scores for the full sample of speakers. The speakers are grouped, as usual, by town, age, and sex, and the mean scores for each group are also shown (marked by plus signs).

TABLE 4.11
Phonological Conditioning of (ɑ)-Shifting: Summary of Effects

Favor Shifting	*Disfavor Shifting*
PRECEDING VOICELESS	PRECEDING GLIDE*
PRECEDING NASAL	Preceding /l/
Following interdental	PRECEDING /r/
Following velar	Following palatal*
FOLLOWING /l/	
Two-syllable words	

NOTE: Categories shown in small capitals strongly favored or disfavored shifting (i.e., their phonological index scores were greater than one standard deviation above or below the overall score). Those marked with asterisks are represented by a limited data set (see discussion in text here and in §5.1.2).

FIGURE 4.5
Indices for the Shifting of (ɑ) across the Sample of Speakers

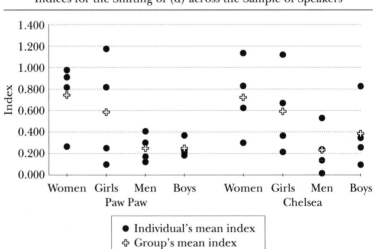

The social distribution of (ɑ) offers a picture rather different than those seen with other vowels. Most notable is the absence of the usual differences between the towns. Instead of the Paw Paw lead that we have come to expect, we find a much greater balance. Also missing are the generational differences, as adults and adolescents of both sexes show roughly the same amount of shifting. The strongest social differences are between the sexes: in both towns and both age groups, females are generally found to lead males in (ɑ)-shifting.

Another view of these social differences is provided by figure 4.6. This figure plots the mean indices for each of the groups defined by the main social factors of town, age, and sex. Because the differences between the sexes are the most dramatic, the data for the town and age factors are further subdivided by sex.

The mean scores confirm the primary importance of the sex differences, which are shown to hold consistently across towns and age groups. The difference is much greater among adults, however, than among adolescents, due to an interesting reversal. Whereas among female speakers, adults (women) lead adolescents (girls), for males the opposite is true. Similarly, the female lead is greater in Paw Paw than in Chelsea, because, while little difference is found between the female means of each town, the Chelsea males show a higher average index than their Paw Paw counterparts.

FIGURE 4.6
Mean Indices for (ɑ) Comparing Social Factors: Town, Age, and Sex

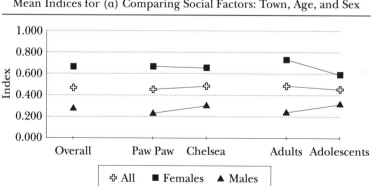

TABLE 4.12
Multiway ANOVA Results for Social Factors in (ɑ) Variation

Factor	F	df	p-value
Town	0.05	1, 24	.823
Age	0.09	1, 24	.726
Sex	11.56	1, 24	.002
Town × Age	0.16	1, 24	.698
Town × Sex	0.08	1, 24	.777
Sex × Age	0.94	1, 24	.342
Town × Age × Sex	0.08	1, 24	.784

Multiple r = .592; multiple r^2 = .351.

The statistical significance of the social patterning was evaluated through a multiway ANOVA of the individual index data. The results of this procedure are listed in table 4.12. The only social factor shown to be significant is sex. This finding confirms the indications of figures 4.5 and 4.6, which suggest shifting was much more common among female speakers than among males. Also, the fact that no interactional effects were identified as significant indicates the consistency of the sex-based pattern and suggests that there is general agreement across the sample that (ɑ) functions as a gender marker.

This section has examined linguistic and social factors shaping the (ɑ) variation. Further consideration of the issues raised here is given in chapter 5. For now, the discussion turns to the final NCS element to be examined, the back vowel (ɔ).

4.3. THE VARIABLE (ɔ)

4.3.1. PHONETIC DESCRIPTION OF THE VARIATION. Our tour through the vowels of the Northern Cities Shift concludes with an investigation of back rounded (ɔ). This vowel is classified by some accounts (e.g., Ladefoged 1982) as mid and by others (e.g., Kenyon and Knott 1953) as low. Regardless of how it is labeled, the vowel (in its conservative state) is distinguished from the maximally low /ɑ/ in height as well as rounding. These distinguishing features are precisely what is lost during the NCS, as the vowel is lowered and unrounded.

The coding system distinguished the usual three degrees of shifting for (ɔ), but the differences coded involved rounding as well as movement of the vowel.[2] The first degree of shifting was used to code tokens that were heard as relatively high and back but only slightly rounded. Tokens judged to be low and slightly rounded were coded as the second degree of shifting. The most extremely shifted tokens were those heard as low and clearly unrounded. These variants are represented phonetically in table 4.13.

In addition to the main path of shifting illustrated by these variants, there were several tokens that appeared to involve a process of fronting without substantial lowering. This process was often accompanied by some degree of unrounding as the vowel approached the quality of [ʌ]. These fronted tokens were coded as shifted only when they included the unrounding. Fronting of (ɔ) was a relatively rare phenomenon compared to the more frequent lowering and is not treated separately in the following analysis, though it certainly merits consideration in future research.

An acoustic representation of the (ɔ) variation is provided in figure 4.7. Shown are formant frequency measures for several tokens of (ɔ) produced by speaker JH (C, f, 16), who had the highest index of shifting for this vowel. For comparison purposes, tokens of (ʌ) and (ɑ) that were judged to be conservative are also shown. All of the (ɔ) tokens marked as shifted come from conversational data, but the unshifted tokens, as well as the examples of (ʌ) and (ɑ), are taken from the word-list reading because this speaker produced so few unshifted tokens in free speech.

These data show more than the usual amount of overlap among categories. The distinction between shifted and unshifted

TABLE 4.13
Coded Variants of (ɔ)

0	1	2	3
[ɔ]	[ɔ̞]	[ɒ]	[ɑ]

FIGURE 4.7

F1 and F2 Frequencies for Tokens of (ɔ) Produced by JH (C, f, 16)

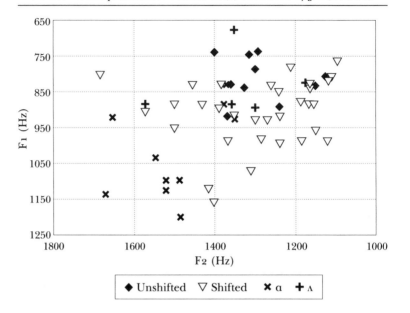

(ɔ) is reflected primarily in the vertical dimension, as most of the unshifted tokens appear in the upper portion of the diagram with F1 values below 850 Hz. Quite a few shifted tokens also appear in this range, though many more are found below it. The distinction is less clear in terms of F2, as shifted tokens appear on both sides of the unshifted. It might therefore be concluded that, in addition to lowering, shifting sometimes involves fronting and sometimes backing. It is more likely, however, that the F2 variation shown here reflects differences in lip rounding in addition to or instead of differences in the position of the tongue body. If this is the case, then the variants showing lower F2 values may simply be (more) rounded without necessarily being more back. It should also be noted that the acoustic effects of lip rounding are commonly seen in the frequency of F3 as well. Because F3 is not represented here, this picture of tremendous overlap among variants may not accurately reflect the perceptual differences among them.

Shifting brings (ɔ) well within the range occupied by (ɑ). For this speaker, we find a few (ɑ) tokens with F1 values in the more conservative neighborhood of around 900 Hz, but most show the extreme lowering that was seen earlier (fig. 4.4). Even these very low variants, however, are rivaled by some of the shifted tokens of (ɔ).

As a final observation on this acoustic picture, we note the high degree of overlap in the (ɔ) and (ʌ) distributions. A similar situation was seen in the discussion of (ʌ)-shifting (see fig. 3.7). While the spectral (F1 × F2) data suggest there is little or no contrast between these vowels, they are perceptually quite distinct. This distinction involves lip rounding and, therefore, may not be fully reflected in the absence of F3 data. Perhaps more importantly, however, the contrast involves temporal differences between the vowels, as /ɔ/ is typically much longer.

4.3.2. PHONOLOGICAL CONDITIONING OF (ɔ). The question of possible influences from phonological factors on the shifting of (ɔ) was examined using the same procedures that were applied for other vowels. Indices representing the amount of shifting occurring in each of several phonological contexts were calculated using pooled data from a subsample of speakers. As before, the 16 most active users of this variable were selected for the subsample. The resulting indices are given in tables 4.14–16. An overall index of shifting across all categories was also calculated (at 1.308) and appears in each figure as a reference point.

For the factors involving the preceding context (table 4.14), the greatest differentiation is found with the manner categories. These indices suggest that shifting is strongly favored by preceding glides (which here are represented only by /w/) and /r/,[3] somewhat less strongly favored by preceding fricatives, and strongly disfavored by preceding nasals and /l/. The place differences appear to have less of an impact, though it does seem that preceding glottals promote shifting, while preceding interdentals have the opposite effect; still, both of these results are based on lexically restricted data sets, with most of the glottal cases involving tokens of *hall* and all of the interdental cases involving tokens of *thought*. Only minor differences are seen with the voicing factor.

TABLE 4.14

Effects of Preceding Phonological Factors on (ɔ)-Shifting:
General Indices, Frequency of Shifting, and Chi-Square Results

	Index	Unshifted	Shifted	Total
Voicing (χ^2 = 1.39; p = .238)				
Voiceless	1.339	52 (15.5%)	284 (84.5%)	336
Voiced	1.235	24 (20.2%)	95 (79.8%)	119
Place (χ^2 = 3.15; p = .534)				
Labial	1.284	50 (17.7%)	232 (82.3%)	282
Alveolar	1.305	49 (15.3%)	272 (84.7%)	321
Interdental	1.219	5 (15.6%)	27 (84.4%)	32
Velar	1.333	11 (11.1%)	88 (88.9%)	99
Glottal	1.393	6 (21.4%)	22 (78.6%)	28
Manner (χ^2 = 17.85; p = .007)				
Stop	1.243	49 (17.0%)	239 (83.0%)	288
Fricative	1.431	27 (16.2%)	140 (83.8%)	167
Nasal	1.031	14 (21.9%)	50 (78.1%)	64
Glide	1.576	2 (3.0%)	64 (97.0%)	66
/l/	1.122	25 (21.7%)	90 (78.3%)	115
/r/	1.532	4 (6.5%)	58 (93.5%)	62
#__	1.324	54 (14.7%)	313 (85.3%)	367
OVERALL	1.308			

The situation with the factors related to the context following the vowel (table 4.15) is largely the reverse, as greater differentiation is found in the voicing and place categories than in those for manner. Shifting is clearly favored by following voiced obstruents, labials,[4] velars, fricatives, and clusters. As for disfavorable contexts, the lowest indices are found with following interdentals and palatals, though both of these scores are based on an unreliably low number of tokens. Though not as low as these, the score for following nasals is more reliable, and it, too, suggests a disfavorable influence on shifting. Among the categories showing little or no impact on shifting is the context of final position, an environment that has not previously been examined because the other vowels never occur word-finally.

Among the word-level categories, none appears to offer a strongly favorable context. Shifting appears to be disfavored in words of three or four-plus syllables, and in medial syllables. The indices for the latter two categories, however, are based on too few tokens to be reliably evaluated.

The significance of these suggested patterns was evaluated through chi-square testing on the distributions of shifted and unshifted tokens in each category. These data are provided in tables 4.14–16.

One important point to note about the data in these tables is that, for (ɔ), unlike for the vowels examined earlier, almost all phonological categories show more shifted tokens than unshifted, and many categories show a great deal more shifted tokens. This is, of course, a consequence of the fact that shifted variants of (ɔ), as

TABLE 4.15

Effects of Following Phonological Factors on (ɑ)-Shifting:
General Indices, Frequency of Shifting, and Chi-Square Results

	Index	Unshifted	Shifted	Total
Voicing				
Voiceless	1.386	51 (12.7%)	351 (87.3%)	402
Voiced	1.850	0 (0.0%)	20 (100%)	20
Place (χ^2 = 11.88; p = .003)				
Labial	1.484	13 (10.2%)	115 (89.8%)	128
Alveolar	1.238	129 (18.2%)	580 (81.8%)	709
Interdental	1.000	0 (0.0%)	1 (100%)	1
Palatal	1.000	0 (0.0%)	6 (100%)	6
Velar	1.446	21 (9.9%)	192 (90.1%)	213
Manner (χ^2 = 8.53; p = .080)				
Stop	1.343	34 (14.4%)	202 (85.6%)	236
Fricative	1.489	17 (9.1%)	169 (90.9%)	186
Nasal	1.167	19 (16.7%)	95 (83.3%)	114
/l/	1.259	93 (17.9%)	428 (82.1%)	521
_#	1.306	12 (16.7%)	60 (83.3%)	72
Cluster (χ^2 = 7.56; p = .006)				
Cluster	1.500	9 (7.1%)	117 (93.9%)	126
No cluster	1.284	166 (16.6%)	837 (83.4%)	1,003
OVERALL	1.308			

NOTE: No test was possible for the voicing factor because of the lack of unshifted tokens for the voiced category. Because there were too few tokens representing the interdental and palatal categories for reliable testing, they were omitted in the place test.

analyzed here, appear so frequently and are much more common than shifted forms of any of the other NCS variables. For this reason, it seems clear that practically all of the phonological categories examined here can be said to promote shifting of (ɔ). Therefore, this analysis indicates which environments are more strongly favorable and which are less strongly favorable to shifting.

For the most part these statistical results in tables 4.14–16 confirm the suggestions made above. In the context preceding the vowel, differences of manner are most important, as indicated by the significant chi-square result (p = .007) associated with these differences, while insignificant results were found for the voicing and place factors in table 4.14. In the following context, however, it is the place differences that play the greatest role, as they were significant (p = .003) while the manner differences were not. The differences related to the cluster factor are also shown to be significant, but those related to the voicing status of the following consonant could not be evaluated due to the low number of tokens for the voiced category. Finally, neither of the word-level categories was found to be significant.

TABLE 4.16
Effects of Word-Level Factors on (ɔ)-Shifting:
General Indices, Frequency of Shifting, and Chi-Square Results

	Index	Unshifted	Shifted	Total
Number of syllables (χ^2 = 1.67; p = .435)				
1	1.314	99 (14.8%)	570 (85.2%)	669
2	1.323	67 (15.7%)	360 (84.3%)	427
3	1.067	7 (23.3%)	23 (76.7%)	30
4+	0.333	2 (66.7%)	1 (33.3%)	3
Syllable position (χ^2 = 2.66; p = .264)				
Initial	1.265	51 (16.5%)	259 (83.5%)	310
Medial	1.000	3 (37.5%)	5 (62.5%)	8
Final	1.394	22 (15.5%)	120 (84.5%)	142
OVERALL	1.308			

NOTE: Because there were too few tokens representing the 4+ syllable category for reliable testing, these data were omitted in the test for syllable number.

The individual categories that likely contributed to the findings of significance have already been discussed. This discussion is summarized in table 4.17.

4.3.3. SOCIAL DISTRIBUTION OF (ɔ). As with all respectable sociolinguistic variables, the (ɔ) variation is shaped by social as well as linguistic factors. Social differences in the use of (ɔ) are evident in figure 4.8, which displays the index scores for the full sample of speakers. The format of this graph is familiar from the discussion of the other vowels. As before, group means are indicated by plus signs.

The social distribution of (ɔ) resembles that seen with (ɑ) and, therefore, is rather different from those of the other four vowels examined. The clear differences between Paw Paw and Chelsea that characterized the distributions of (ε), (ɪ), (ʌ), and (æ) are again absent here. Furthermore, the sex-based distinctions that were seen with (ɑ) are repeated in this distribution.

TABLE 4.17

Phonological Conditioning of (ɔ)-Shifting: Summary of Effects

Favor Shifting	*Disfavor Shifting*[a]
Preceding fricative	PRECEDING NASALS
PRECEDING GLIDES*	PRECEDING /l/
PRECEDING /r/	
FOLLOWING VOICED*	
FOLLOWING LABIALS	
Following velars	
FOLLOWING CLUSTERS	

NOTE: Categories shown in small capitals strongly favored or disfavored shifting (i.e., their phonological index scores were greater than one standard deviation above or below the overall score). Those marked with asterisks are represented by a limited data set (see discussion in text here and in §5.1.2).

a. These categories are more properly interpreted as less strongly favoring shifting rather than actually disfavoring it since shifted variants of (ɔ) are more common than unshifted even in these contexts.

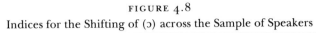

FIGURE 4.8

Indices for the Shifting of (ɔ) across the Sample of Speakers

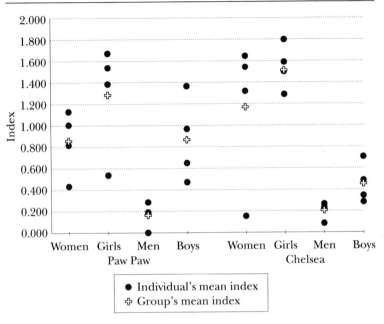

There is, however, one major way in which the (ɔ) distribution differs from that of (ɑ), and that relates to the age factor. Whereas no significant generational differences were found with (ɑ), such differences are evident here. Interestingly, these differences are the reverse of those seen with (ɛ) and (æ), as adolescents generally show greater degrees of (ɔ)-shifting than comparable adults.

These social differences are further explored in the mean indices presented in figure 4.9. As in similar graphs, the means for each of the main divisions (Paw Paw vs. Chelsea, adults vs. adolescents, females vs. males) are plotted, and the town and age data are further subdivided by sex.

These mean scores confirm the earlier observations regarding the sex and age factors. Females consistently lead males. The extent of this lead is roughly the same among adults as among adolescents, though the latter show higher rates of shifting. Comparing the two towns, we find indications of an interesting sex-based reversal. When female speakers are compared, Chelsea is

FIGURE 4.9
Mean Indices for (ɔ) Comparing Social Factors: Town, Age, and Sex

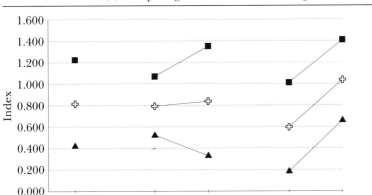

found to lead Paw Paw, but when males are compared, it is Paw Paw speakers who lead. As a result of this reversal, the sex differences are more pronounced in Chelsea.

The individual indices were examined through a multiway ANOVA in order to assess the statistical strength of the patterns suggested by their social distribution. The results of this procedure are summarized in table 4.18.

TABLE 4.18
Multiway ANOVA Results for Social Factors in (ɔ) Variation

Factor	F	df	p-value
Town	0.13	1, 24	.724
Age	11.09	1, 24	.003
Sex	36.34	1, 24	< .0005
Town × Age	0.95	1, 24	.340
Town × Sex	3.12	1, 24	.090
Sex × Age	0.09	1, 24	.768
Town × Age × Sex	0.54	1, 24	.468

Multiple r = .592; multiple r^2 = .351.

The age and sex patterns described here are confirmed as significant through the ANOVA procedure. These results also confirm the insignificance of the differences between the towns; however, there is a hint (p = .090) of an interactional effect between town and sex. This effect was evident in the reversal discussed above, whereby Chelsea females lead Paw Paw females, but Chelsea males show less shifting than their Paw Paw counterparts.

With this discussion of (ɔ), the tour through each of the Northern Cities vowels is completed and with it the main presentation of results. The implications of the observations made in this chapter and in chapter 3 are addressed in the following chapter, which attempts to bring together findings on all the NCS elements.

NOTES

1. The minor tendency of (ɑ)-raising (mentioned above) was not demonstrated by the speaker whose data are represented in figure 4.4.

2. The question of whether the coding scheme for (ɔ) is comparable to those used for the other vowels is addressed in chapter 6.

3. The effect indicated for preceding /r/ may be related to the influence of the environment following the vowel in these items, many of which contained velar nasals or fricatives (e.g., *wrong, strong, cross*), both of which promote shifting (see §5.1.2.2).

4. The effect of following labials is almost certainly related to the effect of following fricatives, since all but 1 of the 128 labial tokens involved the fricative /f/ (e.g., *sophomore, offer*).

5. DISCUSSION

THE PRECEDING TWO CHAPTERS have put forward the primary results of this study by describing the variation associated with each of the NCS vowels. Throughout that discussion, attempts to interpret or explain the findings were kept to a minimum for purposes of presentational clarity. Having examined each vowel individually, we are now in a better position to approach the results from a broader perspective, drawing links among the various results offered here and relating these to findings from other studies.

This chapter adopts such a perspective to consider some of the major issues raised by the present findings. The discussion begins by elaborating and attempting to explain patterns related to the linguistic conditioning of the NCS variation. The focus then turns to questions concerning the social distributions detailed above. The goal throughout this discussion is to clarify the findings and consider their implications for our understanding of the NCS and other language changes.

5.1. ISSUES RELATED TO PHONOLOGICAL CONDITIONING

Language change is, for the most part, an incremental process. Innovations typically do not appear immediately throughout the entire language (nor the entire speech community), but rather have their start in a limited number of linguistic contexts. As the change progresses, the new forms are found in more and more contexts. The investigation of phonological conditioning carried out for the NCS vowels was designed on these principles and sought to identify those contexts most involved in the changes. For each vowel, comparisons were made of the degree of shifting associated with each of several phonological environments, and, based on these comparisons, a number of linguistic factors were judged to either favor or disfavor shifting.

These findings provide important information about how the NCS changes are implemented, and a better understanding of them may offer key insight into the change process. With this in mind, we return to the findings, this time exploring areas of possible explanation for the patterns observed. Several types of explanations are discussed and exemplified through data from the various NCS vowels. This discussion does not attempt to explain all the results presented in chapters 3 and 4. Rather, it focuses on some of the major patterns, and it outlines a series of issues to be considered when addressing such results. Before turning to these issues, however, the findings of previous research on the phonological conditioning of the NCS are reviewed and compared to those of the current project.

5.1.1. COMPARISONS TO PREVIOUS RESEARCH RESULTS. Questions related to the linguistic factors involved in conditioning the NCS changes have been addressed by some of the earlier studies, though this aspect of the shift is not as well documented as one might expect of such a well-known series of changes. The studies that treat this issue have restricted their focus either by considering only a subset of the shifting vowels or by examining only a narrow range of phonological contexts. Still, some patterns have been observed, and a comparison of these with the present findings may prove helpful in evaluating both sets of data.

Before discussing particular findings, some comments about the comparability of results are in order. The most-developed discussion of phonological conditioning of the NCS (and even it is rather limited in scope) is found in the study by Labov, Yaeger, and Steiner (1972). In that work, the progress of the changes was assessed using acoustic measures (F1 and F2 frequencies). The authors compared the influence of consonantal contexts by mapping tokens of the vowel appearing in those contexts in acoustic space (similar to the F1 × F2 figures used here). The contexts that were identified as promoting shifting were those whose tokens were measured to be most distant from "normal" (i.e., unshifted) values. In this way, factors are compared in terms of the degree of shifting they condition—but not in terms of the frequency with which they condition shifting.

The indices used in this study, by contrast, were designed to incorporate both degree and frequency information. Nevertheless, when the degree differences form a continuum, as they appear to do here, they should directly correlate with frequency differences. That is, as shifting of a vowel becomes more frequent, it is predicted to shift further as well and vice versa. We do not expect to find a vowel that shifts very rarely but shows extremely shifted variants when it does. For these reasons, the observations made in this study based on the index data are largely comparable to those based on acoustic data, such as those of Labov, Yaeger, and Steiner (1972), though, as will be described below, the present reliance on measures of frequency of occurrence necessitates consideration of certain other factors when seeking to explain the results.

Turning now to the findings, we begin with (æ), the vowel that has received the most attention, both in general and with regard to questions of phonological conditioning. Research into such questions has focused almost exclusively on the influence of consonants following the vowel; very little attention has been paid to possible effects related to the context preceding the vowel. Among the findings is Labov, Yaeger, and Steiner's (1972) report that following nasals strongly promote (æ)-raising. In the present study, nasals were found to promote shifting, though their index (0.891) was not exceptionally high (cf. overall index of 0.794). However, it is possible that this index is not truly representative of the amount of (æ)-shifting before nasals because of a lexical bias introduced by the large number of tokens of *and*. This possibility is considered in more detail below (§5.1.2.1).

Labov, Yaeger, and Steiner (1972) also investigated the effects of place differences among voiceless stops and concluded that the strongest shifting occurred before palatals, then alveolars, then bilabials, with the least degree of shifting before velars.[1] The examination of place differences in the present study considered all consonants, rather than just voiceless stops, and found a similar hierarchy with the exception that the least amount of shifting occurred with following palatals. However, none of the indices associated with these place differences was exceptional. The indices for following labials (0.790) and alveolars (0.798) were very near the overall index for (æ) (0.794), while those of velars (0.695) and palatals (0.657) were well below it (though within a standard deviation). Interestingly, the only place category to show a really exceptional index was the one not investigated by Labov, Yaeger, and Steiner (1972), namely interdentals, which are indicated by their index of 1.347 to strongly favor shifting.

One area of fairly good agreement between this study and that of Labov, Yaeger, and Steiner (1972) is seen in the effects of preceding liquids (the only prevocalic context discussed by Labov and his colleagues). Both studies found this environment to disfavor shifting of (æ). We have seen here that the disfavoring effect of preceding /r/ was very strong (with an index of 0.505). Preceding /l/ also showed a low index (0.654), though this value was within a standard deviation of the overall index of 0.794.

The only other study to examine the phonological conditioning of (æ) is Callary (1975), who found that shifting was not particularly common before nasals but was strongly promoted by following velars, results that run counter to those reported by Labov, Yaeger, and Steiner (1972) and, to a somewhat lesser extent, to the present study. Callary also examined the effects of voicing differences in following stops, concluding that shifting is more favored before voiceless than before voiced. This finding is consistent with the data reported here, though both the index for following voiceless and that for following voiced are below the overall index and neither is exceptional (voiceless = 0.772, voiced = 0.648).

For the (ɑ) and (ɔ) variables, the only work to examine phonological factors is Labov, Yaeger, and Steiner (1972), and even they restrict their discussion to the effects of following (mostly voiceless) stops. The hierarchy they report for (ɑ)-shifting is similar to that seen with (æ), whereby palatals show the most shifting, then alveolars, then velars, with the position of labials unclear. This picture does not accord well with the results found here, which indicate that following palatals strongly disfavor shifting and following velars strongly favor shifting, while labials and alveolars seem to have little effect either way. Labov, Yaeger, and Steiner's (1972) results for (ɔ) are somewhat more consistent with those seen here. They found, at least among their middle-aged speakers,[2] the most extreme shifting before velars and more conservative variants before alveolars. In this study, velars were found to favor shifting and alveolars to disfavor shifting, though the greatest amount of shifting among place categories was associated with following labials, which were not discussed by Labov, Yaeger, and Steiner.

The phonological conditioning of the upper half of the NCS, the (ı), (ε), and (ʌ) variables, has received less attention than that of the lower half. Eckert (1991) noted that the backing of (ε) was very common before /l/, a finding consistent with the very high index found to be associated with that category in the present study. In another paper, Eckert (1988) reported that backing and rounding of (ʌ) is favored by adjacent, especially preceding, labials. This finding, however, is not supported by the present results, which show that preceding labials have only very slightly positive effects on (ʌ)-backing, while following labials actually have negative effects on this shifting. For (ı), no research on phonological conditioning has been reported in the literature.

Overall, this comparison of results reveals no strong contradictions. Many of the findings that have been reported here are weakly consistent with those of previous studies, while others are weakly inconsistent. The general lack of points of strong agreement may be indicative of the very different types of analysis used, particularly of the great differences in the scope of factors considered. It is worth noting that with only two exceptions—the effects of liquids on (æ) and those of labials on (ε)—previous researchers either have not considered or have considered and dismissed the effects of the environment preceding the vowel, yet for every one of the NCS vowels, the present study identified several categories among the factors related to the preceding context as having a significant impact on shifting.

One of the advantages of examining a broader range of potential factors is the perspective this provides. The analysis pursued here allowed not only for comparisons of categories within a factor (e.g., place differences) but also for comparisons across factors (e.g., place vs. manner effects). In addition, for each vowel there was a benchmark, in the form of the overall index, to which each score could be compared. An example of how the conclusions available from this analysis differ from those of other studies was seen above in comparing the results regarding place effects on (æ). Labov, Yaeger, and Steiner (1972) examined within-factor differences to arrive at a hierarchy with palatals at one end and velars at the other. Much of the same relative ordering of these categories was evident in the data reported here; however, the data also suggested that the effects associated with these place categories were, for the most part, minor, relative to the conditioning influence of other categories (e.g., following /l/, preceding velars). Thus, having a range of effects to compare (including effects related to the consonant preceding the vowel) provides a greater perspective from which to assess the conditioning impact of individual categories.

5.1.2. TYPES OF EXPLANATIONS. The following analysis builds on the discussion of the phonological results by exploring a number of issues that may help explain some of the patterns noted above. Various results are considered in a discussion that is organized by types of "explanations," a term that is used here with some apprehension. Many of the suggestions made simply clarify earlier observations. Even with those suggestions that address the underlying causes for the results, I am making no claim that these explanations account fully for the patterns. While they do have insight to offer in the present discussion, they are mentioned here also as potentially fruitful avenues for future research.

5.1.2.1. *Lexical Bias.* The first of these issues to be explored involves the possibility that certain results are biased by particular lexical items. The index scores on which much of the phonological analysis is based are meant to indicate the amount of shifting associated with categories that are phonologically defined (e.g., following labials, preceding fricatives). In some cases, however, the indices are calculated from a limited variety of words, raising the possibility that they are not representative of the phonological category as much as of the few lexical items sampled. Often, this situation occurs because a particular phonological combination is rare and found in only a few items. Alternatively, the combination may be fairly widespread in the English lexicon (occurring in many different items), but the data sets for the indices may not truly reflect this lexical variety because they are dominated by a few extremely common words containing the combination. Furthermore, the probability for lexical bias may be greater with certain vowels, particularly (ʌ) and (ɔ), which, because of their historical development, occur either in a smaller set of lexical items or in more limited phonological contexts.

A good candidate example of a lexically biased result is seen in the index for (ɛ) in the category of a preceding interdental. The low index for this category (0.190) suggests that it is an environment disfavoring shifting. However, the 147 tokens upon which that index is based involved just two words: *then* (139 tokens) and *them* (8 tokens). In conversational speech, these items, like many short, commonly occurring function words, are frequently unstressed or only lightly stressed and, therefore, are subject to phonetic reduction. As a rule, such reduced variants were excluded from consideration in this study, which meant that only those tokens that were fully stressed could be used in constructing the indices. It is likely that this selection criterion biased the sample toward more conservative variants, since fully stressed tokens might be expected to be articulated more carefully. As a result of this greater care, speakers might be less apt to produce socially marked forms such as the shifted variants of the NCS vowels.

A number of the indices for (ɪ) may have been affected in much the same way. For example, initial position was identified as an environment that strongly disfavors (ɪ)-shifting. However, this index is based mostly on four function words, *it*, *in(to)*, *is*, and *if*, that together account for 486 of the 505 tokens examined. The many tokens of *in* (221), just 4 of which were shifted, also contributed to the low score for the context of following nasals. Similarly, the low index associated with preceding glottals depicts mainly the degree of shifting in the items *him* and *his*, which contributed 56 of the 61 tokens counted. Even less variety is seen in the items from which the indices for preceding and following interdentals were calculated, as the former used exclusively tokens of *this* and the latter used exclusively tokens of *with(in)*.

Some of the (ʌ) data seem to reflect a lexical bias from the very high frequency of the items *was(n't)* and *one(s)*. Shifting in these words was very rare; none of the 147 tokens of *was* was shifted, and only 2 of the 112 tokens of *one* were shifted. The effects of these items are seen very clearly in the extremely low index for the category of preceding glides, since together they account for nearly 86% of the 302 tokens in this category. They also, of course, influence the category of preceding labials. In the original calculation, the index for this category was somewhat surprising. We might expect, for phonetic reasons and on the basis of previous research (Eckert 1988), that preceding labials would strongly favor shifting, particularly backing and rounding. Yet, we found an index that was higher than the overall index, but not by much (0.125 vs. 0.114). When this index is recalculated and the *was* and *one* tokens are excluded, the result is a score (0.215) that ranks as the second highest of all categories examined and suggests that preceding labials are indeed a very important promoter of (ʌ)-shifting.

Such a recalculation is also appropriate to evaluate the effect on (ʌ)-shifting of following nasals. The original index of 0.091 suggests that this environment does not favor shifting. That calculation, however, is based on a sample of 605 tokens, which includes 112 tokens of *one*, 152 tokens of *some* and its compounds (e.g., *somebody, something*), and 48 tokens of *from*. When these items are omitted from the calculation, we find a much higher index for this category (0.174), indicating that this too is an important promoter of the shift.

A similar situation may also help explain why following nasals were not found to overwhelmingly favor the raising of (æ), as had been seen in previous studies (e.g., Labov, Yaeger, and Steiner 1972). Among the 559 tokens used in calculating the index for this category, the largest number from any single item were those from *and*, which contributed 64 tokens. Shifting was not very common in this item, and only 8 of the tokens were coded as raised. When the *and* tokens are removed from consideration, the index for this category rises from 0.891 to 0.986. Still, this score is within a standard deviation of the overall index for this vowel, which is

0.794, and, perhaps more importantly, ranks quite a bit below other categories, including following /l/ (with an index of 1.385) and preceding velars (with an index of 1.217). Thus, even without the potentially biasing effects of *and*, the index for following nasals suggests that this environment favors shifting but not to the powerful extent reported in earlier studies.

There are other cases where the data sets used to construct the indices were dominated by particular lexical items but where these items were not especially prone to reduction. In these cases, interpretation is more difficult, as it is less clear whether the effects demonstrated are peculiar to the words sampled or are really representative of the phonological context involved. An example is seen in the (1)-shifting associated with the category of preceding velars. A total of 99 tokens illustrating this context were examined, 75 of which were tokens of *kid(s)*. This category showed a high index of shifting, though every one of the 21 shifted cases occurred in *kid(s)*. While it is possible that this is indeed a phonological effect (i.e., one conditioned by the velar context), the fact that none of the other 24 cases of (1) after velars was shifted might suggest otherwise. One possible alternative interpretation is that this is a case of lexical diffusion, a process whereby a change becomes established in particular morphemes and spreads by increasing the number of items in which it appears. A more lexically diverse pool of data will be needed to help clarify this issue.

As an addendum to this suggestion, we might consider the results for (1)-shifting following palatals. This context also was found to favor shifting, though again one word seems to have figured heavily in this result, and that item is *children*, which contributed 11 of the 26 tokens, including 5 of the 10 shifted cases. Because of the semantic similarity, it is tempting to see a connection between this result and the shifting in *kid*. This might, for example, suggest that lexical diffusion is sensitive to semantic fields. On the other hand, it might be argued that shifting in the tokens of *children* is really an effect of the following /l/, which generally favors the change. The latter argument seems more plausible, but as with *kid*, more data will be needed to sort out these possibilities.

The situation is unclear in other cases as well. For example, the category of following palatals was found to promote shifting of (ʌ). However, 50 of the 67 items illustrating this context were tokens of *much*, including 7 of the 8 shifted tokens. While this high rate of shifting may really be an effect associated with following palatals, it may also be due to the influence of the preceding /m/ since labials were shown above to favor shifting. There also exists the possibility that this is a lexical effect, that is, a characteristic of the word *much*. Again, more data will be needed.

Some similar cases can be mentioned as other potential instances of lexical bias. Thus, the 50 tokens of *walk* may influence certain (ɔ) indices, especially those related to preceding glides.[3] Also, many of the (ɑ) indices were based heavily on the words *lot*, *not*, and *got*. For *lot*, 206 tokens were counted, of which 57 (28%) were shifted. A similar rate of shifting was seen for *got*, where 37 of the 163 tokens (23%) were fronted, but for *not*, shifting was much more common, occurring in 110 of the 202 tokens (54%).

These cases illustrate one of the ways in which the primary analytical tool used in this study, the vowel shifting index, can be affected by the frequency of particular lexical items. Because very common words may distort the phonological picture represented by the indices, it may seem to be a disadvantage to use such a technique. On the other hand, this type of approach is needed to help illuminate lexically based patterns. Perhaps the lesson to be taken from this discussion is the need for careful examination of the index data to ensure the appropriateness of the claims that are based on them.

5.1.2.2. *Coincidental Effects.* Each word that contributed to the data set for the phonological analysis served as an example of a number of phonological categories. In constructing the phonological indices, aspects of both the preceding and following contexts as well as of the entire word were distinguished, but, of course, these aspects coexist within the word. Thus, for example, the word *cat* serves as an illustration of the categories of preceding voiceless, preceding velars, and preceding stops, as well as following voiceless, following alveolars, following stops, and monosyllables. It is possible for the effects of one category to be reflected in another category simply due to the coincidence of these categories in the data set, that is, simply because the two categories co-occur in the items utilized for the phonological analysis. This type of coincidence is improbable, especially when the input data for an index are numerous, except when it involves lexical biases such as those described above. There are, however, certain cases where such coincidental effects appear to be at work.

One such case involves the category of preceding glottals and their effects on the shifting of (ɛ). The index for this category suggests that it is one that favors shifting; however, this index is not based on a great number of tokens ($N = 24$). More importantly, a review of those tokens reveals that most of them (75%) contain an /l/ following the vowel (e.g., *help*, *held*, *health*). Since a following /l/ also favors shifting, it may be safe to assume that the effect seen with preceding glottals is really due to this co-occurrence. Of course, the reverse is also possible, that is, the effects of following /l/ might be due to its co-occurrence with preceding glottals. However, this seems not to be the case. For one thing, shifting before /l/ is seen in many other examples, several of which do not contain a preceding glottal. Moreover, the tendency for shifting to occur with a following /l/ has already been noted in previous research (Eckert 1991), and, as detailed below, there are solid phonetic reasons to expect greater shifting in this context.

The high rate of (ɔ)-shifting associated with preceding /r/ is another effect that appears to be coincidental. Among the words on which the index is based are several tokens with following velars (16 tokens of *wrong* and 8 tokens of *strong*) as well as several with following fricatives (12 tokens of *cross* and 6 tokens of *across*). Both of these categories of following environment were found to favor shifting, even in cases where the preceding environment does not contain an /r/.

The effects of following fricatives on (ɔ)-shifting appear to also be responsible for the high index found for following labials. All but 1 of the 128 labial tokens involved a following fricative, specifically /f/. The high degree of shifting found before fricatives may be a result of the historical development of the vowel in this context. We will return to this suggestion below.

Many of the apparently significant effects of word-level categories seem also to be due to coincidental effects. For example, words with four or more syllables were found to have an extremely low index for (æ)-shifting. Examining the items upon which this index is based, however, we see words involving many of the categories known to disfavor shifting, including preceding liquids (e.g., *elaborate*, *democratic*), preceding palatals (e.g., *January*, *championship*), and following velars (e.g., *actually*, *manufacture*).

As a final example, we consider a case in which the directionality of effects is less certain. Such is the case for the categories of preceding velars and following interdentals, both of which are shown to strongly favor (æ)-shifting. Their frequent co-occurrence in items such as *Catholic* and *Cathy* raises the question of whether one is a coincidental effect of the other. It is perhaps more likely that the primary influence is that associated with the preceding context because the index for preceding velars is based on many more tokens ($N = 138$) than that of following interdentals ($N = 49$), and several of the shifted tokens among these illustrate different following contexts (e.g., *can't*, *gal*, *capitol*). Still, the index for following interdentals, though based on fewer tokens, takes into consideration (and finds shifted examples of) preceding contexts other than that of preceding velars (e.g., *math*, *path*, *athletes*), suggesting that it, too, has an independent effect of shifting. Thus, despite their co-occurrence in a number of words, it appears that each of these categories is properly interpreted as offering a favorable environment for (æ)-shifting.

5.1.2.3. *Phonetic Motivations.* There is a strong tradition in historical linguistics of seeking phonetic explanations for sound changes. The reasoning is fairly clear: the continuous nature of speech brings segments (sounds) into contact with each other and opens the door for influence of one segment on another. Traditionally, these explanations have relied on articulatory factors, but more recently, awareness of acoustic factors has been greatly increased with the advent of spectrography. In the following discussion, both types of factors are considered as a means of exploring possible motivations for the patterns observed.

A common source of phonetic influence affecting vowel quality is seen in the place differences of adjacent consonants. These differences are organized, for the most part, along the horizontal dimension, and, therefore, they might be expected to show their strongest influence in processes of backing or fronting—or at least this might be expected of consonantal articulations that involve the tongue body, which, of course, is also involved in vowel production. A potential example of this influence is apparent in the findings regarding preceding and following palatals and velars, which were seen to disfavor shifting (especially backing) of (ɛ).[4] From an articulatory perspective, this result makes sense. Palatals are produced with a front tongue body position, as are phonemic velars (in English), when adjacent to front vowels like /ɛ/, and these front articulations might be expected to discourage any backing tendency. A comparable acoustic account might also be offered. Fronted tongue body positions are associated with a high F2 frequency, and the F2 transition into or out of vowels flanking consonants with such articulations (i.e., "fronted velars" or palatals) will be relatively high. These transitions may influence perceived vowel quality, particularly in vowels of short duration, where the transitional period represents a greater portion of the vocalic signal (Olive, Greenwood, and Coleman 1993, 347). Because backing of (ɛ) involves a decrease in F2, it is, it seems, less likely to occur in an environment marked by high F2 frequencies.

A similar case can be made to explain the differing effects of preceding palatals on the (ʌ) and (ɑ) variables. While this context strongly disfavored (ʌ)-shifting, it strongly favored (ɑ)-shifting. For the same articulatory and acoustic reasons just discussed, it makes sense that the change involving backing, as with (ʌ), would be less likely, and the change involving fronting, as with (ɑ), more likely in this environment. The evidence regarding following palatals, however, seems to weaken this argument, as the effects are reversed in this context—(ɑ)-shifting is disfavored and (ʌ)-shifting is favored. Nevertheless, these results probably represent the influence of particular lexical items. As was noted earlier, the vast majority of cases of (ʌ) before palatals involve the word *much*, and the high index of shifting may reflect the influence of the preceding labial rather than the following palatal. Similarly, the data set from which the (ɑ) index for following palatals is drawn contains many tokens of *watch*, an item that might be less likely to undergo fronting for historical reasons discussed below.

This type of account regarding the effects of palatals and velars runs into some difficulties in explaining (æ) variation. Shifting of this vowel, though commonly described as raising, involves a good deal of fronting and, therefore, an increase in the frequency of F2 (see §4.1.1). This movement accords well with the finding that preceding velars (with their high F2 transitions) promote shifting. However, we should expect to find shifting promoted by preceding palatals as well, yet this context is one that strongly disfavors the change. The effects of these consonants when following the vowel do not offer any better support for this phonetic account, as shifting is clearly disfavored by both following palatals and velars. In defense of the phonetic account, it should be noted that the indices for preceding and following palatals may not be wholly reliable, as they are based on fairly low numbers of tokens ($N = 34$ and 35, respectively). Also, there are potentially relevant phonetic differences between these consonants in pre- and postvocalic positions. For example, among the sounds coded as "palatal" are the alveopalatal affricates /tʃ/ and /dʒ/, which begin with an alveolar stop. Thus, the vocalic F2 transitions into these consonants would typically be more like those associated with alveolars, which characteristically have lower transitions (Johnson 1997, 136). Also, unlike when appearing before front vowels, velars when appearing postvocalically (even after front vowels) are not particularly fronted and, therefore, do not involve F2 transitions as high as those seen when preceding front vowels. Finally, it should be noted that (æ) often behaves unusually in the context of following velars and that this may simply be a peculiar feature of English. This point is elaborated below (§5.1.2.4).

Place effects may also be seen in the (ʌ) variation. Among the strongest of these is that of preceding labials, which greatly favor backing and rounding. Articulatorily, it is not surprising that lip rounding for labial consonants may extend into the following vowel. In addition, because the labiovelar glide /w/ was coded as labial, the shifting associated with this category may also reflect coarticulatory effects of tongue body position, whereby the back articulation of the glide is carried over into the vowel. Acoustically, the frequency of the F2 transition out of (and into) a labial, including /w/, is typically low, and, as was mentioned earlier, rounding often has a lowering effect on F2. Thus, articulatorily as well as acoustically, labials seem to set the stage for vowel backing and rounding.

Velars were another category found to promote shifting of (ʌ) when they occurred in either the preceding or the following environment. This might be explained as the result of articulatory assimilation, as was suggested for preceding /w/. It should be noted, however, that these findings seem to run counter to acoustic predictions. The high F2 transition characteristic of velars should function to deter backing of the vowel in this context, just as it appears to do in the case of (ε). It is possible that this apparent discrepancy may be related to the allophonic differences between the palatalized velars that occur before front vowels (like /e/) and the back forms that occur before nonfront vowels (like /ʌ/), though further acoustic research will be needed to explore this issue.

Effects associated with particular manners of articulation are also evident in the data. Some of the most consistent effects are those related to the preceding liquids /l/ and /r/. For the most part, the index results show these consonants favor shifting of (ε), (ɪ), and (ʌ) and disfavor shifting of (æ), (ɑ), and (ɔ).[5] This distinction is interesting because these two sets of vowels undergo different directions of shifting. The vowels in the former group are engaged primarily in backing, while those of the latter participate in fronting—accompanied by raising in the case of (æ) and by lowering in the case of (ɔ). This division appears to fit well with phonetic predictions. Liquid consonants are characterized by very low F2 frequencies and thus could be expected to favor backing and disfavor fronting. Unfortunately, this pattern does not hold as neatly for following liquids, for which only /l/ was examined. There were not enough tokens to evaluate the effects on (ʌ), but this context was found to favor shifting of (ɛ) and (ɪ) and to disfavor, though slightly, shifting of (ɔ). However, it also proved a favorable environment for (æ) and (ɑ). It might seem that the differing effects of /l/ in preceding and following position could be related to the distinction of "light" and "dark" allophones, where the latter designates a velarized variant, though the phonetic basis for this connection remains unclear. The velarization associated with /l/ in postvocalic position is expected to lower F2 even further and, thus, is still predicted to disfavor vocalic changes involving fronting such as (æ) and (ɑ).

Another class of consonants frequently found to affect shifting is the nasals. Acoustically, vowels that are nasalized in the context of a nasal consonant have, in addition to oral formants, nasal formants which result from the additional resonance created by the airflow into the nasal cavity. The lowest frequency nasal formant generally appears in the same range as F_1 and may interact with F_1 perceptually through a process known as spectral integration (Beddor 1991). The theory behind this process states that when two formants are relatively close in frequency (in this case, the nasal formant and F_1), they may be perceived as a single resonance. The perceived frequency of the integrated formant is essentially an average of the two input frequencies. In cases where the original frequency of F_1 is higher than that of the nasal formant, integration will have the effect of lowering the perceived F_1 frequency, while in cases where F_1 frequency is lower than that of the nasal formant, the result will be an increase in perceived F_1 frequency. The prediction, then, is that nasals will promote raising of low vowels (because these are characterized by a high F_1) and promote lowering of high vowels (because these are characterized by a low F_1).

These predictions appear to be borne out by the results for (æ) and (ɪ) in the category of following nasals. This context was shown to promote raising of the low vowel (æ), though, as noted earlier, this effect was not as strong as suggested by earlier researchers. With regard to the high vowel (ɪ), the original indices suggested that following nasals strongly disfavored shifting in general but slightly favored lowering. As discussed above, however, these scores appear to represent a lexical bias from function words like *in* and *him*. When the indices are recalculated without these items, they show lowering to be much more favored. Interestingly, the (1) results for the category of preceding nasals are much stronger and suggest that lowering is greatly promoted in this environment. The argument that this effect is acoustically motivated is more speculative in this case. While nasalization in English affects a large portion of the vowel preceding a nasal consonant, it normally does not extend very far into the vowel following a nasal consonant. Thus, acoustic consequences such as the interaction of F1 and the nasal formant are less likely to result from preceding nasals.

This discussion has examined a number of cases where phonetic factors suggest a plausible account for patterns of phonological conditioning. While these factors have proved useful as a means of better understanding the findings they address, this avenue of inquiry has not led to as many destinations as was originally hoped. Above, we have seen cases where the results are only weakly or partially consistent with phonetically based predictions, and there are other cases for which it is difficult even to arrive at predictions. An example of the latter is seen in the effects associated with the voicing status of the preceding consonant. This factor conditioned noteworthy effects for five of the six NCS vowels, yet phonetic accounts of these effects are lacking. It is reasonable to suppose that aspiration is somehow involved, possibly leading to a decrease in perceived vowel duration due to masking of some of the periodic portion of the vowel. Durational differences (in particular, the shorter vowels heard following aspirated consonants) might, then, be related to differences of perceived vowel quality. Enthusiasm for such an account wanes, however, when the data for postvocalic voicing are recalled, since significant effects related to the voicing status of the consonant following the vowel were relatively rare. The voiced/voiceless contrast is known to condition substantial durational differences in preceding vowels (compare, e.g., *bet* vs. *bed*), and if there is a link between these differences and perceptions of vowel quality, it should be seen in these data as well. Still, while situations like these have been a source of some frustration in this analysis, they have inspired careful examination of the data and consideration of a range of potential explanatory factors, phonetic and otherwise, and, as has been noted on several occasions, they have also signaled many directions for future research.

5.1.2.4. *Peculiarities of English.* A number of the findings regarding phonological conditioning are not traceable to particular lexical items or to any coincidental confluence of categories, nor are they obviously due to phonetic factors. Rather, they appear to involve effects that, for lack of a better description, could be termed peculiarities of English. In some cases these effects seem to stem from historical and/or dialectological developments, while in other cases their motivation is more of a mystery.

Among such mysterious cases is the example of following velars and the effect they seem to have on (æ) and (ɛ). For both of these vowels, the velar context was found to play a conditioning role, disfavoring shifting of (æ) as well as backing of (ɛ), but favoring the lowering of (ɛ). That such a role is demonstrated by following velars is not surprising, as this context is often involved in special vocalic developments in English. It is, however, odd to find these particular tendencies, as more often the velar context is found to condition patterns directly opposite those shown here. For example, as was noted earlier, raising of /æ/ before velars, especially /g/ and /ŋ/, is actually a frequently cited dialectal pattern (e.g., Thomas 1958, 204; see also examples of *bag* in Kurath and McDavid 1961).[6] In Belfast, /æ/, which in most contexts shows a variable pattern of backing, instead appears as raised when followed by velars, a tendency which produces mergers or near mergers in pairs like *pack ~ peck* (Milroy 1981, 74). Raising of /ɛ/ before /g/ is also well attested in the dialect literature and leads to [e]-like pronunciations of items like *egg* and *beg* (Krapp 1919, 70; Thomas 1958, 204). While these dialectal patterns run counter to those observed here, they nevertheless provide evidence of a unique influence of velars on /æ/ and /ɛ/.[7] The motivation for this influence is unclear, but it appears to surface commonly in dialects of English.

The pattern of (æ) before /l/ may also be connected to certain effects particular to English. It might be suggested, for example, that the high degree of raising found in this context is related to the fact that this is phonologically a lax vowel. Tensing and raising of lax vowels (as well as laxing and lowering of tense vowels), especially before /l/, is a common feature in much of the American South and West and has led to near mergers in pairs like *pool ~ pull*, *heel ~ hill*, and *sale ~ sell* (Labov 1994). Though this tensing of mid and high vowels was not observed in this study, the fact that the low lax vowel demonstrated such a clear preference for tensing and raising before /l/ raises the possibility that these two patterns are indicative of a more general feature of the language.

An alternative possibility is that (æ)-raising in the context of following /l/ is motivated by an analogy with the context of following /r/.[8] As noted earlier, the raising of (æ) before /r/ is found commonly in American dialects including those of "the North Central area" (Thomas 1958, 199). In this study, the context of following /r/ was not included in the analysis; however, raised variants of (æ) were commonly observed in this environment. Phonologically, English /l/ and /r/ are classed together as liquids, and acoustically these sounds show very similar effects (e.g., low F1 and F2 frequencies), which makes the possibility of an analogy between them worth considering.

A somewhat more certain suggestion can be offered to explain the results regarding (ɛ)-shifting in the context of following nasals. The fact that this category was found to disfavor shifting may reflect the interaction of the NCS with another dialect pattern, the *pin ~ pen* merger. This pattern involves the raising of /ɛ/ before nasals and eventually leads to the loss of the /ɪ/ ~ /ɛ/ distinction in this environment. This tendency is often associated with Southern dialects, though it is found much more generally across the United States (Labov 1996), including the speech of a few of the individuals sampled in this study. For those speakers, the raising pattern appears to take precedence, and thus the backing or lowering tendencies characteristic of the NCS are not found. Moreover, even for those speakers who did not clearly demonstrate raising of the vowel before nasals, it is still possible that their (ɛ) usage is influenced by this pattern, making other directions of shifting less likely in this context. The very low indices of (ɛ)-shifting before nasals suggest that the avoidance of the regular NCS pattern is not limited to those speakers affected by the merger.

There are other examples suggesting a more historically rooted motivation. Such is the case with a series of words containing low back vowels and initial /w/. There is a tremendous amount of variability between the /ɑ/ and /ɔ/ classes in American English, with many lexical items classified differently in different areas of the country. Chief among these variable items are words deriving from Middle English *wa-*, such as *watch, water, walk,* and *wash,* in which the vowel has undergone a process of backing and, in some cases, rounding. Regardless of their phonemic classification, the vowels in these words often appear in the phonetic middle ground between the clearly unrounded [ɑ] and the fully rounded [ɔ]. As a consequence of this tendency, we might expect that the (ɑ) items among these words would tend to appear as unshifted, whereas the (ɔ) items would tend to appear as shifted, and this is precisely what we find. These tendencies regarding (ɑ) are reflected in the results for preceding glide and for following palatal, which show the lowest indices of any categories. However, these scores are based very heavily on tokens of *watch,* which contributed 20 tokens, only 1 of which appeared with a fronted vowel. For (ɔ), we find the highest index of shifting is that associated with preceding glides. This score is based entirely on *wa-* words, especially on tokens of *walk.*

A similar scenario may account for the finding that following fricatives strongly promote shifting of (ɔ). The majority of words illustrating this category represent cases of Middle English "short-*o*" before voiceless fricatives (e.g., *off, cross, lost*). Like the ME *wa-* items, this set of words has had a unique development. Whereas most ME *o* items were lowered and, in America, unrounded and now constitute the bulk of the /ɑ/ class (e.g., *pot, lock, cot*), those appearing before voiceless fricatives came to join the /ɔ/ class. The details of these developments are a matter of dispute, but the vowel either was never unrounded or was unrounded with the rest of the short-*o* items and later rerounded.[9] In either case, it can be argued that these historical tendencies might be reflected in shifted (i.e., lowered and lightly rounded or unrounded) variants of (ɔ) in this particular environment.

The observation of these connections with historical developments still leaves open questions of how the present results are to be interpreted. Does the (ɔ) variation seen in contexts like preceding /w/ or following voiceless fricatives really represent a change, or is this simply the historical residue of an incomplete transfer of items to the /ɔ/ class? In other words, are these items being unrounded now as part of the NCS, or do the "shifted" variants observed here represent older forms that have long been participating only halfheartedly in the /ɔ/ class while their true intentions lie with /a/? Such questions have important implications for the issue of how the NCS is motivated and will be addressed in chapter 6 in considering aspects of the chain-shift argument.

5.1.3. SUMMARY OF DISCUSSION ON PHONOLOGICAL FINDINGS. The preceding discussion has attempted to add definition to the picture of linguistic conditioning suggested by the findings of this study. These findings have been explored first through comparison with the results of previous research and then through consideration of various factors by which they may have been influenced. This latter discussion has addressed most of the stronger effects identified in this study, though no attempt has been made to offer an account of each individual result. Instead the goal has been to propose broad categories of factors that appear to be involved. In some cases, this discussion served to clarify results by suggesting that they may not be indicative of the general phonological category they are intended to illustrate but instead involve either a bias toward particular lexical items or a coincidence of unrelated effects. In other cases the discussion has accepted the results as accurately representing aspects of the phonological conditioning of the NCS and has suggested factors that may be involved in motivating the observed patterns. There is one important type of factor that was not mentioned among these: the possibility that the linguistic conditioning of a particular element in the NCS is motivated by the conditioning of another element. Such effects could serve as key evidence in establishing the interrelatedness of the

NCS changes, and this is another of the issues considered in chapter 6 in discussing the chain-shift question. For now, the focus moves from the more purely linguistic aspects of the findings to a consideration of elements related to the social distribution.

5.2. THE SOCIAL DISTRIBUTION OF THE NCS

The incremental nature of language change is reflected socially as well as linguistically. Innovations generally spread through the social structure of a speech community just as they spread through the linguistic structure, appearing first among a limited range of speakers before diffusing out in ever-widening circles. Speaker participation in a change is not governed by processes of random selection but rather seems to pattern in socially meaningful ways. This patterning reflects the fact that changes are diffused through interactions among speakers, interactions which are largely dictated by social factors (e.g., where one lives or works, the community organizations in which one participates).

As the linguistic forms involved in the change come to be associated with particular types or groups of speakers, they acquire social significance. It falls to the researcher, then, to try to gain a better sense of this social significance by examining the usage of a variety of speakers. In the present study, speakers were compared along three parameters: town, sex, and age. Obviously, this categorization is very limited and only begins to represent the wealth of significant social groupings that might play a role in shaping linguistic behavior among these speakers. Still, it does provide a frame through which speakers may be viewed, and, as the results show, this frame serves to highlight important differences among these speakers in their usage of the linguistic variables. Of course, identifying patterns of usage is only a first step in understanding the social significance of a variable, and there remain the questions of how and why these patterns came to be. By way of addressing such questions, the following discussion offers elaboration and interpretation of the results reported earlier. This discussion is organized around the three principal speaker factors (town, sex, and age), with each being treated in a separate section.

5.2.1. THE FACTOR OF TOWN. In designing this study, the decision to investigate two different communities, as well as the choice of the particular communities investigated, was motivated by a desire to address issues related to the diffusion question, that is, the question of how the NCS variables spread geographically. Thus, towns located roughly 100 miles apart were selected to provide some indication of the geographic extent of the shift. Furthermore, because previous research, indeed the very name by which it is known, had suggested the NCS is an urban phenomenon associated with major cities including Detroit and Chicago, the selected towns were located between these cities, one (Chelsea) much closer to Detroit, the other (Paw Paw) roughly midway between them. The decision to investigate small towns was also part of the strategy to examine the extent of the shift's diffusion, since smaller communities are predicted to be affected later than larger ones. This prediction is based on the suggestion that this change, like many others, is spreading hierarchically, jumping from city to city before eventually diffusing to smaller communities (Callary 1975; see also §1.2).

Given this research design and the predictions of available models of the diffusion process, the results related to the town factor surely rate among the most surprising findings of this study. The original expectations were that the NCS changes would be much better established in Chelsea than in Paw Paw. After all, Chelsea is much closer to Detroit than Paw Paw is to either Detroit or Chicago and so should be affected earlier, as the shift spreads outward from the cities. Even taking into account the hierarchical pattern that this spread is reported to follow, we expect to find Chelsea more advanced. Both towns are located near midsize cities which could serve as intermediaries between the large metropolitan areas (Chicago, Detroit) and the small towns. However, Chelsea's urban neighbor, Ann Arbor (pop. 109,592), is quite a bit larger than Paw Paw's, Kalamazoo (pop. 80,277), and, therefore, Ann Arbor is predicted to be affected earlier and, in turn, to affect Chelsea earlier.[10]

It might also not be unreasonable to predict that there would be very little difference between the towns. The two communities are very similar; after all, they were selected for their comparability. They are not really that far away from each other; they are similarly situated along Interstate 94, both within 20 miles of a medium-size city; and they are roughly equal in population size and seem to have similar economies.

The great surprise of the data on the town factor is, of course, that what was perhaps the least expected result is the one found in the majority of cases. Significant differences between the towns were seen for four of the six NCS features, and in every case the Paw Paw speakers were found to lead the change. The reasons for this discrepancy between the predicted and actual results remain unclear, though some suggestions can be made that may provide insight into the present findings.

If we assume the validity of the hierarchical model of diffusion, we might consider the possibility that Chelsea and Paw Paw are somehow not as comparably ranked as they appear. There might, for example, be differences in the roles played by the midsize cities. In order for these cities to influence the towns, there must be interaction between the speakers of each. Perhaps, then, Paw Paw speakers have greater contact with Kalamazoo than Chelsea speakers do with Ann Arbor. Judging from the present sample, however, this does not appear to be the case, as most of the speakers from both towns reported making frequent trips to either Kalamazoo or Ann Arbor for shopping, entertainment, and business.

A case could be made that Paw Paw should rank higher up the diffusional ladder than Chelsea, because it is of relatively greater local prominence. Whereas Chelsea is located in the same county as, and is to some extent overshadowed by, the much larger Ann Arbor, Paw Paw and Kalamazoo are in different counties. Moreover, Paw Paw is the county seat of Van Buren County; thus, much of the county government is housed there, and it seems to serve much more as a focal point for its region. In this sense, Paw Paw represents a kind of big fish in a little pond, as compared to Chelsea, where the pond is bigger and has much of the water taken up by the cetacean Ann Arbor. Still, the significance of Paw Paw's county-seat status should not be overplayed. It may reflect a prominence that is more past than present, as today's greater mobility makes the county line less of a barrier and, thus, helps extend the influence of cities like Kalamazoo. In a similar vein, Chelsea's relationship with Ann Arbor should not be misinterpreted. Like Paw Paw, it is an independent town (not a suburban offshoot) with its own industry. Historically, in fact, it, too, functioned as a kind of focal point for its area, due, in large part, to its location on the railroad line. Facts such as these make it harder to argue that there are great differences between Chelsea and Paw Paw in terms of their local status.

Focusing less on the towns and more on their residents, however, there are indications of a certain contrast along the lines of social class. Specifically, residents of Chelsea are generally more affluent than those of Paw Paw. Statistical support for this claim can be found in the 1990 U.S. Census data, which show that the median annual income for families in Chelsea is $45,787, whereas in Paw Paw it is just $25,132. Also relevant are the data on educational attainment, which show that 44.7% of the Chelsea respondents have no more than a high-school education, while 43.1% have at least some college experience, and 12.2% have a postgraduate degree. In Paw Paw, however, the figures are 59.8% with a high-school education or less, 35.1% with some college, and 5.1% with a postgraduate degree.

These class-based asymmetries may have been unintentionally reflected in the sample of speakers used here, particularly among the adolescents. A telling illustration of this is seen in the recruitment approaches used in each town. In both cases, contact was made with some of the adolescent subjects through the local school. However, in Chelsea this was done by soliciting participants during a meeting of the student council, while in Paw Paw the initial contact was through a vocational and technical (Vo-Tech) education program. Not surprisingly, the participants met through these channels were rather different. The student-council members tended to be people actively involved in school activities (sports and clubs) with plans to attend college. Many of the Vo-Tech students, on the other hand, expressed a dislike of official school activities and either had no plans for college or planned to attend a local community college. In the end, the sample of speakers studied was more balanced than these comments suggest, because a number of those vocational students could not be used as participants, and other participants more like the Chelsea students were recruited through different channels.[11] Nevertheless, acknowledging the fact that no systematic investigation of class differences has been attempted here, it is reasonable to say that on the whole the Chelsea adolescents seem to represent a more affluent segment of society than their Paw Paw counterparts.

These differences are, of course, only relevant to the extent that there are class-based patterns of usage of the NCS. As noted earlier, herein lies something of an open question. No broad survey of speakers from a wide variety of classes has been conducted, and there are contradictions between the smaller studies that have considered the issue. If we accept Eckert's (1991) suggestion that the changes have urban, working-class associations, then the town differences seen here could be explained as reflecting the class asymmetries in the sample. This is not, however, an insignificant "if," and there are some indications, as will be seen below, that the changes have associations that are directly opposite those described by Eckert. In any case, such class differences are certainly less apparent in the adult sample, where, for example, we find similar levels of education and similar occupations (mostly small, family-owned businesses) among participants from both towns. Despite these similarities, the adult sample reveals the same linguistic differences as the adolescents, with Paw Paw speakers generally showing much greater influence from the NCS.

As a final suggestion to account for the differences between the two towns, we might consider the possibility of some kind of resistance to the NCS on the part of Chelsea speakers. Perhaps, as the geographic facts predict, Chelsea is squarely in the path of the spreading NCS, but its residents are choosing, consciously or unconsciously, not to accept the innovations. Such a scenario of active resistance to what is reported to be a "change from below"— that is, a change that many speakers show no conscious awareness of—may seem a bit far-fetched. Still, there are aspects of the social dynamics in Chelsea that add a measure of plausibility to this account.

Chelsea, like other towns in the area and elsewhere in the country, has experienced a great influx of new residents in recent years. Many of these newcomers move to Chelsea to "escape" urban areas like Ann Arbor or Detroit. While some Chelsea natives seem to welcome these new additions, others are less enthusiastic about their arrival. Some participants interviewed for this study expressed anger and resentment about how the character of the town was changing because of the newcomers. Clearly the most vocal on this issue was speaker TE (f, 43), whose views are reflected in the following quotes from her interview.

> [re: the local merchants' association] My impression was they would do anything as long as they made money, and that's because in my opinion most of the people who are in this association didn't grow up here and don't have a real . . . don't have a real sense of heart about how they want the community to be.
> [re: the annual sidewalk sale] Now they don't call it sidewalk sale; they call it sidewalk festival and they advertise it in Ann Arbor and all these places and they bring in all these people who don't belong here in my opinion and they try and make a dime off of everybody.
> I love Ann Arbor, and I want it to stay right there. I love it. I go to the plays in Ann Arbor. I go to the, to the concerts. . . . I go to all those things, but I like it right there. I don't like it when we have our library turn into a district library [part of the Ann Arbor library system], because all these people from Ann Arbor move here, and they want the same services from our library that they had at their Ann Arbor library. Well, hun, go back to the Ann Arbor library! Don't change our library!
> Everybody says "well, we don't want to lose our small town ambiance." Well, Jesus, keep it a secret. What do you go advertising it for?

In addition to feelings of resentment toward the newcomers to Chelsea, we see in these statements a kind of protectiveness for the town and its traditional character. It is not unreasonable to suggest that such attitudes could influence speech behavior. If the NCS variants are associated with speakers from cities like Ann Arbor and Detroit, then it is possible that the negative feelings Chelsea natives have toward the newcomers from these cities could carry over to their linguistic features as well. Thus, the low levels of shifting found in Chelsea may represent a reaction to the influx of new residents from the cities. If this is the case, then the conservative forms of the NCS vowels could come to symbolize some aspect of native Chelsea identity in much the same way as the older dialect forms (raised diphthongs) came to symbolize native island identity for residents of Martha's Vineyard (Labov 1963).

It is difficult to assess the extent to which natives of Chelsea (or of Paw Paw) associate the NCS forms with people from the cities. For the most part, speakers, even those who show high levels of shifting, do not seem to be aware of the variation. In many of the interviews, the topic of linguistic differences did come up, but, with one exception, none of the participants made mention of NCS variants, though, of course, they were not questioned directly about these variants. Interestingly, the one speaker who commented on an NCS form was TE (C, f, 43), who referred to raised (æ) pronunciations of *man* and described them as a feature of Detroit.[12] In her own speech, TE did show a fair amount of (æ)-raising, though hers was not nearly at the levels found among Paw Paw women, and for the other three variables where significant town differences were found, (ɛ), (ɪ), and (ʌ), TE showed almost no shifting.

TE's low levels of shifting are rivaled by those of another Chelsea speaker, JE (f, 47), whose use of (æ) was particularly exceptional and showed the lowest index in the entire sample (0.058; cf. mean index for the sample, 0.521). This speaker did not give indications of the same sort of anger or resentment toward the newcomers to Chelsea that TE demonstrated, other than in a mild complaint about the steep rise in real estate prices that they seem to have caused. She did, however, express similar feelings of protective pride in Chelsea's small-town atmosphere, commenting on how safe and fun the thriving downtown area is and on how the town has special traditions (e.g., a Halloween party for children) that are not found in big cities. It is interesting to note that JE was the only speaker in the Chelsea sample to have lived in the Ann Arbor–Detroit area. She spent five years living away from Chelsea but did not like it and decided to move back. Again, we see a parallel to the Martha's Vineyard study (Labov 1963), as JE's situation is reminiscent of a similar case involving a young man who returned to the island after having lived in Boston for a time. The parallel extends to the linguistic behavior as well because that speaker was found to have one of the highest rates of use of the centralized diphthongs, the forms that were associated with traditional island identity. There is a key difference between the Chelsea and Martha's Vineyard situations, however, and that is that the Chelsea speakers seem to be avoiding a socially marked incoming change, whereas the Vineyarders were seen as asserting and even exaggerating localized features.

The above observations have been put forward as suggestions of factors that may have played a role in producing the differences found here between Chelsea and Paw Paw in the use of the NCS variables. Among the more promising suggestions is the possibility that the low levels of shifting heard in Chelsea are related to the tension created by the recent influx of city people into the town. It should be noted that Paw Paw has experienced a similar influx, though not to the same degree as Chelsea, and none of the participants interviewed expressed negative attitudes toward the newcomers. This discussion highlights the potential explanatory value of attitudinal factors and suggests that such aspects of the social dynamics in small towns like Chelsea could serve as a profitable area of future research.

5.2.2. THE FACTOR OF SEX OF SPEAKER. While the discovery of differences between the towns and the particular patterns these differences showed were not anticipated, the findings regarding the factor of speaker sex were much more in line with expectations. Those expectations stem from the reporting of significant sex-based variation in almost every sociolinguistic study of language change over the past three decades. Moreover, in the vast majority of the cases it was found that females lead males in the use of innovative forms. Thus, no presses were called to be stopped when significant sex-based differences indicating a female lead were found in the present study. Such differences were identified for four of the six NCS vowels: (ɪ), (æ), (ɑ), and (ɔ). In the case of (ɛ), the differences did not achieve statistical significance but indicated pretty clearly a female advantage, while for (ʌ), no consistent differences were evident, a finding that is perhaps related to the overall low rate of shifting for this variable.

While sociolinguistic research has produced massive amounts of evidence establishing the ubiquity of sex-based linguistic differences, efforts to explain the underlying causes of these differences have been less common. Much of the difficulty in seeking explanations for the differences lies in the fact that they involve complex, socially constructed notions of gender. While appeals to general principles can provide some insight into these notions, understanding the functioning of gender in any given society requires careful consideration of factors that are determined locally (Eckert and McConnell-Ginet 1992). Although the ethnographic component of the present study was relatively minor, certain observations are available that may add some depth to the quantitative findings.

We begin by considering the findings regarding a particular group of speakers, the adolescent Paw Paw girls. The index scores for this group showed an interesting pattern of distribution for many of the vocalic variables. Two of the speakers had rather high indices (often among the very highest in the entire sample), while the other two had rather low indices. The speakers showing the high rates of shifting are MN and TN, while those showing lower rates are CR and SS (for this discussion, I will employ the pseudonyms Mary, Tracy, Claire, and Sarah, respectively, to refer to these speakers). This pattern of divergence is seen clearly in the data for (ɛ) (fig. 3.2), (ʌ) (fig. 3.8), (æ) (fig. 4.2), and (ɑ) (fig. 4.5), and appears somewhat less clearly in the data for (ɪ) (fig. 3.5). For (ɔ) (fig. 4.8), the pattern is slightly altered, as Claire's score appears at the top with those of Mary and Tracy, leaving only Sarah nearer the bottom. The indices for these four speakers (as well as the mean scores for the entire sample) are shown in table 5.1.

The consistency of this pattern is striking, though not altogether surprising when something is known about their personalities. Both Claire and Sarah were recruited to the study from the Vo-Tech center they attended for half of their school day. Mary and Tracy did not participate in the Vo-Tech program and were met

TABLE 5.1

Indices of Usage of the NCS Variables by the Adolescent Paw Paw Girls
(overall mean indices for all 32 speakers also shown)

	(e)	(ɪ)	(ʌ)	(æ)	(ɑ)	(ɔ)
MN	0.597	0.193	0.356	1.375	1.175	1.538
TN	0.473	0.081	0.221	0.865	0.818	1.386
SS	0.076	0.029	0.024	0.228	0.098	0.538
CR	0.178	0.041	0.014	0.061	0.250	1.673
OVERALL	0.181	0.075	0.055	0.521	0.469	0.815

through an adult contact. These differences in recruitment are emblematic of a series of differences between the two pairs of girls.

One area in which the differences seem quite clear is their relationships to the school as a community. Mary and Tracy are very involved in extracurricular activities at the high school, participating in sports (one as an athlete and one as a cheerleader) and clubs. Both also participated in a program known as Peer Assistant Leaders (PALs), which Tracy explained as follows:

> Tracy: It's like, it's a class you take, you have to get chosen to be in the class and it's like we're there to like, if anybody needs to talk to someone or something like that or if someone has a problem or if there's like a crisis in the school then we're there to like help people and all that kind of stuff so. . . .
> Interviewer: So how did you get interested in that?
> Tracy: I just, I've always, I mean people recommend you and then you have to apply yourself and then you get recommendations and stuff like that but I, it's pretty much from people recommending you and just like if people talk to you and stuff like that then they might recommend you to be a PAL and people recommended me so—
> Interviewer: Like friends of yours?
> Tracy: Yeah people just that I, liked to talk to me, I love helping people, I just love it.

As might be surmised from Tracy's description of the process by which students are selected to be PALs, this is a program whose members are drawn from the "popular crowd," and, in fact, other students have indicated that the recommendation process is widely viewed as a kind of popularity contest.

In contrast to the leadership roles that Mary and Tracy appear to play within the school, Sarah and Claire seem to take very little interest in official school life. The fact that both attended classes at the Vo-Tech center is indicative, and, to a certain extent, is a cause of their lack of involvement in the regular high school. The Vo-Tech is an educational center for high-school students that offers classes in a variety of areas, including carpentry, construction, child care, cosmetology, automotive repair, electronics, marketing, photography, and drafting. It serves the entire county, and so its students come from various high schools. The center itself is located in Lawrence, a town some ten miles away from Paw Paw. Students are bused in and spend half their day (either the morning or the afternoon) at the Vo-Tech and the other half at their "home" school. This setup entails that Vo-Tech students are automatically less involved in the regular high school, simply by virtue of the fact that they attend it for only part of the day.

This status as half-time attendees seems to have contributed to a sense that the Vo-Tech students are not really a part of the high-school community. Many of these students indicated that they had been made to feel unwelcome at Paw Paw High by the other students and even by the faculty. As Claire describes:

> The reason we don't care about school is because they don't make us. I mean they don't try, they don't try to care about us. All they care about is their little star students with their four-points and their everything like that and if you're not like that then they don't want to even try with you.

Given these apparent feelings of rejection, it is not surprising to find that Claire and Sarah, like other Vo-Tech students, are generally not involved in activities and organizations sponsored by the high school. This unwillingness to become involved is even extended to their friendships. Both girls were very candid about their dislike and even distrust of their classmates and indicated that they tended to look outside the school for their friends. As a result, their friends were generally older (late teens to early 20s) people who had already graduated from high school or who had dropped out and were working full-time.

The distinction being described between students like Mary and Tracy, who are very active in official school affairs, and those like Sarah and Claire, who reject such involvement, is a familiar one in American high schools. Eckert (1989b) has detailed various aspects of this distinction based on her ethnographic research in a suburban Detroit school. The social structure of that school was dominated by the primary opposition of the categories Jock and Burnout. This categorization is one constructed by the adolescents themselves, though it generally correlates with the more general socioeconomic distinction of the middle and working classes. It is, however, perhaps better understood as a difference of cultures and attitudes. As Eckert describes, Jocks are characterized by an attitude involving "an acceptance of the school and its institutions as an all-encompassing social context and an unflagging enthusiasm and energy for working within those institutions" (1988, 189). The Burnouts, on the other hand, typically "do not accept the school as the locus of their operations; rather, they rebel to some extent against school activities and the authority they represent and orient themselves to the local, and the neighboring urban, area" (Eckert 1989a, 258).

Elements of the Jock/Burnout distinction are evident in the situation described here for the Paw Paw girls. In their endorsement of and participation in school institutions, Mary and Tracy seem to fit well with Eckert's description of the Jocks. On the other hand, while Sarah and Claire seem to share certain aspects of the Burnouts' attitude toward the school, they are in other respects quite different from such students. For example, both intend to continue their education after high school, Sarah at a four-year college and Claire at a community college. It is, therefore, inaccurate to identify these girls with the Burnout category, though their opposition to the group represented by Mary and Tracy (which is labeled as "Jocks" as well as "Preppies" at Paw Paw High) seems clear.

Returning to the linguistic evidence of this opposition, we find an interesting reversal of the situation reported by Eckert (1989a). Whereas the Burnouts of Eckert's study showed consistently higher rates of shifting than the Jocks, here it is the two Jock-like girls, Mary and Tracy, who show greater shifting. This pattern is not unexpected, however, in the context of the larger social distribution. For many of the NCS variables—for example, (æ) (fig. 4.2) and (ɑ) (fig. 4.5)—the high levels of shifting shown by Mary and Tracy place their indices in the same range as those of the adult women. This linguistic connection to adults may be indicative of a more general affiliation. Eckert (1988, 190) notes that the Jocks' relationships with adults are another element that distinguishes them from Burnouts:

By providing a comprehensive social sphere away from home, the high school offers the opportunity to play adultlike roles away from parental, if not adult, supervision. In return, the student must endorse the corporate norms of the school and the overriding authority of the adults who run it. . . . By and large, this bargain is accepted willingly by those students, particularly the college bound, whose plans for adulthood require the continued sponsorship of adults and adult institutions, and for whom the kinds of corporate roles offered within the school provide preparation for those they anticipate playing as adults.

In addition to this attitudinal connection to the adults, it might be argued that Jocks have greater contact with adults, or at least to those adults affiliated with the school, who serve as coaches and club sponsors. Exploring these suggestions could provide an interesting avenue for future research.

The linguistic evidence from Sarah and Claire suggests a rather different connection. Their low indices indicate that they are not modeling adult linguistic norms (at least not those of women, who were found generally to have the highest rates of shifting), but are instead shifting at rates similar to those seen by their male peers. Such linguistic similarities are intriguing in light of certain remarks they made regarding their relationships with boys and girls.

I have more guy friends than I do girl friends just because girls annoy me. I really don't like girls. . . . I grew up around boys, so I played with boys, you know. Just, like, all my little friends were boys. . . . I wasn't like a little tomboy or anything, I was pretty girly, but I still played with GI Joes and I went out and built forts and swam

in the rivers and rode the boys around on my banana seat bike.
. . . See, I lived in an apartment building and . . . there were no
girls and so I had to play with the boys. [Claire (PP, f, 17)]

I like guys better than girls because girls tend to fight over petty stuff,
so I have more guy friends than girls. . . . I'm probably not your
average girl; I don't really like to do girl things. . . . I don't like to
dress up. . . . I love to gossip though. . . . I love to shoot things, I
don't know why, it's, and I'm probably considered a bit of a
pyro[maniac]. . . . I just find, like, gross, gruesome things just
incredibly hilarious. . . . I was always a real big tomboy. . . . my
friends would play with the Barbies and I would build the house,
so, out of my building blocks. I had building blocks, my sister
had dolls. I ripped the heads off Barbies, my sister would cry. . . .
I never acted like a girl, when I was younger. I got my hair cut
really short like a boy 'cause I hated climbing trees and getting
my hair caught. [Sarah (PP, f, 17)]

It is interesting to find that both of these girls recounted
childhood experiences as a way of explaining their current attitudes. We expect the strongest influence on linguistic patterns to
come through peer interactions, and, thus, we see in these comments suggestions of how Claire's and Sarah's patterns came to
resemble those of the boys. Moreover, in the attitudes expressed
here, we also see a possible motivation for preserving those similarities, because they serve not only to mark Sarah's and Claire's
affinity with boys but also to distinguish them from the other girls.

Before closing this discussion, another, more general point
deserves to be made regarding the nature of the differences observed with the sex factor. In a number of cases and in various ways,
the linguistic data show a greater range of variation among female
speakers than among males. The facts discussed above regarding
the adolescent Paw Paw girls are an excellent case in point. For
many variables, the indices for these girls show a tremendous span,
from the high levels of shifting demonstrated by Mary and Tracy to
the lower levels of Sarah and Claire. Similar distributions are found
with other female groups; see, for example, Paw Paw women's use
of (ɛ) (fig. 3.2) and (ɪ) (fig. 3.5), Chelsea women's use of (æ) (fig.
4.2) and (ɑ) (fig. 4.5), and Chelsea girls' use of (ɑ) (fig. 4.5). In
contrast, the indices of male groups are typically more tightly

clustered. Often these clusters appear along the bottom of the distributions, indicating a lack of shifting, though this is not always the case; see, for example, Paw Paw boys' use of (ɛ) (fig. 3.2) and (æ) (fig. 4.2) and Paw Paw men's and Chelsea men's use of (æ) (fig. 4.2).

One interpretation of these distributional differences is that female speakers are using the linguistic variables to mark social distinctions other than those indicated here. Again, we have already seen hints of such distinctions in the account of the Paw Paw girls, where the linguistic data seemed to reflect a more general set of differences similar to those represented by Eckert's Jocks and Burnouts. Interestingly, the sample of Paw Paw boys also consisted of two speakers who were heavily involved in sports and organizations in the school and two who were not so involved (one of whom even attended the Vo-Tech). Still, despite this parallel composition, the indices for these boys did not show the same split found with the girls. This finding suggests that category distinctions like those illustrated by the girls either were not as relevant to the boys or were marked by other symbolic means.

There is another sense in which the variation associated with female speakers is greater than with males, and that is seen in the use of the directional variants of certain NCS vowels. Recall that three of the vowels examined demonstrated variant trajectories of shifting, sometimes being backed, sometimes being lowered, and sometimes being both backed and lowered. In two of these cases, (ɛ) and (ɪ), the social distributions of such directional variants revealed sex-based differences. The finding was the same in both cases: male usage tends to be centered on one direction (backing), while female usage is more evenly distributed.

This finding of a wider phonetic range utilized by female speakers may be connected to the wider distributions that are typical of the female indices. If, as was suggested here, these wider distributions are a result of the fact that women and girls are using linguistic variables like the NCS vowels to mark a range of social distinctions, then so too may be the wider phonetic variability, since the ability to mark such distinctions would be enhanced by a greater variety of forms in the sociosymbolic arsenal. Conversely, the fact that male speakers seem to have settled on basically a single form of the shifted vowels, (ε) and (ι), suggests that their usage is more constrained. Whereas females may use backing for whatever symbolic needs arise, it seems to have come to serve as a gender marker for males, and, in this sense, it is essentially the only option available to them for shifting. These types of gender-based constraints on linguistic variation have been reported by other researchers, including Milroy and Milroy (1985) and Chambers (1995).

This discussion has explored certain aspects of the findings regarding the factor of speaker sex. One point that has been evident throughout this discussion is that sex-based linguistic differences cannot be adequately treated in isolation and must instead be considered in the context of the full range of variation in a speech community. Such an approach is similar in spirit to the one advocated by Eckert and McConnell-Ginet (1992) and illustrated by Eckert (1989a). The issues that have been discussed here related to the role of gender in shaping linguistic variation are, of course, not intended as an exhaustive list, but rather as indications of the potential benefits of this avenue of research.

5.2.3. THE FACTOR OF SPEAKER AGE. The speaker factor of age, like the others, was treated as a binary opposition, comparing middle-aged adults and adolescents. The motivation for examining speakers of different age groups lies in the fact that the NCS is reported to be a change in progress. Thus, the generational data were designed to provide a kind of apparent-time window onto the diachronic development of the changes. The anticipated view from this window had adolescents showing higher degrees of shifting than the adults, at least, for the putatively more recent NCS variables. For the vocalic variables that have been active for longer periods, we might expect to find less of a generational distinction, though still the adolescents should have some lead.

Given these expectations, the results found here come as somewhat of a surprise. Compared to those of the sex and town factors, these findings offer much more of a mixed bag, indeed a very evenly mixed bag. The differences between adults and adolescents were strong enough to achieve statistical significance in two cases, one of which, (æ), showed an adult lead, and the other of which, (ɔ), showed an adolescent lead. In addition, the data for (ɛ) and (ʌ) indicated fairly clear differences, with adults leading in (ɛ) and adolescents in (ʌ). For (ɪ), the age effects were split along sex lines, and a significant interactional effect was found, showing women leading girls but boys leading men. Only in the case of (ɑ) were no remarkable generational differences apparent.

The implications of these findings bear most significantly on the question of whether the NCS is indeed an ongoing change. The greater use of some of the "innovative" variants among adults would seem to suggest a change in retreat more than in progress. Such findings are made harder to dismiss by the fact that similar patterns have been reported elsewhere. As was noted earlier (§1.4.3), the only other study to consider a systematic sample of speakers of different ages was that of Herndobler (1977), who compared three generations of Chicagoans and found the highest rates of shifting among the middle generation for both of the NCS variables she examined, (æ) and (ɑ). In Labov, Yaeger, and Steiner's (1972) study, there were also hints of age effects that are inconsistent with the change-in-progress interpretation. For example, they reported that the lowering of (ɪ) and (ɛ) in Detroit was seen in older speakers but not in younger speakers (121).

Closely connected to the change-in-progress question is the matter of the relative chronology of the individual elements in the NCS. This issue is fundamental to the interpretation of the NCS as a chain shift and is considered more fully in chapter 6. Still, a few points are worth mentioning as preliminaries to that discussion. For example, the chronology proposed by Labov (1994, 195) receives some support here in the case of the (ʌ) findings. This is one of the variables that appeared to be more active among adolescents, a pattern consistent with the proposal that it is the most recent development. On the other hand, adolescents were also found to lead, to a statistically significant degree, in the use of (ɔ), yet according to Labov's chronology, this is one of the older elements in the shift. Similarly, we might be willing to dismiss the significant adult lead in (æ)-shifting as somehow a product of the fact that this is the oldest of the NCS features; yet, adults appear to be leading in the shifting of (ɛ) as well, and this is reportedly a more recent aspect. Finally, there is the case of (ɑ), which showed no age differences despite the fact that it is purported to be linked on either end to (æ) and (ɔ), which showed the most dramatic, though countervailing, age effects of all the vowels. Thus, the data on the age factor are only partially consistent with expectations based on the chronology of the NCS changes suggested by Labov.

In addition to these chronological considerations, the age findings may also have implications for an understanding of the diffusion process. If we assume that the NCS changes are spreading (rather than receding), then we might view the adult lead in certain of these changes as somehow a product of this spread. One possible interpretation is that adults are functioning as the conduits through which the changes flow to new communities. Typically, adults have greater mobility and contact with people outside their local communities than do adolescents. This would, perhaps, especially be the case for adults still active as part of the workforce, such as those sampled here and those of Herndobler's (1977) middle generation. Many of the adults in the present study have friends or business contacts or have themselves worked outside their towns, often in such nearby cities as Kalamazoo or Ann Arbor. Such connections expand the geographic extent of these speakers' social networks and, thus, may be expected to increase their exposure to supralocal linguistic patterns like the NCS.

Clearly, confirmation of these suggestions will require a more systematic analysis of social network patterns than was attempted here, though some supportive indications are available in the present results. We might consider, for example, the case of BG (C, f, 44). Among her fellow Chelsea women, BG stands out as having the highest index of shifting in three cases: (æ), (ɛ), and (ɪ). Interestingly, these are the three variables for which adults were found to be more advanced.[13] BG is also distinguished from the other Chelsea women (and men) by the fact that she has worked for the last ten years in Ann Arbor, living in Chelsea and commuting daily to her job in a retail store.[14] For this reason, BG suggests an interesting parallel to the case described by Milroy (1980) of the young Catholic women who were found to have linguistic patterns that were more commonly associated with the Protestant section of the city. These women were distinguished by the fact that they worked outside their local area in a retail store in the city's downtown, where both Catholics and Protestants shop.

This suggestion that adults, particularly those with supralocal social connections, are playing a key role in the diffusion of the NCS is offered as an account of the present findings that is still consistent with the interpretation of the shift as an ongoing change. It should be remembered, however, that a slightly different picture was suggested by the distribution of the directional variants. Particularly interesting are the data related to (ε). While the general indices for this vowel indicated an adult lead in shifting, it was demonstrated above (§3.1.3.2) that this lead applies only in the case of backing. For the other directions of shifting, higher rates were found among the adolescents.

The most straightforward interpretation of such findings is that these variants, the forms that are lowered or both backed and lowered, represent the latest trends; that is, the original backing pattern is being supplemented or even supplanted by these others. If true, this would directly contradict the chronology proposed by Labov (1994, 195), who suggests that the original direction of shifting was one of lowering but that this was later redirected into a backing tendency. Nevertheless, this development seems to make a good deal of sense from a sociosymbolic perspective. If backing of (ε) is fairly common among adults, we might expect adolescents to explore new directions of shifting as a way of drawing a distinction between themselves and their parents. Such motivations are a critical aspect of the adolescent experience, as Eckert (1988, 187) explains:

As they enter secondary school, American youth recognize that they are making a formal transition into a life stage in which they are expected to accomplish a separation from the family and parental authority. For most, this separation is achieved communally with the age cohort as it develops a social structure that provides the means for the development of an identity independent of the family structure.

A key component of adolescents' independent identity is linguistic, choosing and establishing patterns of usage that help them define their separateness. In the case of (ɛ), as we have seen, separateness is found in lowering, or backing with lowering. These directional variants are not the tendencies of adolescent choice in the case of (ʌ), however, where adolescent preferences focus on backing. Still, the motivation appears to be the same, as this trend serves to mark their usage as distinct from the adults, or at least from the adult women, who tend to use lowering for this vowel.

This discussion has considered some of the issues raised by the findings regarding the age factor. These findings were much more varied than those of the other speaker factors, as some of the NCS vowels indicated an adolescent lead over adults while others illustrated the reverse pattern. The latter results are of particular relevance and present a challenge to the interpretation of the NCS as an active change. The discussion here has offered suggestions aimed to account for the apparent contradictions of an adult-led change in progress. There is, of course, a simple alternative to this pursuit, and that would be to interpret the decreased shifting found among adolescents as indicating a recession of earlier changes. While the discussion has not focused on this possibility, it certainly cannot be dismissed. Ultimately, it seems that a clearer picture of these issues will emerge only when sufficient real-time evidence is available.

5.3. SUMMARY

The discussion in this chapter has sought to add greater definition to the results presented in the previous two chapters. Various issues raised by those results have been considered. The findings concerning the phonological conditioning of the NCS were examined in comparison to those reported in previous studies. This examination revealed some areas of weak disagreement as well as some of weak agreement, though no strong contradictions were indicated. The phonological findings were also addressed through a discussion of various types of "explanations," some of which were intended to clarify the interpretation of certain results (e.g., the cases for which the index scores are based on a limited range of lexical items), while others offered suggestions related to the underlying motivations for the observed patterns (e.g., the cases in which phonetic factors, either articulatory or acoustic, appear to have an influence). The findings concerning the social factors were also given consideration. Each of the three main factors (town, sex, and age) was treated individually, though connections among them were also noted.

Throughout this discussion, both of the phonological and of the social factors, the goal has been to elaborate and interpret the largely quantitative picture drawn in chapters 3 and 4. Thus, in some cases, evidence of a more qualitative nature has been introduced to support the claims being made, such as in the discussion of the town-based differences, where speakers' attitudes were considered as a possible factor influencing their adoption of the linguistic features. An attempt has also been made to draw comparisons among the findings for the different NCS variables and to consider both the similarities and the differences in their sociolinguistic patternings, since these variables were discussed separately in chapters 3 and 4. This approach has been taken as a means of drawing a broader perspective from which to view the individual findings. The discussion is continued along these same lines in chapter 6, and, in fact, many of the points raised thus far are brought together there, as consideration is given to an issue that is central to the interpretation of the variation associated with the NCS: the chain-shift question.

NOTES

1. Actually, this pattern held for their Buffalo and Detroit speakers, but for the Chicagoans they found following velars to be the strongest promoter of shifting among the stops (Labov, Yaeger, and Steiner 1972, 80).

2. Labov, Yaeger, and Steiner (1972, 119) discussed one younger speaker for whom the order appeared to be reversed.

3. This case may also be motivated by particular historical developments (see discussion in §5.1.2.4).

4. Actually, following velars were found to promote lowering of (ɛ), a result that is discussed below.

5. The finding on preceding /r/ for (ɔ) actually suggests that this context favors shifting, but this result was discussed earlier as a case of probable coincidence. Similarly, preceding /r/ was found to disfavor (ʌ)-shifting, but this result probably reflects a lexical bias from the word *from*, which is rarely shifted.

6. In the present study, tokens of (æ) in the context of following velar nasals (e.g., *bang*, *language*) were omitted from consideration, because raising appeared to be so common that some speakers had reclassified such items as members of the /ɛ/ class.

7. As a more general tendency, it is worth noting that most of the English tense/lax contrasts (e.g., /e/ ~ /ɛ/, /i/ ~ /ɪ/) are neutralized before the velar nasal /ŋ/.

8. A similar analogy is considered by Labov, Yaeger, and Steiner (1972, 237) to explain the near merger in the *pool* ~ *pull* pairs and others discussed above.

9. Pilch (1955, 82) and Wyld (1927, 181) held that these items were unrounded, then later lengthened and rounded again, whereas Moore and Marckwardt (1951, 135) seem to suggest that rounding was never lost in these items.

10. The status of the NCS in these cities was not investigated for this study; however, my impression, based on several years of living in Ann Arbor, is that the shift is fairly well established there.

11. In many cases the interviews were not long enough to produce enough reliable data, and in other cases speakers were excluded because they had not lived in Paw Paw for their entire lives.

12. TE mentioned other features as well, including the use of multiple negation, and later in the interview she even commented on the ubiquitous use of *like* by the interviewer.

13. Actually, for (ɪ) the adult lead only applies to women (see §3.2.3.1).

14. Speaker JE, discussed earlier, worked and lived in the Ann Arbor area for some five years, but that was nearly 20 years ago.

6. IS THE NORTHERN CITIES
SHIFT A CHAIN SHIFT?

THE CONCEPT OF CHAIN SHIFTING offers a powerful explanatory model that accounts neatly for the co-occurrence of a set of sound changes. The model provides a wide range of explanations for why particular changes take the form they do (e.g., why a vowel undergoes backing rather than fronting) as well as for the broader social and historical distribution of the changes (e.g., why they are found together in the same dialect at the same point in time).

The question of whether the NCS constitutes a chain shift is of fundamental importance, yet it seems not to have been posed by previous researchers. In the major theoretical works dealing with the NCS (Labov, Yaeger, and Steiner 1972; Labov 1994), the shift is offered as an example illustrating certain basic principles of chain shifting, though no explicit defense of the applicability of the chain-shift model to the NCS changes is offered. These works assume that the NCS changes form a chain shift and examine them for what they reveal about chain shifting in general. Labov and his colleagues should not be faulted for relying on such an assumption, since their focus was not on the NCS but rather on the general principles. Besides, had these authors sought to establish the NCS as a chain shift, it is doubtful that firm conclusions could have been drawn, given the sparseness of empirical research that was available.

The chain-shift question poses a substantial methodological and analytic challenge. How does one test whether a series of changes are participating in a chain shift? Is it even possible to recognize a chain shift in one's midst? To begin to face these challenges, we look to the heart of the chain-shift concept. The theoretical underpinnings of chain shifting were outlined above (§1.3), and from that account, two definitional criteria seem to emerge as crucial: (1) a chain shift involves a series of (at least two) interrelated changes, and (2) these changes do not result in any loss of contrast in the phonemic system.

The greatest complexity of this definition lies in the notion of interrelatedness. On the one hand, interrelatedness has spatial implications, including the occurrence of the changes in the same dialect and (though this might be disputed) in the same speaker. A kind of linguistic space is also at issue here, as the changes must involve related sounds, those that are near each other either physically (i.e., according to their articulation) or structurally (i.e., according to their phonological categorization). On the other hand, interrelatedness also involves a temporal component, as the chain is formed by a sequential appearance of the changes in time.

The second criterion, that the changes do not result in the loss of phonemic contrasts, is, in some respects, more straightforward. If distinctions are preserved through the shifting, then this criterion may be considered met. Such preservations have often been seen as the motivating force behind chain shifting, though this teleological interpretation is not a necessary part of the definition. Of concern here are the outcomes of this process of contrast preservation: the extent to which the sounds involved in the changes maintain their perceptual distance.

6.1. ARE THE NCS CHANGES INTERRELATED?

6.1.1. GENERAL SPATIAL CONNECTIONS. As noted above, the question of the connectedness of the NCS changes in space involves both a geographic aspect (do the changes occur in the same dialect area?) and a linguistic aspect (do the changes occur in the same "area" of the phonological system?). The response to the former question seems to be pretty clear. Certainly based on the limited geographic investigation conducted here, it appears that the changes do occur together in the same locations. They were not found to occur to the same degree in both towns examined (they were generally more common in Paw Paw than in Chelsea), but evidence of each of the changes was heard in both research sites. The larger geographic picture seems to indicate a connectedness to the changes as well. The changes are reported to co-occur across a wide section of the northern United States, from western

New England to Chicago and beyond into the upper Midwest (Labov 1994, 185).[1] Perhaps more significantly, we do not seem to find the NCS changes occurring in isolation. Where one of the changes occurs, it is accompanied by others. There are, of course, many historical and dialectal precedents for these patterns in which a change similar to those seen in the NCS occurs in isolation, but these examples are not directly related to the NCS changes. We do not find cases of individual parts of the NCS (i.e., changes that are directly related) being adopted without others.[2] These facts seem to reinforce the notion that the NCS changes are connected by suggesting that they come as a kind of package deal. This point would also appear to be relevant to how individual speakers are affected by the NCS, and the extent to which the same picture emerges from the usage data of individuals is addressed below.

The other aspect of spatial connectedness at issue for chain shifts pertains to the linguistic system. Essentially, the issue is whether the changes involve related sounds. This question is complicated, however, by the fact that varying degrees of relatedness may apply. In the case of the NCS changes, the affected sounds are certainly related in the sense that all are vowels. Furthermore, most of them are related as members of the subgroup of short (or lax) vowels. This is not the case, however, for (ɔ), which historically belongs to the class of long (or tense) vowels. The matter is further complicated by the suggestion that some of the "short" vowels in the NCS, specifically (æ) and (ɑ), assume certain phonetic properties (e.g., peripherality) of the long vowels as a consequence of their shifting (Labov 1994). Thus, from a phonological perspective, the relatedness of the NCS vowels can only be partially confirmed.

There is also a phonetic dimension to this issue, as the changes involved in a chain shift are expected to be articulatorily (and/or possibly acoustically) related. In the case of a vocalic shift, this means that the changes affect items contiguous in vowel space and are linked by one vowel entering the space previously occupied by another. This is the image portrayed in the standard representation of the NCS, as shown in figure 6.1.

FIGURE 6.1
One View of the NCS
(based on Labov 1994, 191)

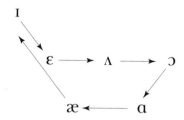

The connections between the NCS changes seem quite clear from this diagram as the vowels are linked into a complete circuit by the shift. This view of the NCS does not, however, reflect all of the variation demonstrated by the shifting vowels. The findings of the present study suggest a picture that is much more complicated and might more accurately be represented as in figure 6.2.

The links between NCS vowels are less obvious in this representation. In some cases the shifting does not seem to bring the vowel into the range of another vowel, as with the backing of (ɪ),[3] and in other cases the shifting seems to bring two vowels into the same range, as with the lowering of (ɛ) and the fronting of (ɑ). These observations are certainly relevant to the issue of maintaining phonemic contrasts, a matter that is addressed below. For now, it is important to note that the spatial connectedness of the NCS

FIGURE 6.2
A View of the NCS Showing Directional Variants

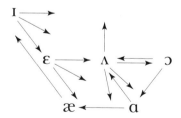

changes is made less clear when the full range of variation is considered.

Evidence of the relatedness of changes can also be sought among the factors that condition the changes. Before turning to consider the effects of the NCS on individuals, two brief observations about its sociolinguistic conditioning should be made. The first relates to phonological conditioning, a topic that has been discussed extensively in this study. If a particular phonological environment (e.g., following nasals) is found to promote one of the changes in a chain shift, it may be expected to show similar effects on the changes contiguous to that change. Such expectations are ultimately based on the idea that the maintenance of distinctions operates on an allophonic level; thus, the ranges of two shifting vowels may overlap, but the distinction is preserved through the consistent effects of particular environments that either favor or disfavor both changes. The question of whether such consistency is found among the NCS changes is addressed below. The point is raised here as a possible source of explanation for certain of the findings on phonological conditioning. It was noted above (§5.1.2.3) that many of the conditioning patterns observed seemed, somewhat unexpectedly, to have little if any phonetic motivation. This finding might be taken as supporting the claim that the changes are connected, since phonetic factors could be expected to be less important in the case of related changes where the phonological conditioning of one change is, to some extent, determined by the conditioning of another. Of course, this suggestion will only be valid if it can be shown that similar conditioning patterns hold across putatively related changes, an issue taken up below.

The final observation to be made here pertains to the social conditioning of the changes. We might expect related changes to show similar patterns of social distribution, just as we expect them to show similarities in their phonological distribution. These expectations are really just an extension of the idea that chain-shift changes will be geographically related. Thus, spatial connectedness applies to social space as well. In this study, there was a fair degree of similarity in the social distributions of many of the NCS changes. The data on the town and sex factors were particularly consistent, showing many of the changes to be more common in Paw Paw than in Chelsea and among females than among males. Perhaps more significant are cases where contiguous vowels show similar conditioning, as was found with (æ) and (ɛ), both of which were seen to be more common among Paw Paw speakers, females, and adults. Similarly, it is interesting that the only two examples of vowel shifting found to be more common among adolescents were (ʌ) and neighboring (ɔ). Still, there are a number of cases where contiguous vowels do not have the same social conditioning; for example, shifting of (ɛ) is led by adults, whereas shifting of (ʌ) is led by adolescents. Thus, the social data provide, at best, a mixed bag of evidence for the relatedness of the NCS changes.

6.1.2. IMPACT OF INDIVIDUAL SPEAKERS. The logic that changes involved in a chain shift must co-occur in space can be carried even further by suggesting that they should co-occur in the usage of individual speakers. Although some linguists (e.g., Lass 1978) would argue against a speaker-based approach to change, claiming instead that the language system is the proper object of study, most accounts of the functioning of chain shifts suggest that individuals play a role. Such a role is evident in Martinet's discussion of "the basic necessity of securing mutual understanding" (1952, 126) that motivates these changes. Even the antifunctionalist account offered by Labov (1994), which focuses on the mechanical process of probability matching (see §1.3), seems to rely on the interactions of individual speaker/hearers, and, of course, acoustic representations of the vowel systems of individuals are commonly used by Labov to illustrate the inner workings of various shifts. Thus, if one accepts the basic premise of chain shifting that the elements involved are in some way causally connected, then it is not unreasonable to expect that connections among the elements in a chain shift should be reflected in the speech of individuals.[4]

As a way of investigating such connections, we can compare the extent to which the various changes are used by individuals. If two changes are related, then we expect to find them used to similar degrees. We also expect the relative usage of such changes to be more or less consistent across individuals; that is, we do not expect to find one speaker using a lot of Change A and very little of Change B, while another speaker uses a lot of Change B and very little of Change A.

For the present changes, such a comparison is available through each speaker's indices for the six NCS variables. These indices are plotted in figures 6.3 and 6.4 for the Paw Paw and Chelsea speakers, respectively.

The initial impression from these data is that there is tremendous interspeaker variation in the use of the NCS variables. Some caution is advised, however, in approaching these figures. First, it should be noted that the comparability of the indices for different vowels is somewhat of an open question. Although the same basic coding scheme was used for each vowel and the degrees of shifting involved roughly equal distances in vowel space, it is not a given that these codes represent equivalent measures of the significance of shifting for each vowel (in terms of its perceptibility, its consequences for the vowel system, etc.). It is difficult to say, for example, whether shifting an (ɪ) by two degrees is somehow equivalent to shifting an (æ) by two degrees. The issue of comparability may be particularly important in the case of (ɔ), where the coding scheme involved unrounding as well as lowering and fronting. It is best, therefore, to approach the indices in relative rather than absolute terms, to compare a speaker's usage of the variables by considering the index for each vowel in the context of the indices from other speakers for that vowel.

On another cautionary note, it should be remembered that these data reflect the social differences discussed earlier. Thus the scores tend to be higher among Paw Paw speakers and among females, and, for some variables, there are generational differences. It is perhaps best, therefore, to compare speakers within the socially defined categories used here (e.g., Paw Paw women, Chelsea boys), and it is for this reason that the speakers have been separated as they are in these figures.

Even when these speaker factors are held constant, however, we find indications of differential use of the NCS vowels. Such indications are found, for example, in the usage patterns of the overall most active group of shifters, the Paw Paw women (fig. 6.3).

FIGURE 6.3
FIGURE 6.3
Mean Indices of Shifting of the NCS Vowels for Paw Paw Speakers

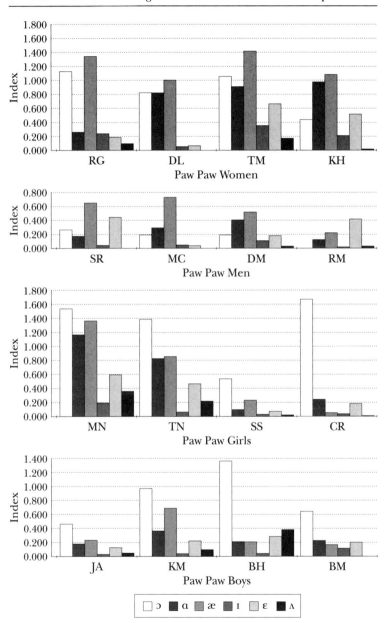

FIGURE 6.4

Mean Indices of Shifting of the NCS Vowels for Chelsea Speakers

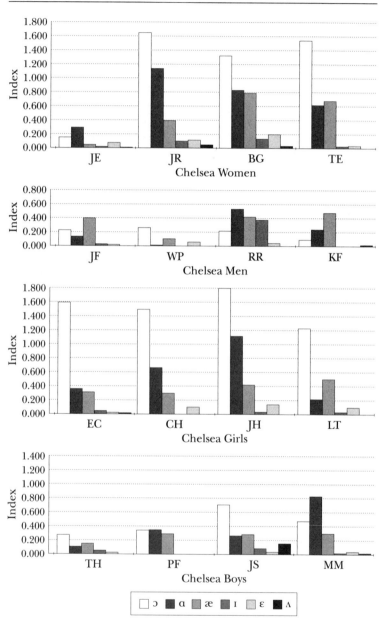

The indices for this group show that all four women are active users of shifting for (æ); however, there is much less consistency in the use of the other vocalic variables. Speakers DL and TM show roughly the same rates of shifting for (ɑ) as for (ɔ), but KH is seen to shift (ɑ) quite commonly and (ɔ) much less so, whereas RG shows a high rate of shifting for (ɔ) but very little for (ɑ). The pattern seen with RG is particularly important for the question of the relatedness of the changes, because she shows high levels of shifting for the front (æ) and the back (ɔ), but somehow (ɑ), which lies between these, is left relatively unaffected.

Many of the female speakers show fairly high levels of shifting for each of the variables in the lower half of the NCS: (æ), (ɑ), and (ɔ). With the exceptions noted above, this appears to be the case for the Paw Paw women, and a similar pattern is seen with two of the Paw Paw girls, TN and MM (discussed as individuals in §5.2.2). There are, however, many speakers who show a very high index for one (or two) of these variables but have less remarkable indices for the other(s). Most often the high index is found with (ɔ), as is the case for speaker CR (fig. 6.3) and for the Chelsea girls EC and LT (fig. 6.4). Other speakers show fairly high indices for both (ɔ) and (ɑ), but show much lower rates of shifting for (æ), as seen with the other two Chelsea girls, CH and JH, and the Chelsea woman JR (fig. 6.4). These patterns are of particular relevance to the issue of the chronology of the NCS changes and are discussed further below.

Among male speakers, there are also a number of cases where an exceptionally high index is found for one vowel but not for others. Two Paw Paw men, SR and RM, were shown to shift (ɛ) at relatively high rates, but they shifted neighboring (ɪ) and (ʌ) very little. One Paw Paw boy, BH, showed a fairly average amount of shifting for (ɛ) but had the highest index in the entire sample for (ʌ). Like some of the female speakers, BH also has a fairly high index for (ɔ), but he has (æ) and (ɑ) indices that are rather low. Among the Chelsea men, the exceptional (ɪ) index for RR was noted earlier (chap. 3), and here we see that this speaker shows little shifting of (ɛ) and absolutely no shifting of (ʌ). Finally, among the Chelsea boys, we note the exceptional (ɑ)-shifting seen with

MM, which is accompanied by only moderate shifting for (æ) and (ɔ). Also, with JS, we find an interesting pattern for the vowels of the upper half of the NCS, as he shows very little shifting of (ɛ) but a fairly high degree of (ɪ)-shifting and the highest index of (ʌ)-shifting of all Chelsea speakers.

As the focus here has been on exceptional cases, it should be acknowledged that there are many cases illustrating the expected patterns. Still, the findings raise questions about whether the NCS changes are related—or at least about the nature of any relations among them. It is harder to argue for a necessary connection between two changes if, for some speakers, one of the changes is very common and the other is uncommon, while for other speakers the pattern is reversed, and for still others both changes are very common.

As a final observation on these findings, we might consider the possibility that the inconsistency seen here is in some way a product of the process of diffusion of the changes. It might be argued that the forces of chain shifting—those factors (whatever their nature) by which the individual changes are connected—guide the initial development of a shift, but their influence wanes once the pattern of the shift has been established. If this is the case, then the correspondences among the links may become blurred as the shift diffuses beyond its point of origin. New speakers may encounter the shift as an assembled whole from which they may choose to adopt individual pieces. At least in the initial stages, these speakers will be relatively free to select from the available variation without concern for the repositioning impact of the changes on their personal vowel systems. Even in this scenario, however, it seems that the forces that shaped the original shift must eventually catch up to their wandering offspring and intervene to readjust the system so that the patterns of usage by speakers in these new locations will come to reflect the connections that were involved initially. Perhaps, then, we might explain the findings presented here as characteristic of a relatively early stage in the diffusion of the NCS to these communities, suggesting that relations among the changes will become clearer once the shift is more firmly established.

6.1.3. TEMPORAL RELATEDNESS. In addition to spatial considerations, there is a temporal dimension to the relations among members of a chain shift. These are presumed to be cause-and-effect relations and, thus, rely crucially on sequential ordering. In the present case, the investigation of this ordering necessarily proceeds through indirect means, given that the results of this study represent a synchronic slice in the life of the NCS. Thus, much of the discussion relies on apparent-time reasoning, though some connections are made to the scarce real-time evidence of the shift that is available. It is important to bear in mind the limitations of this method, which, in Labov's (1975) words, "uses the present to explain the past." Some of the dangers involved in this kind of reasoning have been mentioned above (§1.1), including the fact that the method relies on the assumption that basic speech patterns are not significantly altered over the course of a person's life. Also of particular concern here is the assumption that changes proceed (through the language and through the speech community) at roughly the same rate, since in the following discussion comparisons of the current degrees of usage of innovative forms are taken as indicating the time depth of the innovations. Despite these potential difficulties, the method is still the best available approach to questions of the chronology of the NCS and does seem to shed light on these issues.

As a preface to this discussion, we might briefly review the chronology of the NCS changes that has been proposed by Labov (1994, 195), the only researcher to have made such a proposal. According to Labov, the first element in the shift was the raising of (æ), which created a void that (ɑ) then fronted to fill. This, in turn, spurred the lowering and fronting of (ɔ), which moved to fill the space left by (ɑ). Thus, the bottom half of the shift is claimed to be a drag chain. Labov acknowledges that the ordering of changes in the upper half is less clear, but he suggests that the first to shift was (ɛ), which was initially lowered. This movement inspired a drag chain as (ɪ) was then lowered. Later, it is claimed, (ɛ) changed courses and became backed, which led to a push chain in which (ʌ) was also backed. Thus, Labov's chronology of the shifting elements from first to last is: (æ) > (ɑ) > (ɔ) > (ɛ) > (ɪ) > (ʌ).

An initial approach to the chronology question can be made by simply comparing the average index of each NCS variable across the sample of speakers. These indices are listed in table 6.1.

If we assume that these indices provide comparable measures of the degree of shifting found with each vowel (an assumption that, as noted above, may be open to debate), then we can use them as apparent-time indicators of the history of the NCS. Higher indices denote more established changes which are presumed to have been active longer. Following this reasoning, the data in table 6.1 suggest the following chronology from oldest to youngest: (ɔ) > (æ) > (ɑ) > (ɛ) > (ɪ) > (ʌ). This ordering shows a close resemblance to Labov's, but it differs in one very significant respect, the position of (ɔ). This difference is of great relevance to the chain-shift question, not only because it suggests that the shift began in the back rather than the front, but also because it makes it harder to argue for causal relations among the variables of the lower half of the shift.

Before exploring the implications of these findings for the lower vowels, however, a few comments about the upper half of the shift should be made. First, it should be noted that there is fairly good support elsewhere in the data for ordering these vowels (ɛ) > (ɪ) > (ʌ). Thus, most of the data on individual speakers conform to the general pattern. There are, of course, exceptions, some of which have been noted above. For example, speaker BH (PP, m, 16) showed an exceptional rate of (ʌ)-shifting, speaker RR (C, m, 51) showed an exceptional rate of (ɪ)-shifting, and speaker JS (C, m, 18) showed a fair amount of shifting of both (ɪ) and (ʌ) but almost no shifting of (ɛ). Despite these exceptional cases, generally it seems that (ʌ)-shifting appears only if (ɪ)-shifting is present, and (ɪ)-shifting only if (ɛ)-shifting is present. Furthermore, whereas (ɪ) and (ʌ) are often shifted at roughly the same (generally low) rate,

TABLE 6.1
Mean Indices of Shifting for the NCS Variables

	(ɛ)	(ɪ)	(ʌ)	(æ)	(ɑ)	(ɔ)
Mean index	0.181	0.075	0.055	0.521	0.469	0.815

there is commonly a pretty clear separation between the rate of (ε)-shifting and the rates at which either (ι) or (ʌ) is shifted, as reflected in the mean indices in table 6.1: (ε) = 0.181 versus (ι) = 0.075 and (ʌ) = 0.055). This pattern is interesting in light of the scenario proposed by Labov (1994, 195) for these vowels, whereby both (ι) and (ʌ) were set to shifting by the movement of (ε).

The chronological picture for the variables in the bottom half of the NCS, (æ), (ɑ), and (ɔ), is much more complicated. One of the first things to note is the great discrepancy between the rates of shifting found with these variables and those of the upper half. The lowest average index for the lower vowels, the score of 0.469 for (ɑ), is over 2.5 times that of the highest average index for the upper vowels, the 0.181 for (ε). Thus while these data suggest that, in terms of the relative order of the changes, those in the lower half of the shift precede those in the upper half, they also suggest that the former set of changes is quite a bit older than the latter.

As noted above, the only point of difference between Labov's chronology and that suggested by the mean indices in table 6.1 pertains to (ɔ). The suggestion that this is the oldest of the NCS changes has troubling implications for the chain-shift argument if, as indicated by these data, the ordering of (æ) before (ɑ) holds. It is highly implausible that shifting of (ɔ) could be directly related to shifting of (æ) without the involvement of (ɑ), which lies between them.

Perhaps, then, the sequence of the (æ) and (ɑ) changes needs to be reexamined. The mean indices for these variables indicate a fairly small difference between them, 0.521 for (æ) and 0.469 for (ɑ), so it is not unreasonable to suggest that shifting appeared in (ɑ) before, or at roughly the same time as, it did in (æ). Certainly, many of the data from individual speakers support this possibility, particularly the indices of the women and girls of Chelsea (see fig. 6.4). Further support can be found in Herndobler's (1977) finding that (ɑ)-fronting was more common among her older speakers than (æ)-raising. This ordering is also consistent with some of the real-time evidence reported above (§1.4.4.1), such as the early descriptions of (ɑ)-fronting by Pilch (1955), Thomas (1958), and Kurath and McDavid (1961).

Given that the issue raised earlier about the comparability of the indices appears to be of particular importance in the case of (ɔ), we might reasonably question the inference that the high average index for this vowel is an accurate reflection of its time depth. Just as with (ɑ), however, there is certain real-time evidence to support the suggestion that this change has been active for some time. For example, DeCamp (1940) reports lowering and unrounding of (ɔ) as well as fronting of (ɑ) in a description of Scranton, and Marckwardt (1941, 1942) details the tendency for lowering and reduced rounding of (ɔ) across a great section of the Northern dialect region. It is important to emphasize that this shifting of /ɔ/ is apparently separate from and historically unrelated to the phonetically similar pattern in which /ɔ/ is lowered and unrounded as part of the merger of this class with the /ɑ/ class (the *cot ~ caught* merger) (cf. Stockwell and Minkova 1997).

The fact that Marckwardt's research concentrated on the development of words deriving from ME short-*o* and *wa-* (e.g., *off, long, wash, water*) raises another interesting set of possibilities. It was observed earlier (§5.1.2.4) that shifting of (ɔ) was found to be particularly frequent in items of these Middle English origins. Marckwardt's (1941, 563) work was based on a survey of "the oldest stratum of native speech" and so used speakers who were at least 70 years old. His findings, therefore, suggest that this pattern has been in operation for at least a century. One interpretation of these findings, then, is that the lowering and unrounding of (ɔ) is not part of a change in progress but is actually a relic pattern. However, apparently contradicting this suggestion is the finding of significant age differences for this variable, with adolescents showing more shifting than adults. This was, in fact, the only variable for which such a pattern was found to be statistically significant in this study. More importantly, for today's speakers, the lowered and unrounded variants of (ɔ) are clearly not restricted to items representing ME short-*o* and *wa-*. Marckwardt did not report other items (e.g., *caught, thought, talk*), so we do not know whether they, too, were lowered and unrounded at that time; however, if they were not, then the current distribution would certainly represent an expansion of the earlier pattern. Actually, in either case, it might still be suggested that variants associated with the ME short-*o* and *wa-* words were crucially involved in the origins of the change to (ɔ). They might have served as the first members of the class to undergo the shift, inspired in some way by a desire to reunite with their historical cousins who had remained in or joined the /ɑ/ class (e.g., *cot, watch,* etc.). On the other hand, if the lowered and unrounded variants in the ME short-*o* and *wa-* items represent an earlier pattern that was not originally part of the NCS, they might still have played a role in spurring the NCS, as they could have provided a phonetic model for the shifting of (ɔ), serving as a kind of allophonic bridge between /ɔ/ and /ɑ/. Regardless of these details, the points to be taken from these observations are that lowering and unrounding of (ɔ) appears to have a fairly long (by American standards) history in the Northern dialect region and that certain facts involved in the historical development of the /ɔ/ class suggest a reasonable scenario for the initiation of movement of this vowel.

This discussion has considered the issue of the temporal relatedness of the NCS changes by examining some of the evidence regarding the chronology of these changes. There seems to be fairly strong support for the chronological ordering proposed by Labov (1994, 195) for the changes in the upper half of the shift, (ɛ) > (ɪ) > (ʌ), but the situation in the lower half is less clear. The present data suggest that (ɔ) is the oldest element in the shift, and there is real-time evidence to support this proposal. This means, of course, that if the changes in the lower half of the NCS form a chain shift, then it seems to be a push chain begun in the back, rather than a drag chain begun in the front, as Labov proposes. As was noted earlier (§1.4.4.2), the case for (æ) serving as the initiating element in the NCS is open to debate. With the possible exception of Thomas's (1935–37) description of upstate New York, there is no real-time evidence of (æ)-raising in this dialect area, and the apparent-time data (such as those offered by Labov, Yaeger, and Steiner 1972) do not give clear indications that (æ) was the first element to shift. It is worth considering that this aspect of Labov's chronology may have been influenced by early research (e.g., Bailey 1973) that mistakenly viewed the NCS pattern of (æ)-raising as historically related to the raising found in the Middle Atlantic area, as well as by Labov's own theoretical proposal that /æ/ is one of the "pivot points" in the English vowel system "that determine the dynamics of chain shifting" (1991, 12). At the very least, then, this discussion suggests that the temporal relations among (æ), (ɑ), and (ɔ) are unclear and need to be given greater consideration by future research.

6.2. ARE CONTRASTS PRESERVED BY THE NCS CHANGES?

The second major definitional criterion of chain shifting is that the changes do not result in any loss (or gain) of phonemes but only alter the phonetic realizations associated with the original set. This aspect of the definition is, in large part, an elaboration of the nature of the spatial connectedness of the changes. Vocalic chain shifting, as noted above, implies a relationship between two contiguous vowels whereby one vowel leaves a space and the other moves into that space, either in that order, as in a drag chain, or in the reverse order, as in a push chain. It is by this departure of the original occupant that a chain shift is distinguished from a merger, and this fact has led to the functionalist interpretation that chain shifting is motivated by an avoidance of merger (e.g., Martinet 1952). The merits of such teleological explanations will not be addressed here; rather, the notion of an avoidance of merger will be approached as a potentially observable result of sound change (regardless of its underlying motivation), and evidence bearing on its observation will be considered.

The discussion offered here is much less extensive than the preceding account of the issues involved in the relatedness question. This is due in part to the nature of the evidence needed to address these matters. The issue of whether contrasts between vowels are preserved or threatened by shifts like those of the NCS is fundamentally a phonetic question, one that needs to be approached through systematic acoustic and perceptual research. Given that such research was not a principal concern in this project, the discussion here is necessarily limited by the types of evidence available from the present study.

With that caveat, however, there are some interesting aspects of the present findings that seem to bear on these issues. An initial approach to these matters has already been seen in portrait of the NCS variation offered earlier (fig. 6.2). In that representation the changes of the lower half of the shift seemed to conform well to the standard image of a chain shift. The main directions of change show that the back (ɔ) drops and fronts into the space originally occupied by (ɑ), while (ɑ) fronts toward the (æ) space, and (æ) exits up the front path. The acoustic data presented above (chap. 4) suggests only slight modifications of this impressionistic description. For example, the shifting of (æ) was seen (fig. 4.1) to involve a substantial increase in the frequency of F2, suggesting that it undergoes fronting as well as raising. Likewise, the shifting of (ɑ) seems to be marked by an increase in F1 as well as F2, which indicates that its fronting is accompanied by lowering. The combined effects of these two changes seem to preserve or possibly even to increase the acoustic distance between the vowels. F2 of both vowels is increased by comparable degrees, but F1 is decreased for (æ) (as the vowel is raised) and increased for (ɑ) (as the vowel is lowered). Thus, what seems to have been originally (i.e., before the vowels are shifted) primarily a distinction of F2 is supplemented as a result of the shifting by an increase in the F1 difference.

The preservation of vocalic contrast is less obviously the result with many of the other changes shown in figure 6.2. The less common tendencies demonstrated by (ɔ) and (ɑ), for example, seem to lead these vowels head on into the path of shifting (ʌ) as it is backed or lowered. Actually, the lowering of (ʌ) is problematic even without the complication of occasional raising by (ɑ). This tendency brings (ʌ) into an area of vowel space that is occupied by conservative tokens of (ɑ) as well as by shifted tokens of (ɔ) (see fig. 3.7). Still, this situation may not lead to as much perceptual confusion as the spectral picture suggests, since some of the contrast may be maintained through durational differences. Such differences may not, however, be available in another potential trouble spot, one created by the lowering of (ɛ). This movement drops the vowel into a range where conservative tokens of (æ) and shifted tokens of (ɑ) may be found (see fig. 3.1).

It is difficult to see how the patterns of shifting seen with (ɛ) and (ʌ) could be fully accounted for by the chain-shift model. The lowering of (ɛ) may serve to increase the contrast with (ɪ) when it, too, is lowered, but it also seems to endanger certain other contrasts, such as that with (æ) and (ɑ). Labov (1994, 588) suggests that this potential for confusion with (ɑ) is what led to a redirection of (ɛ)'s shifting toward the back. However, as noted earlier (§5.2.3), this study found the lowering of (ɛ) to be more common among adolescents, suggesting that it is the more recent trend. It is much harder to see a chain-shift connection between the lowering of (ɛ) and any movement of (ʌ). Ignoring the generational differences, however, the overall pattern of shifting shows backing to be the more common direction taken by (ɛ). Backing of (ɛ) certainly does encroach on the vowel space of (ʌ) and therefore could inspire shifting of the latter, as the standard scenario claims (Labov 1994, 95). Nevertheless, while backing of (ʌ) seems a plausible course of retreat in response to the (ɛ) invasion, lowering is certainly a less obvious choice. Though technically this direction of change does not produce any loss of contrast, it is not clear that the maintenance-of-distinction argument offers the best account of this tendency or others. In order to deal with difficulties such as these, a different proposal, one based on analogy, is put forward below.

As a different approach to the issue of phonemic contrast, we might examine evidence related to the phonological conditioning of the changes. As noted above, the maintenance of distinctions between vowels might be expected to show context-sensitive effects. These expectations are based on the idea that avoidance of homophony plays a key role in preserving vocalic contrasts. Thus, given that vowels tend to shift at differential rates according to phonological contexts, the distinction between two shifting vowels will best be maintained if they respond similarly to their contexts.

For example, if the shifting of both (ɔ) and (ɑ) is favored by a following /t/, then *caught* can be pronounced with an [ɑ] without being confused with *cot*, since *cot* is pronounced with something closer to [æ]. This is true even if (ɑ) items representing other contexts are still pronounced with [ɑ], as long as the (ɔ) items in those same contexts are still pronounced with [ɔ]. Thus, the phonemes can have overlapping allophonic distributions without necessarily losing the contrast between them. Following this reasoning, we can compare the conditioning patterns of putatively related vowels as a means of investigating the extent to which contrasts between those vowels are maintained during the shift.

Mention should be given to some of the more robust results suggested by the phonological index data, though an absolutely thorough comparison along these lines is not attempted here. Beginning in the low, back region of the shift, we find very little similarity in the conditioning patterns for (ɑ) and (ɔ). The phonological indices suggest that both of these changes are favored (though not necessarily strongly so) in the context of following velars as well as when followed by a tautosyllabic cluster.[5] There are other contexts that have a strong influence on one of the vowels but appear to have little influence on the other, as in the case of following labials, which strongly favor (ɔ)-shifting but seem to play no role in (ɑ)-shifting. Still other contexts have strong effects on both the vowels but show opposing tendencies, as in the case of preceding nasals, which favor (ɑ)-shifting but disfavor (ɔ)-shifting, or the case of preceding /r/, which disfavors (ɑ)-shifting but favors (ɔ)-shifting. The latter example is particularly important for the issue at hand, since it suggests that the vocalic contrast is reduced in this context as /ɔ/ is shifted toward [ɑ] without /ɑ/ shifting away.

Greater consistency is seen in the conditioning patterns of (ɑ) and (æ). Both changes are disfavored by preceding /r/ and following palatals, and both are favored by preceding voiceless obstruents, following interdentals, and especially following /l/. The only major discrepancy is found with preceding palatals, which strongly disfavor (æ)-shifting but seem to favor (ɑ)-shifting, though there were too few tokens to verify this latter tendency statistically (see table 4.8). Nevertheless, this case is important because it seems to lead to a reduced contrast in that environment, as (ɑ) fronts while (æ) remains in place.

There is also a fair amount of consistency between the conditioning of (æ) and (ɛ). The favorable effects of following interdentals[6] and following /l/ and the unfavorable effect of preceding palatals are also found to apply to (ɛ)-shifting. There is an apparent point of discrepancy seen with preceding velars, which strongly promote (æ)-shifting but strongly disfavor (ɛ)-shifting. Interestingly, this unfavorable effect applies only in the case of (ɛ)-backing, and lowering of this vowel is actually somewhat favored by this context. This is interesting, of course, because the lowering brings the vowel into an area near [æ], which has been left vacant by the shifting of (æ).

A comparison of the conditioning of (ɛ) with that of (ɪ) reveals a great degree of discrepancy. For example, shifting of (ɪ) appears to be strongly favored by preceding palatals or velars,[7] both of which strongly disfavor shifting of (ɛ). On the other hand, preceding glottals strongly seem to favor (ɛ)-shifting while having the opposite effect on (ɪ)-shifting.[8] The two changes do respond similarly to an adjacent lateral, however, as both are favored by either a preceding or a following /l/. Furthermore, the discrepancy may not be as great as the general patterns suggest. For example, as noted above, preceding velars disfavor the backing of (ɛ) but slightly favor lowering of this vowel. Importantly, lowering (sometimes with backing too) is also the preferred direction of shifting for (ɪ) in this environment. Similarly, the context of a preceding nasal is also seen to promote lowering of both these vowels.

The conditioning data for (ʌ) also offer mixed results when compared with the (ɛ) data. Both changes are disfavored by preceding palatals and favored by preceding /l/; however, preceding velars are found to favor (ʌ)-shifting while disfavoring (ɛ)-shifting, and preceding glides (at least /w/) disfavor (ʌ)-shifting[9] while favoring (ɛ)-shifting. Perhaps more significantly, among the strongest promoters of (ɛ)-backing, none is found to clearly promote backing of (ʌ).

Finally, comparing (ʌ) to (ɔ), we find almost no common patterning other than the fact that both changes seem to be favored by the presence of a following tautosyllabic cluster. The phonological indices suggest that preceding glides, preceding /r/, following voiced obstruents, and following fricatives all favor (ɔ)-shifting and disfavor (ʌ)-shifting. On the other hand, many of the contexts that favor (ʌ)-shifting, even those that favor backing of the vowel, seem to have little effect on (ɔ) (e.g., preceding velars, initial position, following voiceless obstruents).

These comparisons of conditioning patterns are intended to provide indications of the degree to which the NCS changes are coordinated in their passage through the phonological system. Such coordination might allow the changes to proceed without jeopardizing phonemic distinctions. As with much of the other evidence on the chain-shift question, the findings here offer a mixed bag of results. Some of the comparisons reveal fairly consistent patterning across vowels, as with (æ) and (ɑ), while others show very little common ground, as with (ʌ) and (ɔ). These findings are suggestive even though, as an approach to the issue of whether perceptual contrast is maintained, the methods employed are admittedly rather indirect. As a next step for future research, the suggestions made here can be pursued through a more direct line of investigation, one involving a more systematic acoustic and perceptual analysis.

6.3. CONCLUSIONS

Considering all the evidence discussed in this chapter, the answer to the question posed by its title seems to be a resounding "maybe." Some aspects of this evidence offer support for the interpretation of the NCS as a chain shift, while others challenge that interpretation. In truth, it is difficult to imagine what kind of evidence would prove satisfactorily that a certain set of variable features did indeed constitute a chain shift. The situation is made all the more challenging by the fact that most of the available evidence on the NCS is synchronic, while the concept of chain shifting (as an instance of language change) is inherently diachronic. As noted earlier, previous researchers of the NCS have not attempted to establish the validity of the chain-shift interpretation but seem rather to have operated with this interpretation as an assumption. There has not been, therefore, a concentrated effort to produce evidence bearing on this issue. More generally, there seems not to have been much consideration of whether, and if so, how, the process of chain shifting should be evident in any ongoing change.

For these reasons, the efforts made here to address the chain-shift question are clearly preliminary. Nevertheless, there do seem to be some conclusions that can be drawn from this discussion. One point that has been evident throughout much of this account is the primary division of the NCS changes into an upper half, (ε), (ɪ), (ʌ), and a lower half, (æ), (ɑ), (ɔ). This separation is suggested by the discrepancies in the apparent ages of the changes (the lower changes are all much more established and, therefore, probably older) as well as in their directional behavior (the upper changes all show variant trajectories of shifting). The evidence for a chain-shift connection between the two halves is, at best, mixed. The data related to phonological conditioning show a fairly consistent patterning at one proposed point of connection, between (æ) and (ε), but very little consistency at the other, between (ʌ) and (ɔ). Even the (æ)/(ε) connection, however, may be questioned on perceptual grounds. Shifting of (æ) involves raising, but it may also involve tensing and the development of an inglide, by which the raised variants should be kept quite distinct from [ε] or even [ɪ] (but cf. Labov 1994, 196–99).

The evidence regarding the changes in the lower half of the NCS is largely consistent with the interpretation that they form a chain shift. If this is the case, however, it is not, as suggested by Labov (1994, 195), a drag chain led by the raising of (æ), but rather a push chain initiated by the lowering and fronting of (ɔ). The apparent-time evidence of this study corroborates the real-time reports that the change to (ɔ) is well established in this region, and, in the absence of indications to the contrary, this change appears to be the oldest in the NCS. As an alternative interpretation of this evidence, it might be suggested that the change to (ɔ) is actually not related, or at least not originally related, to the (æ) and (ɑ) changes. Phonological support for such a proposal was seen in the data on conditioning, which indicated very little coordination in the shifting of (ɔ) and (ɑ), and, of course, these vowels represent different phonological classes, as /ɔ/ is grouped among the tense vowels and /ɑ/ among the lax. If the (ɔ) change is not connected to the others (either historically or at present), then the drag chain scenario proposed by Labov (1994, 195) for (æ) and (ɑ) may hold. Certainly, the evidence for a connection of these two seems fairly strong (e.g., the data on phonological conditioning).

The evidence regarding the changes in the upper half of the NCS offers much greater challenges to the chain-shift argument. The apparent-time data on the relative chronology of these changes, (ɛ) > (ɪ) > (ʌ), and some of the data on the patterns of phonological conditioning support the interpretation that these changes are related, but it is not clear that this relationship has been forged through chain shifting. Particularly troubling for the chain-shift interpretation are the variant trajectories demonstrated by the shifting vowels. The difficulties posed by the lowering of (ʌ), for example, have already been mentioned. Equally problematic is the backing of (ɪ), which, despite being the most common tendency demonstrated by this vowel, has no obvious connection of a chain-shift nature to any other element in the NCS. One of the most interesting aspects of the variation associated with the vowels of the upper half of the shift is that, although each vowel was found to shift in multiple directions, they all illustrated the same basic pattern: mostly backing, but sometimes lowering and at other times combining backing and lowering. This tremendous similarity suggests the possibility that, rather than having developed via chain shifting, the links among these changes stem from a kind of parallelism, whereby a pattern of multidirectional variation has been analogized to three phonologically similar vowels. This pattern might be original to (ɛ), as the apparent-time evidence suggests, in which case another interesting possibility is raised, namely, that the development and spread of the pattern—at least the spread to (ɪ)—may have been aided by preexisting variation associated with these vowels. Centralized forms of (ɛ) and (ɪ) are, after all, common in unstressed syllables as a product of phonetic reduction, and it is possible that having such forms in the allophonic repertoire somehow played a role in establishing the generalized pattern of variation seen today. This proposal is admittedly speculative, but it is intended not so much to answer questions as to raise them, to offer an alternative account that will encourage more careful consideration of the chain-shift assumptions that have guided previous thinking about the origins of the NCS variation.

On a more general note, throughout this study, attempts to seek explanations for the patterns observed have frequently led in various directions, and for many of these patterns, plausible accounts have been found down a number of different explanatory avenues. This wealth of possibilities is undoubtedly due in part to the rather limited amount of empirical research conducted on the NCS, as some of these possibilities might appear less plausible were better documentation of the shift available. Still, it would be a mistake to think that more research would necessarily point toward a single explanation for any one of the patterns. As Malkiel (1976) and others have made clear, language change is not brought about as the product of factors operating in isolation; rather, it stems from a kind of harmonic convergence of multiple influences. Thus the suggestions that have been offered here are probably best viewed not as alternatives, though they have occasionally been described that way, but rather as potential pieces of a larger puzzle, the puzzle of how and why the changes we call the Northern Cities Shift have come to assume their current sociolinguistic distribution.

The mechanisms and processes at work in the actuation and diffusion of linguistic innovations are among the most challenging issues facing researchers. Nevertheless, through the study of changes in progress we are presented with an opportunity to investigate these mechanisms and processes while they are active, and thus we are brought closer to the heart of language change and perhaps closer to an understanding of its functioning.

NOTES

1. Unpublished materials from the Phonological Atlas of North America project at the University of Pennsylvania suggest that elements of the NCS are found as far west as the Dakotas (see Labov 1996).

2. It is possible that such isolated cases could occur and simply not be recognized as related to the NCS because they do not reflect the entire pattern. However, no such cases were identified in reviewing the dialect literature for this study.

3. Some speakers do have a high central vowel, [ɨ], though only in unstressed positions.

4. In cases where multiple changes are active in a community but where these changes are not involved in a chain shift, this expectation would not necessarily hold. In fact, if two changes acquire opposing social meanings (e.g., they differ along gender lines), then it seems likely that they would most often not co-occur in the usage of any individual speaker. Such cases serve to illustrate the distinction between speaker- and system-based accounts of language change (see Milroy and Milroy 1985).

5. The chi-square results regarding the cluster factor for (ɑ) showed that it fell just short of statistical significance ($p = .055$), though the index score associated with the presence of a following cluster was rather high (0.841; cf. overall index = 0.664).

6. Again, there were too few tokens of (ɛ) before interdentals to verify this apparent trend statistically.

7. As discussed above (§5.1.2.1), the results regarding these categories are based on a lexically restricted set of data.

8. The possibility that the findings regarding these categories are not representative of broad phonological trends was discussed above (§§5.1.2.1 and 5.1.2.2).

9. This finding, too, may reflect a lexical bias rather than a phonological tendency (see §5.1.2.1).

APPENDIX A: WORD LIST

about	Bob	dog	hodge-podge	launch
aid	bomb	doll	hoe	law
am	book	dollar	honey	lawn
ant	boot	Don	hood	laws
apple	bought	dumb	hop	leapt
as	box	ebb	house	Leslie
babble	boy	edge	how	less
back	bum	egg	hub	lesson
bad	bus	enact	Huck	limb
badge	but	English	huddle	lip
bag	buy	ever	huff	little
bait	cab	fall	hug	live
ban	calm	father	hull	log
banana	camera	feather	hum	long
bang	casual	fog	hummer	longer
bash	caught	fond	hung	lot
bat	cause	gem	hush	loud
batch	chemist	glad	hut	love
bead	chip	Glen	hutch	ma'am
beat	chop	gone	if	map
bed	chopper	gong	is	member
beg	clip	gull	itch	men
bell	closet	hall	jab	mesh
bend	clump	ham	jam	mint
bent	coffee	hand	jaw	miss
best	come	handler	jeopardy	mock
bet	common	have	Jim	mode
Beth	cop	hawk	John	mom
bib	cot	hay	Josh	mood
bid	cough	he	jut	mop
big	cut	help	keg	moth
bike	dawn	hem	kept	must
Bill	Deb	hill	kibble	nab
bit	deputy	him	Kim	net
bite	dish	hip	lab	nip
boat	doesn't	hockey	lamb	noise

numb	path	planet	Sam	Tim
nut	pauper	planter	says	tip
odd	pawn	pleasure	sissy	Tom
office	pebble	plumb	sister	top
on	peck	pod	sketch	toss
other	pen	pop	song	trauma
ought	pep	possible	stem	under
pal	pick	pot	tab	up
Pam	pimple	poverty	talk	wash
pass	pin	profit	talked	watch
passage	ping	put	talking	who
past	pip	sad	taught	yum
pasta	plan			

APPENDIX B: ITEMS OMITTED FROM CODING

As explained in §2.3.1, various items were excluded from analysis in this study because they are commonly involved in patterns of phonetic variation that are unrelated to, but potentially confusable with, the variation associated with the Northern Cities Shift. These items are listed here, along with a brief explanation of why they were excluded.

Variable	Item	Reason for Exclusion
(ɪ)	*been*	[ɪ] ~ [ɛ] variation
(ɪ)	*until*	[ɪ] ~ [ɛ] variation
(ɪ)	*since*	[ɪ] ~ [ɛ] variation
(ɪ)	*milk*	[ɪ] ~ [ɛ] variation
(ɪ)	*real(ly)*	[ɪ] ~ [i] variation
(ɪ)	*again*	[ɪ] ~ [ɛ] variation
(ɪ)	*Illinois*	[ɪ] ~ [ɛ] variation
(ɪ)	any word with /ɪŋ/	[ɪ] ~ [i] variation (exception was made for *English*)
(ɛ)	*any*	[ɪ] ~ [ɛ] variation
(ɛ)	*get*	[ɪ] ~ [ɛ] variation
(ɛ)	*well* (discourse marker)	[ɛ] ~ [ʌ] variation (adverb *well* was counted)
(æ)	*can* (aux.)	[æ] ~ [ɛ] variation (*can't* did not show this variation and was counted)
(æ)	*than*	[æ] ~ [ɛ] ~ [ʌ] variation (usually very reduced)
(æ)	*that* (conj.)	[æ] ~ [ɛ] variation (usually very reduced)
(æ)	*have* (aux.)	[æ] ~ [ɛ] variation (usually very reduced)
(æ)	*an*	[æ] ~ [ɛ] ~ [ɪ] variation (usually very reduced)
(æ)	*catch*	[æ] ~ [ɛ] variation
(æ)	*calculus*	[æ] ~ [ɛ] variation (demonstrated by one speaker)

(æ)	*algebra*	[æ] ~ [ɛ] variation (demonstrated by one speaker)
(æ)	any word with /æŋ/	[æ] ~ [ɛ] ~ [ɛ] variation
(ɑ)	*want*	[ɑ] ~ [ʌ] variation
(ɑ)	*what*	[ɑ] ~ [ʌ] variation
(ɔ)	*because*	[ɔ] ~ [ʌ] variation
(ɔ)	*Chicago*	[ɔ] ~ [ɑ] variation

REFERENCES

Anttila, Raimo. 1972. *An Introduction to Historical and Comparative Linguistics.* New York: Macmillan.

Bailey, Charles-James N. 1973. *Variation and Linguistic Theory.* Washington, D.C.: Center for Applied Linguistics.

Bailey, Guy, Tom Wikle, Jan Tillery, and Lori Sand. 1993. "Some Patterns of Linguistic Diffusion." *Language Variation and Change* 5: 359–90.

Beddor, Patrice S. 1991. "Predicting the Structure of Phonological Systems." *Phonetica* 48: 83–107.

Borden, Gloria J., and Katherine S. Harris. 1984. *Speech Science Primer: Physiology, Acoustics, and Perception of Speech.* 2d ed. Baltimore: Williams and Wilkins.

Bronstein, Arthur J. 1960. *The Pronunciation of American English.* New York: Appleton-Century Crofts.

Callary, Robert. 1975. "Phonological Change and the Development of an Urban Dialect in Illinois." *Language in Society* 4: 155–69.

Chambers, J. K. 1995. *Sociolinguistic Theory.* Oxford: Blackwell.

DeCamp, L. Sprague. 1940. "Scranton Pronunciation." *American Speech* 15: 368–71.

Deser, Toni. 1991. "Dialect Transmission and Variation." Ph.D. diss., Boston Univ.

Eckert, Penelope. 1987. "The Relative Values of Variables." In *Variation in Language: NWAV-XV,* ed. Keith M. Denning et al., 101–10. Palo Alto, Calif.: Dept. of Linguistics, Stanford Univ.

———. 1988. "Adolescent Social Structure and the Spread of Linguistic Change." *Language in Society* 17: 183–207.

———. 1989a. "The Whole Woman: Sex and Gender Differences in Variation." *Language Variation and Change* 1: 245–67.

———. 1989b. *Jocks and Burnouts: Social Identity in the High School.* New York: Teachers College Press.

———. 1991. "Social Polarization and the Choice of Linguistic Variants." In *New Ways of Analyzing Sound Change,* ed. P. Eckert, 213–32. San Diego: Academic Press.

———. 2000. *Linguistic Variation as Social Practice.* Oxford: Blackwell.

Eckert, Penelope, and Sally McConnell-Ginet. 1992. "Think Practically and Look Locally: Language and Gender as Community-based Practice." *Annual Review of Anthropology* 21: 461–90.

Emerson, Oliver Farrar. 1891. "The Ithaca Dialect: A Study of Present English." *Dialect Notes* 1: 85–173.

Fasold, Ralph. 1969. "A Sociolinguistic Study of the Pronunciation of Three Vowels in Detroit Speech." Unpublished MS.

Ferguson, Charles A. 1975. "'Short a' in Philadelphia English." In *Studies in Linguistics in Honor of George L. Trager*, ed. E. Smith, 259–74. The Hague: Mouton.

Frazer, Timothy. 1993. "Problems in Midwest English." In *"Heartland English": Variation and Transition in the American Midwest*, ed. T. Frazer, 1–19. Tuscaloosa: Univ. of Alabama Press.

Gordon, Matthew J. 1997. "Urban Sound Change Beyond City Limits: The Spread of the Northern Cities Shift in Michigan." Ph.D. diss., Univ. of Michigan.

———. 2000. "Phological Correlates of Ethnic Identity: Evidence of Divergence?" *American Speech* 75: 115–36.

Herndobler, Robin. 1977. "White Working-Class Speech: The East Side of Chicago." Ph.D. diss., Univ. of Chicago.

———. 1993. "Sound Change and Gender in a Working-Class Community." In *"Heartland English": Variation and Transition in the American Midwest*, ed. T. Frazer, 137–56. Tuscaloosa: Univ. of Alabama Press.

Johnson, Keith. 1997. *Acoustic and Auditory Phonetics*. Oxford: Blackwell.

Kenyon, John Samuel, and Thomas Albert Knott. 1953. *A Pronouncing Dictionary of American English*. Springfield, Mass.: Merriam-Webster.

King, Robert D. 1967. "Functional Load and Sound Change." *Language* 43: 831–52.

Knack, Rebecca. 1991. "Ethnic Boundaries in Linguistic Variation." In *New Ways of Analyzing Sound Change*, ed. P. Eckert, 251–72. San Diego: Academic Press.

Krapp, George Philip. 1919. *The Pronunciation of Standard English in America*. New York: Oxford Univ. Press.

Kurath, Hans. 1949. *Word Geography of the Eastern United States*. Ann Arbor: Univ. of Michigan Press.

Kurath, Hans, and Raven I. McDavid, Jr. 1961. *The Pronunciation of English in the Atlantic States*. Ann Arbor: Univ. of Michigan Press.

Labov, William. 1963. "The Social Motivation of a Sound Change." *Word* 19: 273–309.

———. 1966. *The Social Stratification of English in New York City*. Washington, D.C.: Center for Applied Linguistics.

———. 1971. "Methodology." In *A Survey of Linguistic Science*, ed. William Orr Dingwall, 412–97. College Park: Univ. of Maryland.

———. 1972. *Sociolinguistic Patterns.* Philadelphia: Univ. of Pennsylvania Press.

———. 1975. "On the Use of the Present to Explain the Past." In *Proceedings of the 11th International Congress of Linguists,* ed. L. Heilmann, 825–51. Bologna: Il Mulino.

———. 1981. "Field Methods Used by the Project on Linguistic Change and Variation." Sociolinguistic Working Paper 81. Austin, Tex.: Southwestern Educational Development Laboratory.

———. 1987. "Are Black and White Vernaculars Diverging?" *American Speech* 62: 5–12.

———. 1990. "The Intersection of Sex and Social Class in the Course of Linguistic Change." *Language Variation and Change* 2: 205–54.

———. 1991. "The Three Dialects of English." In *New Ways of Analyzing Sound Change,* ed. Penelope Eckert, 1–44. San Diego: Academic Press.

———. 1994. *Principles of Linguistic Change. Vol. 1: Internal Factors.* Oxford: Blackwell.

———. 1996. "The Organization of Dialect Diversity in North America." Paper presented at the Fourth International Conference on Spoken Language Processing, Philadelphia, 6 Oct. Online version at http://www.ling.upenn.edu/phono_atlas/ICSLP4.html.

———. 1997. "Locating the Leaders of Linguistic Change." Paper presented at the annual meeting of the Linguistic Society of America, Chicago, 2–4 Jan.

Labov, William, Malcah Yaeger, and Richard Steiner. 1972. *A Quantitative Study of Sound Change in Progress.* Philadelphia: U.S. Regional Survey.

Ladefoged, Peter. 1982. *A Course in Phonetics.* New York: Harcourt Brace Jovanovich.

Laferriere, Martha. 1977. "Boston Short *a:* Social Variation as Historical Residue." In *Studies in Language Variation,* ed. Ralph Fasold and Roger Shuy, 100–107. Washington, D.C.: Georgetown Univ. Press.

Lass, Roger. 1978. "Mapping Constraints in Phonological Reconstruction: On Climbing Down Trees without Falling out of Them." In *Recent Developments in Historical Phonology,* ed. Jacek Fisiak, 245–86. The Hague: Mouton.

Malkiel, Yakov. 1976. "Multi-conditioned Sound Change and the Impact of Morphology on Phonology." *Language* 52: 757–78.

Marckwardt, Albert H. 1941. "Middle English *o* in American English of the Great Lakes Area." *Papers of the Michigan Academy of Science, Arts, and Letters* 26: 561–71.

————. 1942. "Middle English *wa* in the Speech of the Great Lakes Region." *American Speech* 17: 226–34.

Martinet, Andre. 1952. "Function, Structure and Sound Change." *Word* 8: 1–32. Repr. in *Readings in Historical Phonology*, ed. P. Baldi and R. Werth, 121–59. University Park: Pennsylvania State Univ. Press, 1978.

————. 1955. *Economie des changements phonétiques*. Bern: Francke.

Milroy, James. 1981. *Regional Accents of English: Belfast*. Belfast: Blackstaff.

Milroy, James, and Lesley Milroy. 1985. "Linguistic Change, Social Network and Speaker Innovation." *Journal of Linguistics* 25: 339–84.

Milroy, Lesley. 1980. *Language and Social Networks*. Oxford: Blackwell.

————. 1987. *Observing and Analysing Natural Language*. Oxford: Blackwell.

Monroe, B. S. 1896. "The Pronunciation of English in the State of New York." *Dialect Notes* 1: 445–56.

Moore, Samuel, and Albert H. Marckwardt. 1951. *Historical Outlines of English Sounds and Inflections*. Ann Arbor, Mich.: Wahr.

Olive, Joseph P., Alice Greenwood, and John Coleman. 1993. *Acoustics of American English Speech: A Dynamic Approach*. New York: Springer.

Pederson, Lee A. 1965. *The Pronunciation of English in Metropolitan Chicago*. Publications of the American Dialect Society 44. Tuscaloosa: Univ. of Alabama Press.

Peterson, Gordon E., and Harold L. Barney. 1954. "Control Methods Used in a Study of the Identification of Vowels." *Journal of the Acoustical Society of America* 24: 175–84.

Pilch, Herbert. 1955. "The Rise of the American English Vowel Pattern." *Word* 11: 57–93.

Shuy, Roger, Walter A. Wolfram, and William K. Riley. 1968. *A Study of Social Dialects in Detroit*. Final Report, Project 6-1357. Washington, D.C.: Office of Education.

Stockwell, Robert, and Donka Minkova. 1997. "On Drifts and Shifts." *Studia Anglica Posnaniensia* 31: 283–303.

Thomas, Charles K. 1935-37. "Pronunciation in Upstate New York." *American Speech* 10: 107–12, 208–12, 292–97; 11: 68–77, 142–44, 307–13; 12: 122–27.

————. 1958. *An Introduction to the Phonetics of American English*. 2d ed. New York: Ronald.

Trager, George L. 1930. "The Pronunication of 'Short *A*' in American Standard English." *American Speech* 5: 396–400.

Trudgill, Peter. 1974. *The Social Differentiation of English in Norwich*. Cambridge: Cambridge Univ. Press.

————. 1983. *On Dialect: Social and Geographical Perspectives.* New York: New York Univ. Press.

————. 1988. "Norwich Revisited: Recent Linguistic Changes in an English Urban Dialect." *English World-Wide* 9: 33–49.

Vincent, Nigel. 1978. "Is Sound Change Teleological?" In *Recent Developments in Historical Phonology*, ed. Jacek Fisiak, 409–30. The Hague: Mouton.

Wang, William S-Y. 1969. "Competing Changes as a Cause of Residue." *Language* 45: 9–25. Repr. in *Readings in Historical Phonology*, ed. P. Baldi and R. Werth, 236–57. University Park: Pennsylvania State Univ. Press, 1978.

Weinreich, Uriel, William Labov, and Marvin Herzog. 1968. "Empirical Foundations for a Theory of Language Change." In *Directions for Historical Linguistics*, ed. W. P. Lehmann and Yakov Malkiel, 95–188. Austin: Univ. of Texas Press.

Wolfram, Walt, and Natalie Schilling-Estes. 1998. *American English.* Oxford: Blackwell.

Wyld, Henry Cecil. 1927. *A Short History of English.* 3d ed. New York: E. P. Dutton.

————. 1936. *A History of Modern Colloquial English.* 3d ed. Oxford: Basil Blackwell.

PUBLICATION OF THE AMERICAN DIALECT SOCIETY

Editor: RONALD R. BUTTERS, *Duke University*
Managing Editor: CHARLES E. CARSON, *Duke University*

THE AMERICAN DIALECT SOCIETY

Membership is conferred upon any person interested in the aims and activities of the Society. Dues are \$35 annually for regular members, \$20 for students, and \$5 extra for members outside the United States. Life membership is available to individuals for \$700. Members receive all publications: *American Speech*, its monograph supplement Publication of the American Dialect Society (PADS), and the *Newsletter*. Institutional subscriptions are also available. Address payments to Duke University Press, Journals Fulfillment, Box 90660, Durham NC 27708-0660; phone (888) 387-5687 or (919) 687-3617. Questions concerning membership or the Society should be addressed to the Executive Secretary, Allan Metcalf, Department of English, MacMurray College, Jacksonville IL 62650 (e-mail: AAllan@aol.com).

Officers for 2001

President: DENNIS R. PRESTON, *Michigan State University*
Vice President: MICHAEL B. MONTGOMERY, *University of South Carolina*
Past President: RONALD R. BUTTERS, *Duke University*
Executive Secretary: ALLAN METCALF, *MacMurray College*
Delegate to the ACLS: JOAN H. HALL, *Dictionary of American Regional English*
Executive Council Members: LISA ANN LANE, *Texas A&M University* (2001); WILLIAM A.
 KRETZSCHMAR, JR., *University of Georgia* (2002); KIRK HAZEN, *West Virginia University* (2003); BEVERLY FLANIGAN, *Ohio University* (2004)
Nominating Committee: WALT WOLFRAM, *North Carolina State University* (chair); RONALD
 R. BUTTERS, *Duke University*; JOAN H. HALL, *Dictionary of American Regional English*
General Editor, ADS Publications, and Editor, PADS: RONALD R. BUTTERS, *Duke University*

STATEMENT FOR AUTHORS

The object of the American Dialect Society, as stated in its constitution, "is the study of the English language in North America, together with other languages influencing it or influenced by it." The monograph series Publication of the American Dialect Society (PADS) publishes works by ADS members in (1) regional dialects, (2) social dialects, (3) occupational vocabulary, (4) place-names, (5) usage, (6) non-English dialects, (7) new words, (8) proverbial sayings, and (9) the literary use of dialect. Models for these kinds of studies may be found in issues of PADS. PADS does not publish articles on general grammar without dialect emphasis or articles on literary figures not known as dialect writers.

The general policy of PADS is to devote each issue to two or three long articles or, more commonly, to a single study of monograph length. Shorter articles and book reviews should be submitted to *American Speech*, the journal of the American Dialect Society.

Manuscripts submitted to PADS and *American Speech* should be styled following *The Chicago Manual of Style* (14th ed., 1993). Documentation must be given in the text itself using the author-date system (chap. 16), with the list of references at the end prepared in the humanities sytle (chap. 15).

Manuscripts for *American Speech* and PADS may be submitted to Charles E. Carson, Managing Editor, American Dialect Society Publications, Duke University Press, Box 90018, Durham NC 27708-0018. Telephone: (919) 687-3670. E-mail: carson@duke.edu.

DATE DUE